"Juliet B. Schor and her team have created the most comprehensive and in-depth account of the 'sharing' or 'gig' economy. This book tells the story of how and why this troubling, insecure model of work attracted so much investment, so many workers, and so many customers."

—SIVA VAIDHYANATHAN, author of *The Googlization of Everything: (And Why We Should Worry)*

"Before the pandemic, the gig economy was structurally racist, ecologically destructive, and profoundly exploitative. There's every danger that the reconstruction will be worse. Yet this nuanced and sophisticated study also shows, through the analysis of gig economy workers themselves, that flexibility, a shared sense of purpose, and a commitment to sharing more is well within our grasp. As we turn to imagine what kind of economy and society we want after COVID-19, the work of Schor and her students will be indispensable."

—RAJ PATEL, Research Professor, Lyndon B. Johnson School of Public Affairs at the University of Texas at Austin, and author of *A History of the World in Seven Cheap Things*

"While others have batted around the gig economy with melodrama and polemic, Schor comes to the subject with incisive, challenging questions for both the alarm raisers and the boosters. As a partisan in these debates myself, I've trusted no scholar as much as Schor to keep me honest."

—NATHAN SCHNEIDER, author of *Everything for Everyone: The Radical Tradition That Is Shaping the Next Economy*

Named in remembrance of

the onetime *Antioch Review* editor

and longtime Bay Area resident,

# the Lawrence Grauman, Jr. Fund

supports books that address

a wide range of human rights,

free speech, and social justice issues.

*The publisher and the University of California Press Foundation gratefully acknowledge the generous support of the Lawrence Grauman, Jr. Fund.*

*After the Gig*

# After the Gig

## HOW THE SHARING ECONOMY GOT HIJACKED AND HOW TO WIN IT BACK

### Juliet B. Schor

*and collaborators*
William Attwood-Charles
Mehmet Cansoy
Lindsey "Luka" Carfagna
Samantha Eddy
Connor Fitzmaurice
Isak Ladegaard
Robert Wengronowitz

UNIVERSITY OF CALIFORNIA PRESS

University of California Press
Oakland, California

© 2020 by Juliet B. Schor

Library of Congress Cataloging-in-Publication Data

Names: Schor, Juliet, author.
Title: After the gig : how the sharing economy got hijacked and how to
    win it back / Juliet B. Schor with William Attwood-Charles, Mehmet
    Cansoy, Lindsey "Luka" Carfagna, Samantha Eddy, Connor
    Fitzmaurice, Isak Ladegaard, Robert Wengronowitz.
Description: Oakland, California : University of California Press,
    [2020] | Includes bibliographical references and index.
Identifiers: LCCN 2020001754 (print) | LCCN 2020001755 (ebook) |
    ISBN 9780520325050 (hardback) | ISBN 9780520974227 (epub)
Subjects: LCSH: Precarious employment—Case studies. | Self-
    employed—Case studies. | Cooperation. | Sharing—Economic
    aspects.
Classification: LCC HD5706 .S314 2020 (print) | LCC HD5706
    (ebook) | DDC 331.25/729—dc23
LC record available at https://lccn.loc.gov/2020001754
LC ebook record available at https://lccn.loc.gov/2020001755

Manufactured in the United States of America

29  28  27  26  25  24  23  22  21  20
10  9  8  7  6  5  4  3  2  1

For Krishna and Sulakshana

# Contents

# Acknowledgments

The research team and I have incurred many debts in the almost ten years since we began this project. First and foremost we would like to thank the John D. and Catherine T. MacArthur Foundation, which generously supported our research through the Connected Learning Research Network. We are deeply grateful to the convener, Mizuko Ito, and to our colleagues in the network—Jean Rhodes, Sonia Livingstone, Craig Watkins, Dalton Conley, William Penuel, Kris Gutierrez, Vera Michalchik, Katie Salen Tekinbaş, Amanda Wortman, Julian Sefton-Green, Richard Arum, Kylie Peppler, Ben Kirschner, and Nichole Pinkhard. They provided years of intellectual engagement, suggestions for our research, and friendship. From the Foundation, we thank Connie Yowell, Julia Stasch, and Jennifer Humke. At Irvine, Courtney Santos and Anita Centeno were always helpful. For me, the network was an entrée into the study of digital technology and social life that has been enormously stimulating.

At Boston College, our work has been graciously supported by department chairs Sarah Babb and Andrew Jorgenson, Dean Gregory Kalscheur, and Provost David Quigley. I am grateful to them, as well as to my colleagues in the sociology department and the grants office. I would also like to thank the Radcliffe Institute for Advanced Studies, where I had the privilege of being a fellow in 2014–15. It was a highly productive year, and we had a great cohort. I enjoyed being back at Harvard and am especially grateful for the opportunity to spend time with Judith Vichniac, the fellowship director, and an old friend.

The team benefited from the work of many undergraduates, some of whom took on important parts of the research, including interviewing and coding. We would like to thank Abigail Letak, Alison Wawrzynek, Alex Moscovitz, Lea Oriol, Hahnsol Kang, Elizabeth Jiang, Nathan Schwan, Carolyn Ruh, Cristina Zubizaretta, Alison Grewe, Gloria Kostadinova, John Deacon, Sergio Farina, and Michael Griglak. Your contributions were invaluable.

Because this is a new area of study, I have had the privilege of being at a number of early scholarly gatherings. At each of these I met scholars whose research I already admired, and I was introduced to new people and their work. One of these workshops was the First International Workshop on the Sharing Economy organized by Koen Frenken at Utrecht University in 2015. In 2016 Kathleen Thelen and Peter Hall organized a Radcliffe Ventures meeting on the Politics of Work and Welfare in the Platform Economy, which significantly expanded my understanding of the sector. A third was the Sharing Cities Summit in Barcelona. Most recently, it has been a privilege to participate in the Political Economy and Justice Workshop at the Safra Center for Ethics at Harvard, organized by Danielle Allen, Yochai Benkler, and Rebecca Henderson. Many thanks to all the participants in those gatherings.

I have presented this research to colleagues at many universities and conferences, where I received valuable feedback and encouragement. I am grateful to participants in seminars and workshops at Harvard, Harvard Business School, the Berkman Center, MIT, Northwestern, Boston College, Bentley University, Microsoft Research, Berkeley, Barnard College, New York University, Michigan, Rhode Island School of Design, Brown University, Boston University,

CUNY Graduate Center, Connecticut College, University of Toronto, University of Massachusetts, Northeastern University, New School for Social Research, University of Maine, University of Central Arkansas, Tellus Institute, Utrecht University, Hamburg University, and University of Paris-Dauphine. I also presented our work at a variety of institutions and conferences, including the Annual meetings of the American Sociological Association, the Eastern Sociological Society, the American Anthropological Association, and the Society for the Advancement of Socio-Economics. I presented to the National Economic Council of the White House, the European Commission in Brussels, a joint workshop of the Royal Society and the American Academy of Arts and Sciences, the Division of Consumer Economics of the Federal Reserve Board, the Inaugural US conference of CoreEcon, the Institute for Work and the Economy, the Environmental Law Institute, the New Economy Coalition, the Digital Media and Learning Conference, the Sharing Cities Summit, the Re-Shaping Work Conference, the Women's Forum, the National Institute for Public Policy Analysis (Italy), the Feltrinelli Foundation, the Milan EXPO2015, and the OIKOS Think Tank in Antwerp. I presented at the SHARE conference which I discuss at the end of chapter 1. I was hosted by the Comillas Pontifical University in Madrid for a week in 2017.

I have had transformative conversations with many people over the years about this work. I would particularly like to thank Benjamin Edelman, John Zysman, Martin Kenney, Alex Rosenblat, Michelle Miller, Mary Gray, Sarah Babb, Gali Racabi, and Jerry Davis. Fellows at the Radcliffe Institute were also important sources of inspiration. At Boston College, Sarah Babb and Natalia Sarkisian were indispensable members of the dissertation committees of a number of the team members, and I am fortunate to have them as colleagues. I also am indebted to collaborators outside the team, including Alexandrea Ravenelle, Koen Frenken, Hege Westskog, Stefan Kirchner, and

Elke Schuessler. I have also begun collaborating with a great team at Northeastern, made up of H.C. Robinson, Ozlem Ergun, Michael Kane, and Steven Vallas.

Veena Dubal, Naomi Schneider, and an anonymous reviewer gave me excellent comments on the manuscript and improved it enormously. Susan Rabiner, who has guided me in publishing since the 1990s, made a crucial intervention. Thanks also to the staff at UC Press, including Benjy Malings, Summer Farah, and Emilia Thiuri. For many years I have wanted to publish a book with Naomi Schneider and am privileged to have had the opportunity. It has been a great pleasure to work with her.

There are a few people whose work and colleagueship has been especially important and to whom I have a special debt—Jean Rhodes, Veena Dubal, Krishna Dasaratha, Steve Vallas, and Yochai Benkler. Yochai's writings have been inspirational for me, and our conversations no less so. Yochai, Jean, Krishna, and Prasannan Parthasarathi read the manuscript, and I am grateful to them for doing so. Finally, I would like to thank my family, who are always a source of love and support—David, Jon, Jim, Sharon, Indira, Niranjana, Dan, Lizzie, and Josh. Every day I am grateful for and to my children, Krishna and Sulakshana. Prasannan is my North Star.

The text draws on material from the following published journal articles and book chapters:

In chapter 1: Connor J. Fitzmaurice, Isak Ladegaard, William Attwood-Charles, Mehmet Cansoy, Lindsey B. Carfagna, Juliet B. Schor, and Robert Wengronowitz. 2018. "Domesticating the Market: Moral Exchange and the Sharing Economy." *Socio-Economic Review* (Feb. 16): doi:10.1093/ser/mwy003.

In chapter 3: Juliet B. Schor. 2017. "Does the Sharing Economy Increase Inequality within the Eighty Percent? Findings from a Qualitative Study of Platform Providers." *Cambridge Journal of Regions, Economy and Society* 10 (2): 263–79.

In chapter 5: Juliet B. Schor, Connor Fitzmaurice, Lindsey B. Carfagna, Will Attwood-Charles, and Emilie Dubois Poteat. 2016. "Paradoxes of Openness and Distinction in the Sharing Economy." *Poetics* 54:66–81.

# Note: This Book Has Been Coproduced

This book is the product of a thoroughly collaborative effort among a team of researchers. All (except Juliet) were PhD candidates in sociology. Individuals took responsibility for many of the cases, doing the data collection and case analysis. But we did much of the work as a team, including the choice of sites, discussion of methods, and cross-case analysis. We cowrote many articles and chapters, including cross-case studies, which we have included in the notes where appropriate. The original team, in 2011, consisted of Juliet, Lindsey "Luka" Carfagna, and Emilie Dubois Poteat. Connor Fitzmaurice came on later that year. In 2013 William Attwood-Charles and Robert Wengronowitz joined—then, in 2014, Mehmet Cansoy and Isak Ladegaard. Samantha Eddy is our most recent member, having joined in 2017. Taylor Cain and Xiaorui Huang also participated. We have not put individual names on chapters because so much of the work was done collaboratively. We do, however, want to acknowledge contributions by chapter. Luka worked on the Time Bank case and was the sole researcher for Open Learning (chaps. 1, 5). In addition, her dissertation included a similar historical discussion to the account in chapter 1. Emilie Dubois Poteat was lead researcher on the Time Bank. Connor did the Food Swap research and co-led our analysis of the domestic imaginary with Isak (chaps. 1, 5). Will did two cases—the makerspace and delivery couriers (Postmates/Favor) (chaps. 1, 2, 5). Among the for-profit cases, Robert took the lead on TaskRabbit and our consumer interviews. Isak did Airbnb and ride-hail driver interviews (Uber and Lyft). Juliet was a lead researcher for the for-profit cases (chaps. 1, 2, 3). Samantha did the Stocksy case (chap. 6). Mehmet did all the quantitative analysis of Airbnb (chap. 3), as well as qualitative analysis of Airbnb interviews. He also managed the data and documentation for the team, which was an enormous and at times thankless job. We are especially grateful to him for that work. Methods for each case are discussed in Appendix A. Juliet did the actual writing of this book.

# Introduction

## The Problem of Work

As long as capitalism has existed, it has had a problem with work. Laboring can be degrading, arduous, and dangerous. Wages may not be sufficient to live on. At other times the work itself is boring, and alienation sets in. Sometimes work disappears, as in the 1930s, or in the artificially intelligent future that some envision. Jobs take too many hours. The nine-to-five is a grind. The boss is a jerk.

I've spent much of my professional life studying these issues. When the financial system crashed in 2008, a powerful idea emerged from the rubble: digital technology could solve the problem of work. This is not because machines will replace people but because algorithms and crowdsourced information can make bosses redundant. Software can reorganize economic activity into a person-to-person structure. This empowers individuals to take control of their lives. Vast swathes of the economy, especially in services, are ripe for this transformation. This vision came to be called "the sharing economy."

I became intrigued by the possibilities of sharing while writing a book—*Plenitude: The New Economics of True Wealth*—during the crash. I advocated for a world in which people worked less for companies—a lot less. They'd do more for themselves and use technology to make their labor more satisfying and productive. So when I finished the book, I gathered a team of researchers, and we began studying the "sharing economy." It didn't have a name yet, but it had captured our imagination. As it turned out, we weren't the only ones who were excited about it. Eventually, many people would look to sharing as an alternative to corporate-dominated capitalism. This was especially true of the young adults who were becoming economically independent just as the global system collapsed. They were hopeful that sharing would not just solve the problem of work but would also cure social disconnection, inequality, and environmental degradation.

You will know by now that things haven't turned out exactly as expected. The big platforms—Uber, Lyft, and Airbnb—have been exposed for paying poverty wages, destabilizing urban neighborhoods, and accelerating carbon emissions. Many argue that rather than ushering in an alternative, these companies are intensifying the worst features of global capitalism. The critics blame platform founders and venture capitalists for corrupting a good idea. And there's plenty of evidence to support that charge. But curiously, faith in the positive possibilities of digital sharing got its start in Silicon Valley, among just those people. They believed their technology would automatically yield decent work and good social relations.

Although things haven't turned out as predicted, the Silicon Valley discourse was right about one thing. Technological innovation and cultural change *have* put a person-to-person economy, with its solution to the problem of work, within reach. That's the view we started with, and after a decade of research we still believe in it. We discovered that achieving the potential of platforms requires specific conditions. They won't be met if today's corporate elites are in control. But they can be. I wrote this book to explain how things went wrong and how we can make them right.

## Work under Capitalism

A central question facing our economic system is whether it can provide ordinary people decently paid, meaningful work with reasonable freedom. During the twentieth century it mostly did not. For African Americans the dehumanization of enslavement persisted for decades in most occupations, especially sharecropping and domestic service. In the early decades, for all workers, manufacturing labor was unsafe and poorly paid. Hours were long. In the 1930s the paramount problem became mass unemployment, which spread around the world. A quarter of the labor force was out of work in the United States. People became desperate for any kind of paying job. The post-WWII era prosperity in the West, and the U.S. in particular, resulted in a different kind of problem. White-collar "Organization Men" chafed under the conformist corporate culture.[1] By the late 1960s, alienation had spread to the factory floor. Consumerist lifestyles fueled by high wages proved unable to overcome widespread dissatisfaction. Detroit's autoworkers became the most visible symbols of this period of labor unrest.[2] At the same time, suburban homemakers were also trapped by meaningless domesticity.[3] Psychologists and sociologists got busy trying to provide "quality of work life." But before they figured things out, workplaces changed. Employers abandoned the stability of the postwar period. Beginning in the 1980s, they ushered in a regime of precarious, insecure employment. People once again became grateful for any steady paycheck. Throughout the century, addressing one problem of work under capitalism resulted in another. The job security that solved unemployment led to meaninglessness. When unions achieved high wages, employers outsourced. And when the Great Recession hit, the problems surfaced together: unemployment, inadequate pay, alienation, and precarity.

That's the point at which the sharing economy was born.[4] It promised a new kind of work experience. First and foremost, it offered freedom—the chance to control one's destiny. No boss. Work when you want, as you want. Estrangement, discipline, and overwork would vanish. In the early days the pay was generous. The platforms took care of finding customers and electronic payments. It was turnkey self-determination. As a bonus, it foretold social and environmental benefits. Devon, a self-described Jamerican (Jamaican American) from a diverse inner suburb of Los Angeles, was totally on board when we interviewed him in 2013.

## A New Way to Work

Devon had a career as a national tour manager for global brands, such as Nike and PlayStation, that market themselves at sporting events. The work allowed him to travel, which he loved, and to take time off when he wanted to. Devon was curious, generous, and culturally open. He was into Capoeira, making movies, wrestling, volunteering, nutrition, and professional tutoring. When we interviewed him, he was on a break from touring and had started earning on TaskRabbit, an errands site. He quickly became the number-one-ranked tasker in Los Angeles. He was handy and enjoyed helping others. Part of his success, he believed, was because he'd grown up poor, which led him to develop a lot of skills: "Jamaicans have, like, a hundred jobs. And I'm not far from that stereotype. . . . If you look at my TaskRabbit profile, I'm in a lot of the categories."

Devon also rented on Zipcar and used Couchsurfing, a site that arranged lodging between individuals, without payment. When he heard about Airbnb, he began hosting on that platform, too, figuring he'd make some money doing what he'd been doing for free and really enjoyed. He was also in the middle of building a gadget to test soil moisture and water his plants while he was on the road, using an open-source Arduino digital controller. He was excited about doing it himself rather than buying off the shelf or paying a lot for a custom system. He likened his Airbnb and TaskRabbit work to this "little project": "I'm now having more control over what I'm doing, and not needing to have the other burdens that come with accepting a benefit [i.e., a job] from somebody else." Devon was enthusiastic when we asked if he planned to do more peer-to-peer activity in the future.

When the sharing economy launched, it was heralded with what we call the "idealist discourse"—a rhetoric that framed platforms as bringing economic, social, and environmental benefits. Devon's desire to earn while still retaining "control"—of his schedule, work process, and life—was a key motivator, as it is for many participants. But there were other pluses too. Airbnb seemed like a way to "experience the world without leaving your home." He'd recently hosted a couple of Belgian guys for a few weeks and became friendly with them. TaskRabbit also had social aspects. Given that "Los Angeles is one of the most segregated cities there are," he likened the work to a "microlevel" version of international travel, with strangers' homes being like other countries. He loved getting to meet people and see places he wouldn't otherwise have access to. Devon is also into permaculture and deep-green thinking. Advocates argued that sharing spare rooms, cars, and possessions reduces new purchasing and avoids carbon pollution and resource use. They predicted a revolution from an "ownership" to an "access" society.

Yes, the money mattered to Devon. He was temporarily substituting TaskRabbit for his usual job, and it was paying the rent. But he wasn't mercenary about his participation. He let his new Belgian friends know they could stay with him free on Couchsurfing. He was more excited about the possibility of changing the world, which he thought sharing was already doing: "Things are going full-circle. In the beginning we used to do everything for ourselves and we were very hospitable towards each other. And then . . . corporations started moving in . . . and everyone went there . . . and now [due to corruption] people started being anticorporation. People are going back to helping each other again because it's easier, especially with the advent of the internet. . . . So here we are." For Devon, sharing was an alternative to capitalism. "We don't need these big companies. Even though there are companies in the background that host these sharing things, on the front . . . it doesn't feel like that to the average consumer."

A decade in, tens of millions have earned on platforms. Hundreds of millions have stayed at Airbnbs, gotten into Ubers and Lyfts, and hired labor from apps.[5] Many share Devon's optimism. But there's an opposing view, which focuses on the companies Devon minimized as in the "background," unnoticed by the average person. They are seen as profit-hungry predators, using the idealist discourse as a fig leaf. Airbnb has commercialized, with unlicensed "ghost" hotels taking over neighborhoods and driving up rents. Companies have become notorious for mistreating workers and offering substandard wages. Even more ominously, some contend that the use of algorithms to control workers has become an alienating, almost totalitarian, nightmare. These criticisms have been present from the beginning but are gaining credibility, given mounting worker and popular discontent. As some of the earliest researchers to study the sharing economy we have plenty of evidence to support both points of view. We will introduce you to over-the-moon earners and customers, as well as struggling workers who describe themselves as "wage slaves," their situations as "scary." But the point of this book is not to stake out the empirical middle ground between the boosters and the critics. It's to show that the future that Devon foretold really is possible.

Devon's conversation focused on cultural change, perhaps because as a technically savvy type he took the technology for granted. But the digital tools matter. The platforms use algorithms and maps to match buyers and sellers, collect customer ratings to ensure quality, and offer electronic payment systems. These practices solve the problems of trust, search time, and quality that have long plagued person-to-person markets, what I've called "stranger sharing."[6] They make it feasible to cede significant authority back to individuals. In fact, the platforms already have stepped back from orchestrating the labor process in important ways. That's the control that Devon delighted in having gained. And the fact that he and others can work for themselves raises an existential question for the companies. Is the most revolutionary thing about the algorithms not their ability to control workers, as many have argued, but to make management obsolete? Could owners have invented a pathway to their own extinction? To see how we came to ask these questions, let's step back a bit, to revisit the early days of the sector and see what went wrong.

## The Promise of Sharing

The idea of sharing emerged from the financial collapse. That debacle caused a loss of faith in work, the economy, and the political system, especially among the young people whose futures it put in jeopardy. By 2011 a majority of eighteen- to twenty-nine-year-olds surveyed said they preferred socialism to capitalism.[7] Protests erupted around the world, including the Occupy movement in the U.S. They targeted the elites who were fueling extreme inequality. Given widespread skepticism of state-based solutions, sharing seemed a viable alternative. Leah, a special education teacher, yoga instructor, and Airbnb host and guest, explicitly linked the growth of the sharing economy to this agitation: "The whole Occupy Wall Street movement, and people identifying as being the 99 percent and not wanting to just support that 1 percent. And I think the shared economy is a way where we can get around being dependent on the 1 percent to produce everything and give us all of our media, and all of our food, and all of our oil. So I think there is some unrest that's kind of boiling up. And I think that that partially feeds it." Part of the attraction of sharing was to build a better world. And part was that the labor market was failing young people. Tyler, an aspiring musician and student who turned to TaskRabbit to make ends meet, bemoaned how difficult it was to secure a job. "Graduating with a piece of paper that said you did college doesn't really mean the same thing as it did ten years ago."

For-profit platforms were not the only sharing entities that were remaking work. There was also an upsurge of community initiatives that aimed to transform economic relations, build connections, and reduce eco-footprints. Socially motivated young people joined time banks, food and clothing swaps, and tool libraries. Repair collectives held pop-up events where they fixed appliances to save people money and obviate new purchasing. Communal batch cooking helped give "mamas" a break. These efforts offered ways to access goods and services with little or no money, via barter, loaning, gifting, and secondhand markets. Here, too, freedom was important. If people had less need for cash, they could reclaim their time and engage in socially productive work.

Most accounts of the sharing economy ignore these community initiatives. Some observers cynically think they have nothing in common with the commercial players. Others don't see enough scale to warrant attention. But the nonprofits have been integral to the sharing community and its discourse from the beginning. The proliferation of modes of exchange they are pioneering has contributed to a blurring of the line between the two groups. Olio is a food-waste app that uses a donation model, but it's a for-profit. So is TimeRepublik, a no-cash time bank. For many, the hybrid nature of the sector has been crucial to believing that a progressive transformation is under way.[8]

Before long, sharing platforms were reaching beyond social-change activists into mainstream America, attracting people like Bev—a thirty-year-old, married white woman with an MA in education. Platform work offered her the chance to leave an insecure employment situation, pursue her personal dream, and do good in the process. Bev had been working at a family-support organization when the recession hit and her hours were cut back. Looking to replace the lost income, she "stumbled" on TaskRabbit. It proved to be "empowering" on a personal level and "perfect" for its flexibility. She earned a good hourly wage—eighteen dollars was the lowest she would accept—and loved the variety of "cool tasks" and "really interesting people" she met. Customer support from the platform was great. Before too long, Bev decided to quit her regular job and start her own business. She'd grown tired of the nine-to-five lifestyle, and "knowing [she] had TaskRabbit to fall back on" allowed her to follow her "passion"—making jewelry. She loved being creative and working with her hands.

Bev's experience was similar to many of our interviewees. The money ranged from good to excellent, they loved the control over scheduling and the fact that they didn't have a boss, and they believed that the platforms had their backs. Many talked about the social and environmental benefits of the work. Their stories resonated with much of what the platforms promised: good earnings, flexibility, and the chance to be an entrepreneur. The public vibe was similarly upbeat. Sure, there were sporadic protests from taxi drivers, but as Uber cofounder Travis Kalanick rightly recognized, Taxi is the industry everyone loved to hate.[9] Sharing was cool.

Ten years later, there are still plenty of people who love the platforms, especially consumers and those with valuable assets to rent. But the gauzy optimism of Devon and Bev has been tempered by the ways companies have prioritized growth and profitability. When we reinterviewed Bev two years later, we found that despite being one of the earliest and best workers, she'd been "suspended" for failing to accept enough jobs. The company had changed its system in ways that pumped up sales and took away autonomy from the "rabbits." (Mercifully, they did rename them "taskers.") Bev downgraded her rating of the platform from an eight to a three. "I don't feel that they value individual rabbits the way they used to." Earners on lower-wage platforms also began registering their distress, as companies cut wages and overhired. The experience of Abigail, a gig worker juggling multiple jobs, suggested the chance to remake work might be slipping away.

Abigail was a twenty-eight-year-old white woman, originally from New Hampshire. She's a free spirit, who'd spent much of her twenties backpacking, hiking, even living in a van. She returned to Boston because her family needed her. Like many, she was attracted to the promise of work-life freedom that the platforms offered. But Abigail was struggling financially as she combined sporadic gigs (dog training, catering) with delivery apps DoorDash and Postmates. "No one here is making a living wage off of this app [Postmates] as far as I'm defining it. If you know you can work between thirty and forty hours a week and pay a really modest rent and put gas in your car and eat, that would be making a living wage. Working sixty hours a week is not making a living wage if you have to do that just to meet your basic expenses and you're not saving money." The problem, she noted, is "no savings, no safety net, nothing. There's no job security with these, which does sort of suck in a way." Edward, another Postmates courier, explained the dilemma: "You can have a great week or you can have a slow week. . . . You dedicate ten hours a day of your time, and you get two orders, and you make twenty-five dollars." As the decade progressed, that $2.50 an hour sat uneasily next to the millions and billions being made by platform owners and investors. "We're getting pocket change thrown at us . . . compared to how much money these people are making off of it," observed Abigail. And as unsustainable as her situation was, the stories coming from ride-hail were worse. Uber became notorious for luring drivers with false promises of earnings,[10] repeatedly squeezing pay, and deactivating workers.[11] Newspaper articles about drivers sleeping in their cars, working seventy to eighty hours a week, and earning below minimum wage became common.[12] While proponents of the platforms, such as economist Arun Sundararajan, had optimistically predicted "an end to employment,"[13] some companies seemed to be turning people into serfs.

Abigail's reference to the bottom of the pyramid highlights our finding that there's a hierarchy of platforms in terms of satisfaction, wages, and working conditions. Airbnb is at the top; Uber and Postmates are at the bottom. Discussions of "the sharing economy" often lump all platforms together or assume Uber is representative of the whole sector. Because we studied so many platforms, we saw these distinctions. But we discovered another divide, even among earners on the same platform. It's whether or not they rely on the platform to pay for basic expenses. Devon and Bev, who had good experiences, had diverse income sources and didn't need the money to live. Abigail and Edward, who are trying to eke out a living on the apps, were struggling. This analysis has been key to our understanding of the pitfalls and possibilities of platform work.

By 2018 other cracks were appearing in the facade of the idealist discourse. The "revolution" in goods sharing turned out to be a bust.[14] Studies of Uber and Lyft show that they cause congestion, increase air and carbon pollution, and pull people off public transportation.[15] These findings put the lie to the sector's green promises. Short-term rentals are contributing to gentrification, as they lead to reductions in the supply of rental housing, rising rents, and tourist takeover of central neighborhoods.[16] The platforms also raise privacy concerns. Uber execs were caught spying on critical journalists whose whereabouts they could track through their app.[17] And there's evidence that rather than leveling social differences, platforms are reinforcing them. Profile pictures enable Airbnb hosts to refuse accommodation to people of color, without fear of repercussion. #AirBnbWhileBlack surfaced widespread evidence of racial refusal.

The ambitions of community-based start-ups to solve the problems identified by the idealist discourse have mostly gone unfulfilled, especially in the United States. None has scaled like the big platforms. Many have folded. Others are viable, but we find they are reproducing aspects of the conventional economy they were hoping to escape, including race, class, and gender exclusion. By the end of the first decade, New York City, San Francisco, the state of California, and government entities around the world began passing laws to rein in companies, especially in ride-hailing and lodging. And as they did, they fed controversies that have accompanied the sector since its earliest days.

## Debating the Sharing Economy

There are already a number of books on the sharing economy. They fall into two camps—supportive and critical. The former are mainly written by industry participants, economists, and management scholars. Titles include Rachel Botsman and Roo Rogers's paean to access over ownership *(What's Mine Is Yours),* Gansky's broader take on digital innovation *(The Mesh),* and Robin Chase's *Peers, Inc.* Arun Sundararajan's *The Sharing Economy* is in this group and provides a valuable overview of the basic economics of platforms.[18] While these accounts include some discussion of potential problems and remedies, they welcome the growth of the sector and make their case largely with examples and anecdotes.

Books in the second group are written mainly by sociologists, journalists, and activists.[19] They paint Dickensian pictures of the degradation of work and the growing power of the companies. Trebor Scholz *(Uberworked and Underpaid)* looks broadly at digital labor and argues that workers are being subjected to escalating levels of insecurity and "crowd-fleecing." Steven Hill's *Raw Deal* ties platforms to a larger shift to a "freelancer society" in which workers bear all the risk and owners amass unprecedented wealth. *Gigged,* by journalist Sarah Kessler, also focuses on precarity but ultimately provides a more hopeful view with her description of a platform that opted to employ, rather than contract for, its workers. Like Scholz, Nick Srnicek *(Platform Capitalism)* situates platforms within the larger tech sector and argues that a monopolistic, rapacious "platform capitalism" is on its way. These contributions make the argument for reversing concentrated private ownership of platform capital and restructuring the economy from the bottom up.

Two recent books provide excellent, deeply researched, ethnographic accounts of the platform labor experience—Alex Rosenblat's *Uberland* and Alexandrea Ravenelle's *Hustle and Gig.* Ravenelle studied workers on four platforms and focuses mainly on the precariousness of these arrangements; the core of Rosenblat's analysis is Uber's use of algorithmic control. I engage with their findings in chapter 2. There are also books that offer alternatives—Nathan Schneider's *Everything for Everybody,* Duncan McLaren and Julian Agyeman's *Sharing Cities,* and Scholz and Schneider's *Ours to Hack and Own.* My discussion in chapter 6 owes a great deal to them. The contribution that is probably closest in spirit to this book is Tom Slee's *What's Yours Is Mine.* It's a smart and prescient account of both Airbnb and Uber. While Slee's critiques may be more biting than ours, we both believe that the ideals of sharing can be realized in a more democratic society.

How is this book different? With the exceptions of Ravenelle and Rosenblat, the aforementioned accounts are not based on primary research. We also cover a wider terrain and have a less one-sided picture than most previous accounts. But the most important difference lies in our research findings—a novel explanation of what's unique about platform labor. That analysis provided the grounds for recognizing the democratic possibilities that platforms offer.

## The Connected Consumption and Connected Economy Project

This book is based on seven years of data collection (2011–17) from the Connected Consumption and Connected Economy Project. We have done this work as a team. Core members are Will Attwood-Charles, Mehmet Cansoy, Lindsey "Luka" Carfagna, Connor Fitzmaurice, Isak Ladegaard, Robert Wengronowitz, and Samantha Eddy.[20] In some ways the trajectory of our research provides a genealogy of the sector. We started with nonprofits because we were interested in innovations that could dramatically change the experience of work. Our first case was a time bank, or task-bartering site. We added a food swap, a makerspace, and a study of people who were learning skills on platforms. As the for-profits scaled, we wanted to understand their attractions and how earners experienced working on them. Focusing on consumer services, we added Airbnb, TaskRabbit, and Turo (then called RelayRides, a peer-to-peer car rental site). We moved on to delivery (Postmates and Favor) and ride-hail (Uber and Lyft). For all these cases we mainly spoke to earners, but we also interviewed a small number of consumers. We did big data analysis on Airbnb. By this time it was 2016, and the idea of worker-owned platforms was gaining traction. Our final case was Stocksy United, a photography platform owned by the artists. Altogether, we've done thirteen cases.[21] We adopted a flexible research strategy that allowed us to parallel the growth of the sector, studying new issues as they arose.

We have done 309 formal interviews with 278 respondents across all our cases. At the nonprofits we logged hundreds of hours of ethnographic observation. We've had meetings with platform founders and employees. We've attended onboarding sessions for apps. Luka and Connor did actual trades, including two years of preparing homemade foods for a swap. Will took a class in woodworking at the makerspace and "hung out" there for a year and a half. Mehmet scraped and we later purchased large quantities of Airbnb data. I helped field the first national random sample poll on the sharing economy. We've attended multiple sharing economy conferences. Throughout the book we present this interview and ethnographic data. Where we do not provide notes citing other sources, the information comes from our own research. All quotes without accompanying notes are from our interviews.

Our quantitative analyses of Airbnb are national, but most of our interviews and all of the ethnography was done in the Boston area. Boston is a medium-sized city with a metro population just under five million. Compared to the country as a whole, it is average in terms of age and gender but has a high median household income (currently $85,691, about 1.4 times the national level) and a low poverty rate (9.6 percent). It's also whiter (70 percent) and less African American and Latinx than the general U.S. population. Another key difference is that almost half (47.6 percent) of residents have a bachelor's degree, 1.5 times more than the national average.[22] In 2006 the state of Massachusetts shifted to a health care system that insured almost everyone. It also has relatively generous assistance for people in financial need. While it suffered during the Great Recession, the presence of medical and educational institutions and the absence of a building boom spared it the severity of the downturn seen in other parts of the country.

What are the implications of our focus on one area? For qualitative data collection, knowledge of the study site is extremely valuable. Having one site also controls for factors unrelated to the platforms that vary across multiple locations. One place, however, is never representative of the whole. But is it close enough? We are confident Boston was a good choice because it avoids the extremes of San Francisco and New York—two other major places where it was possible to study sharing activity when we began. (Platforms rolled out city by city.) Because Boston is a less forbidding place to earn a living on an app than San Francisco or New York, it is more like the smaller cities platforms expanded into over the first decade. Therefore, we think it is more representative of the sector. Where we can, we augment our qualitative evidence by discussing the work of other scholars, most of whom conducted their research elsewhere.[23]

We have a wealth of findings on many issues. We have analyzed the experiences of workers on for-profit platforms and investigated the relationship between technology and the labor process. We have studied participants' motivations, including for making social change. Our research includes analyses of racial discrimination, social class exclusion, and gentrification. We have findings about the ratings mechanisms used by digital sites. We have explanations for why the nonprofit sites have been unable to grow like the for-profits. Appendix A includes more detail on our research methods, and throughout the book we provide references to the journal articles, book chapters, and other pieces we've written, most of which can be found on our project website.[24] These writings include individual cases and cross-case analyses. We were among the earliest, if not the earliest, groups to start a formal research program on this sector. Now, after nearly a decade of research, we've written this book to share what we've learned.

Finally, a word about terminology. The earliest branding of the sector was by a management consultant named Rachel Botsman, who called it "collaborative consumption."[25] Within a few years it was rechristened as the less clunky, more evocative "sharing economy." We also use that term but in a specific way. For us it denotes peer-to-peer sites serving individuals (consumers) in offline exchanges. We include both profits and nonprofits. Nonprofits have been part of the story since the beginning, and to write them out helps foreclose the future that they are working toward. That aspiration is also why we continue to use the term *sharing,* despite the many ways in which "Big Sharing" platforms are violating its meaning. According to our usage, the makerspace, the platform cooperative, and some sites in the open learning case are not technically part of the "sharing economy." In Appendix C we discuss other scholars' terminological choices and their critiques of the term, as well as why we included these cases.

## Plan of the Book

The book consists of six chapters. Chapter 1 covers the founding of the sector, including its prehistory in the counterculture of the 1960s. The early period is relevant because it's the ground in which the optimistic claims of a new way to work and the idealist discourse were seeded. This chapter also covers basics like the economics of sharing platforms and the demographics of users. We introduce our primary data in this chapter in a section on how ordinary users feel about their participation. In chapter 2 we dive into the nitty-gritty of platform labor, discussing our interviews with earners on seven commercial apps. Here we emphasize the differences among them, both within and across platforms, as well as the downward trajectory that has been occurring on some of the low-wage sites. In chapter 3 we address issues of inequality that have plagued the platforms. Our main focus is racial inequality, for which we have quantitative findings from Airbnb. We also use our interview data to discuss social class differences and how the platforms may have exacerbated them, particularly between those of high and low educational attainment. Chapter 4 takes stock of the whole, a decade into this experiment. Has the sector lived up to expectations? Relying on our own findings and those of others, we assess the major claims of economic, social, and environmental benefits. In chapter 5 we turn to our nonprofit cases. Understanding why this segment of the sector failed to scale is crucial for those who hope to exploit the real potential of sharing economies. We identify three major barriers to success for the community sites: status positioning by participants, the lack of sufficient value for users, and a "diversity fail." In chapter 6 we turn to the future, beginning with possible pathways, dystopian and utopian. We consider regulation—the dominant approach to reforming the sector—and its possibilities and obstacles. We then turn to the option of more far-reaching change, through the creation of commons and cooperatives. These are economic entities that deploy digital technology to empower workers, users, and citizens. Our final case study, a photography co-op owned by the artists, is an example of such an effort.

# 1  *From the Counterculture to "We Are the Uber of X"*

From the beginning the buzz surrounding the sharing economy was that it was about more than money. It was also a social project, a chance to remake work and build a humane alternative to global capitalism.

Mark, a twenty-five-year-old white management consultant from Boston's Back Bay neighborhood, was a true believer from the very start. "I first heard about the service while reading Rachel Botsman's *The Rise of Collaborative Consumption* [*sic*] . . . and I thought, 'Wow, this makes sense.' . . . I think it is transformative. . . . And I have enjoyed its disruptive power. . . . Right now we're seeing it in Boston with the new taxi service [Lyft] coming online." Mark loved all the new services available to him as a consumer. "[If] I need an executive assistant, I'll go to TaskRabbit and hire someone to do five hours' worth of work for me. If I need a car, I'll go to Zipcar. If I need a bike, I use Zagster—rental bikes that are in the building—or Hubway [the municipal bike-sharing service]."

Mark bought into the rhetoric about the shift from an "ownership" to an "access" economy. "So people all the time ask me why I don't get a bike. . . . It's not about whether I can afford a bike or want a bike. It's about the fact that I'm able to share fifteen hundred bikes with thousands of other people. And that I don't have to take care of it. And there's joy in pulling up to a Hubway station and you see someone waiting, and you give them that bike, and they can go on with their trip."

Like many others, Mark loved the lack of encumbrance and convenience. He also believed these services were leading people to reduce their purchases of new cars and bikes. He was an ardent environmentalist, and these things were important to him. But his main involvement in the sector was as an Airbnb host. Mark rented out his luxury apartment on a regular basis, even making it onto Airbnb's Boston "top twenty" list at one point. When we talked, he had earned $34,000 on the platform. This allowed him to remain in a place he'd originally leased when he had a partner to share the rental payments. Now he was "sharing" with strangers—in his mind, helping them when they needed a place to stay and allowing guests of modest means to enjoy the amazing location and amenities of his home. "Because life's not about money, life's about experience, life's about making this world a better place. . . . This is just my feelings about what priorities should be. Mine at my core is helping other people. This is just one medium through which I can do that and benefit financially." Throughout the interview Mark minimized his monetary motives. (We found his performance somewhat unconvincing, given the large sums he was pulling in.)

We'll return to Mark's story later, as renting got a bit more complicated than he'd bargained for. Here our point is that he believed strongly in the good that sharing represented, a view that was widely held among our respondents. Like Mark, Jason was a twentysomething single white man. We recruited him as someone who rented out his car on Turo, but he was also an employee of the platform. "When I graduated college, I wanted to work for a company that I felt was really kind of doing something, at least, somewhat good. I wasn't necessarily out to save the world. I wanted . . . something that I really believed in and didn't really want to be in a large sort of faceless corporation. I definitely feel that when I'm at Turo and it's great."

Stephanie, a former special education teacher and caterer, believed that fate had brought her to TaskRabbit after she successfully used the platform to start her own personal assistant business. She loved "being able to help other people," especially the "strong, amazing women" who became her clients.

Devon (the Jamerican we met in the introduction), Mark, Jason, Stephanie, and many of our respondents believed in the "idealist discourse."[1] Its major tenets are efficiency and economic empowerment, lower eco-impact, and social connection—benefits that were widely touted. Why was the idealist discourse so compelling, especially when its "everyone will win" claim was implausible on its face? Yes, it jibed with self-interest, as we saw with Mark. And the presence of nonprofits allowed the corporate players to bask under the moral halo of sharing.[2] But the hegemony, or commonsensicalness, of the discourse also drew on a powerful faith in technology. For centuries new machines and methods of communications have arrived with outsized hopes about their ability to change the world.[3] Sharing initiatives were mainly greeted with technological enthusiasm, which attracted users and propelled growth.[4] This technophilia wasn't just a passion of the moment. It can be traced back decades, to the invention of personal computers and belief in their social powers.[5] Understanding this history helps explain why platforms raised such hopes and went so wrong.

## The Californian Ideology

The 1960s counterculture that was centered in San Francisco is now mostly famous for psychedelic drugs, "flower power," and the Grateful Dead. But in its heyday it posed a profound challenge to modern society, in the form of a critique of concentrated power and a desire for egalitarian social relations. Fred Turner, in his book *From Counterculture to Cyberculture*, has identified two strains of the counterculture—antiwar and free speech activists such as Berkeley's Mario Savio, who helped form the New Left, and the "New Communalists," who decamped to rural sites around the West to form small-scale communities. Both groups were rooted in an antibureaucratic ethic, but they took different paths. The New Left retained a political focus—opposing the military, the corporations that supported it, and the U.S. government. They viewed technology through the lens of war, as a destructive, dehumanizing force.[6] New Communalists rejected politics as part of the problem and saw technology as a solution. Their bible was Stuart Brand's *Whole Earth Catalog,* which was known for its innovative gadgets and technical offerings. When personal computing and the internet developed in the 1990s, New Communalists hailed them as the route to the ecotopias they had failed to create in their back-to-the-land phase.

The New Communalists' views morphed into what became known as the Californian Ideology.[7] It combined libertarian politics, countercultural aesthetics, and techno-utopian visions.[8] Its core belief was that technology would yield personal liberation and egalitarian community. Individuals could now determine their own fates, as personal computers plus the internet offered ways to earn money without relying on a bureaucratic institution.[9] The financial accessibility of computers meant that everyone could join in as equals. The vision was of a high-tech Jeffersonian world[10] populated by small-scale asset-holders who self-govern in "harmonious community."[11] Many of these ideas would carry over into the original discourse of the sharing economy—personal empowerment through decentralized task-based work, egalitarianism, and community. An additional dimension of New Communalist thinking—cybernetics, the study of machine-based control—is also present in the design of sharing platforms. It focused on information, feedback loops, and self-correcting mechanisms, which appeared as dynamic algorithms, surge pricing, and crowd-sourced data.[12]

As it happened, the gelling of the Californian Ideology coincided with the neoliberal policy turn of the 1980s. Cyberutopians jumped on the "free market" bandwagon,* combining "the free-wheeling spirit" of hippies with the "entrepreneurial zeal" of yuppies.[13] In the process they came to believe in what Thomas Frank calls "market populism," the view that "markets enjoyed some mystic, organic connection to the people while governments were fundamentally illegitimate."[14] Technology corporations were heralded as agents of revolution,[15] and the task of those in the digital vanguard was to free the companies from the pesky regulations of government bureaucrats.[16] The crucial intellectual move here was the conflation of individual liberty with freedom for corporations, an equivalence that made sense to cyberutopians who had been heavily engaged with Silicon Valley companies for years.[17] The 1996 Telecommunications Act deregulated the sector, and platforms such as Google, Facebook, and Amazon morphed into monopolies with virtually no opposition. Twenty years later, sharing platforms, many of which have been funded by the tech giants, would adopt the same antiregulatory stance and also become monopolies. While the path from New Communalism to the sharing economy is yet to be fully researched, there is a through line of location, people, and ideology.[18]

For some, the history of Silicon Valley is a case of genuinely transformative ideas and technologies gone awry. But it's a more complicated story. From the beginning many believed that the software itself would ensure good outcomes—a strong technological determinism. It's now clear this view was wrong. Unregulated markets frequently lead to monopolies, particularly in tech.[19] The popular equation of democracy and the internet is also fatuous, as recent political

---

* I use the term *free market* somewhat ironically here because most markets are heavily structured by government policy, and many are subsidized. The "free" part mostly refers to the freedoms of companies.

events have made clear.[20] And in retrospect we can see that entitlement played an important role in solidifying the Californian Ideology. Adherents were mostly white, highly educated, well-off men who lived in a bubble of privilege they failed to recognize. It's not surprising they came to believe that technology would be sufficient to solve the problem of social inequality.

Even as massive corporations came to dominate Silicon Valley, there was another option. Some programmers were building free and open-source software in a digital commons, engaging in what came to be known as peer production.[21] This community avoided the determinism that had misled cyberutopians, holding instead to a middle ground in which digital tech made new social relations possible—but only if we chose to create them. These ideas animated many of the nonprofit alternatives that became part of the sharing economy, often under the rubric of the collaborative commons movement. But commons thinking was not influential among the for-profit sharing companies. They were more embedded in right-wing libertarian ideology, a positioning that would prove fateful as they scaled.

## Founding the Platforms

Some years ago, I collaborated with colleagues from Harvard Business School to figure out what makes consumers trust companies with idealist discourses.[22] One answer was a humble origin story. We found lots of "I accidentally discovered this recipe in my garage . . ." tales in the grocery store. Sharing platforms also adopted these origin stories to sell their brands. The best known is from Brian Chesky, a cofounder of Airbnb. In 2007, a few years after graduating from the Rhode Island School of Design as an industrial designer, Chesky quit his stable job. Short on cash to make rent on his loft in pricey San Francisco, he and his roommate bought some air mattresses to rent out in their living room. They threw up a website and targeted visitors to the upcoming Industrial Designers of America conference, who were facing a problem of sold-out hotels. As they say, the rest is history. TaskRabbit innovator Leah Busque claims to have thought up her company's model one cold Boston evening when she had run out of dog food for her pet lab, Kobe. "Wouldn't it be nice if there was a place online I could go to connect with my neighbors—maybe one who was already at the store at that very moment—who could help me out?"[23] Like many other founders, Busque draws on tropes of efficiency, neighborliness, and common sense.

Fitting with its brand, Uber has a less populist origin tale, but it also draws on a relatable consumer dilemma. In the late 2000s, San Francisco software entrepreneur Garrett Camp was at war with the taxi industry. He couldn't find rides, had been blackballed by dispatchers for his frequent cancellations, and got charged $1,000 for a private driver on New Year's Eve. Before long, he teamed up with fellow entrepreneur Travis Kalanick to found Uber.[24] Lyft's story started in Zimbabwe, where Logan Green saw passengers using shared minivan taxis, a common practice in many Global South countries, as well as some low-income neighborhoods in the U.S. Impressed by this example, Green and John Zimmer started Zimride (from Zimbabwe), focusing on long-distance travel to and from college campuses. They debuted at Cornell, a famously isolated university. The platform was more convenient than bulletin boards for matching riders and drivers and preferable to Craigslist because it linked users to Facebook, which allowed them to research each other before committing. In 2012 Green and Zimmer started Lyft, which offered short rides in urban areas. The company emphasized its friendliness and adopted the idealist discourse, promising lower carbon emissions and good treatment of drivers.

While 2008–9 is generally considered the beginning of collaborative consumption, some platforms were already operating. Couchsurfing began in 1991 after Casey Fenton, needing lodging for a trip to Iceland, hacked into the university database and sent fifteen hundred emails to students asking for a place to stay.[25] Craigslist and eBay were founded in 1995 and prefigured key features of later platforms—the peer-to-peer (P2P) structure and ratings systems.[26] Other goods exchanges debuted soon after, including Freecycle, a gifting site. In 2000 Zipcar was founded by Antje Danielson and Robin Chase, with the aim of reducing environmental impact by getting urbanites to forgo car ownership.[27] (In the end Zipcar didn't reduce carbon emissions because it facilitated access to cars and pulled people off public transportation, in a classic case of unintended consequences.)[28] Chase had originally planned a P2P structure but couldn't get insurance companies to cover the rentals. In 2010 three Harvard Business School students went ahead with the P2P model anyway and started RelayRides.[29]

## We Are the "Uber of X"

Within a few years startups were being founded at a frenzied pace, with many describing themselves as "the Uber of x."[30] Investors poured an astonishing $23 billion into the sector between 2010 and 2017.[31] Researchers began predicting that Uberization "might replace the modern corporation."[32] One journalist cataloged 105 American "Uber for x's" founded between 2009 and 2019.[33] Transportation sites offered real-time ridesharing (with drivers who were making trips for their own purposes rather than to earn), jitney services, and apps that promised to treat drivers better than Uber and Lyft. Peer-to-peer rental schemes emerged for boats, airplanes, bicycles, and cars left at airports while their owners were traveling. In lodging, the offerings were less varied, perhaps because Airbnb had hit upon a winning formula.[34] Platforms specializing in "idle capacity" grew, offering parking spaces, yards (for gardening), attics, and storage space. Sites to trade, loan, rent, buy, sell, or give away personal goods appeared, including specialized apps for camping gear, textbook rental, electronics, and tools. In 2012 former Sierra Club president Adam Werbach and colleagues founded Yerdle, which used a hip vibe to appeal to young adults who might be willing to borrow or rent rather than buy new.

There were also platforms that offer labor services to individual customers. TaskRabbit provided "rabbits" who would do any (reasonable and legal) task a "poster" (client) needed done. While rabbits did all sorts of things, common tasks were delivery, house cleaning, home repair, driving, and IKEA furniture pickup and assembly.[35] (IKEA bought the platform in 2017.) Delivery apps such as Postmates, Caviar, UberEats, DoorDash, and Grubhub concentrated on restaurant food. Favor debuted by offering to deliver anything for five dollars, plus a two-dollar tip.[36] Platforms provided artisanal food prepared in the customer's home (Kitchensurfing, now shuttered) or delivered. EWSAs, or Eat With Strangers Apps, organized meals at the cook's dwelling (Feastly and Eat With). The sector also offered household repair (Takl), house cleaning (Handy), babysitting (Sitter-City, UrbanSitter), pet care (DogVacay, Rover), and human care (Care.com is the industry leader). Suddenly there were platforms for just about everything—sports coaching, tutoring, tour guiding, at-home beauticians, line cooks, laundry and dry-cleaning pickup. There are even dedicated apps for alcohol purchase and delivery.[37]

## Ordinary Users and the Idealist Discourse

As platforms proliferated, users flocked to them in hopes that while they were earning or saving, they were also helping to change the world.[38] Our informants repeated the "scripts" we heard from consultants and companies, referencing the three categories of benefit (economic, social, and environmental). This optimistic spin was partly attributable to the fact that participants on both sides of the market were young, highly educated, and relatively privileged.[39] Courtney, an Airbnb host who worked at an environmental nonprofit, explained that although money was her motive, "first and foremost . . . I think also just in terms of how it aligns with my values. . . . I get all my books from the library, I value shared resources, I think the bike share programs are awesome. I just love all those kind of sharing, anticonsumerism, not-wasting-resources things." Like Courtney, many of our interviewees were entranced with the idea of preventing waste and using resources more efficiently, which they saw as the route to less production and environmental impact. Amelie, an Airbnb host, explained the logic: "If you use Turo you're not paying Avis—a car rental agency—you're paying the person whose car you're renting, which was probably sitting around anyway. So it's just a more efficient system." We pressed her to explain the reasoning: "Well, because Avis probably buys thousands and thousands of cars to rent out to people, and then they just sit around. But if I have a car, it's sitting in my driveway all day and I can rent it to somebody else, then that's reducing the need at Avis to purchase those cars. So it's using the resources we have more efficiently."

Respondents were emotionally invested in the idealist discourse, so with few exceptions, they ignored logics and evidence that undermined it. Most failed to think through the environmental impacts of the incipient commercialization of activity. If people buy additional apartments or vehicles for the purpose of renting them out or drivers acquire new cars to stay compliant with platform requirements, the ecological savings are muted. When we challenged Jason on his environmental claims by pointing out that Turo offered easier and cheaper access to cars, he admitted: "I never really thought about it. That's an interesting question."

The appeal of personalized exchange came up repeatedly in our data, most often in relation to Airbnb but also on TaskRabbit and even Turo, where personal contact was fairly minimal. Margaret, a

TaskRabbit earner, took great satisfaction in the social aspects of the work: "I like to serve but I love people. I don't just want to do a good job at the end of the day. . . . I like the connection I have with people. . . . It's very relational for me." Barb, who was also on Task-Rabbit, summed up her view: "Yes, you're getting paid for it, but it's also people helping other people where they have a need." And of course on some platforms there was always the possibility of developing lasting relationships. Peter, an Airbnb host, recalled his favorite guest—an immigration lawyer from Paris who stayed for six weeks. He and his wife had become "kind of like family to her. . . . We're actually still really good friends with her." Hope, a twenty-nine-year-old white teacher, contrasted the authenticity of the sharing economy with the ersatz and coerced social interaction at her previous job as a supermarket cashier. With TaskRabbit "I can be that nice girl, and be myself, and not be, like, Trader Joe's fake nice, where they were like, you need to be more talkative with the customers blah blah blah."

Platforms also offered an escape from the corporate grind and an alternative to an unappealing nine-to-five job, as we saw with Abigail. Our respondents value autonomy and personal agency. Eric was attempting to survive without going back to a corporate world that he found alienating by being active on a number of different platforms. "I haven't worked in several years, and I kind of like that. . . . I'm hoping that I can design a lifestyle where I work a modest amount and receive, okay, obviously a modest amount. . . . And collaborative consumption is a way actually to do that." Leah, who was both an Airbnb host and guest, saw sharing entities as a cure for corporate alienation: "I know so many people today who work jobs where they're kind of isolated. They're in a cubicle with a box, their computer, all day long. And I think that [the sharing economy] provides an outlet as we continue to upload our lives online. It is another opportunity to connect with people." While almost no one used the language of microentrepreneur, quite a few saw platforms as the route to independence, autonomy, and freedom.

Some even went further, seeing platforms as the antidote to big corporations or even to capitalism itself. Suhani, who was active on many platforms, explained her preference for Airbnb: "If I took a hotel, say, Marriott in Texas, right? It's fine. But Marriott has got a board of directors sitting somewhere in a million-dollar house. But this lady is a photographer who owns this house. And as a photographer, maybe she's not earning that much. It'll help her house payment if I was supporting the local business. . . . The Marriott guys don't really need it. They have a lot of money." Like many of the people we interviewed, Suhani prefers to keep money in the local economy. "So that was my idea—support local." Natasha, a Turo renter and Airbnb customer, summed up the rhetoric: "We're putting money right in the pocket of the community we were visiting, skipping the middle man. So that felt good." Participants in the nonprofits also saw their activities as an alternative to capitalism, especially those in the time bank.

Across both types of sites our informants criticized global supply chains, corporate conformity, and exploitative and alienating social relations. We found an inchoate but powerful nostalgia, in which the sharing economy was envisioned as a household space, what we term a "domestic imaginary."[40] Production takes place within the home, social relations are familial, and the aesthetic is cozy. In contrast to the cold and impersonal corporation, this new market operates like a family, rooted in a past place and time.

Overall, the platforms and their boosters did a good job of convincing early users that there was nothing ahead but win-wins. Their rhetoric tapped into common sense so effectively that few applied basic critical thinking to recognize that the future held far more complexity than the cheerleading allowed. This was less true of platform employees, who were more aware of problems, and researchers, who from the beginning debated the pros and cons of sharing platforms, especially their economics.[41]

## The Economics of the Platforms

The conversation about what is propelling the growth of the platform sector has broken down along familiar lines. One group—mainstream economists, management scholars, and the companies—points to digital innovation and market structure, in particular algorithms, crowdsourced information, and network effects.[42] Sociologists, legal scholars, and political economists point to platforms' ability to exploit the labor and capital of sellers and to evade regulation. Both sides have a point.

Sharing platforms are "two-sided markets," whose function is to coordinate individual buyers and sellers.[43] Traditionally, anonymous person-to-person markets have been stymied by the time involved in searching for the right match (think yard sales) and the risk of transacting with an unknown individual. Platform technology solves both problems. Algorithms reduce or eliminate search time by creating matches and filtering options. In ride-hail, algorithms can also cut costs by reducing what economists call "wild goose chases,"[44] as drivers roam around looking for passengers.[45] While our respondents didn't complain too much about the algorithms, they can make mistakes, which can cost earners valuable income. Vinni, a Postmates bicycle courier, recounted landing up at a high-end restaurant one evening: "They hand me these big orders. . . . I'm on a bike and I can't take like five boxes of pizza." Don, another cycle courier, explained that the app can't keep things straight between bikes and cars: "A week and a half ago I had an order come in for two hundred bottles of Fiji water. There's no way I'm going to be able to get that."

The second mechanism that enables P2P markets is the crowdsourcing of ratings. In the sharing economy, exchanges take place among strangers, often in intimate settings, which raises issues of quality, safety, and malfeasance. In the conventional economy, trust is produced either via brand reputation (for large companies) or local knowledge (for neighborhood businesses), neither of which is present with stranger sharing.[46] Ratings and reputational data (and, in some cases, insurance) give people the confidence to enter into trades with people they don't know.[47] Of course, not everyone is convinced. Tawana, a young African American blogger who used sharing sites as a consumer, explained: "'Oh, don't worry. If you rate your Lyft driver then you'll be safe.' But what if they kill me before I can rate them?"

There has been a lot written about the ratings systems,[48] and we'll have more to say about them later. While most of our informants didn't have issues with ratings, a few were tyrannized by them. Karim, a down-on-his-luck young immigrant, was deactivated by Uber after customer complaints. He couldn't figure out how he was supposed to act, as the company told him not to talk and also to be friendly. "You drive me crazy! What you like? Like white or black?" Karim ended up purchasing a camera to protect himself against passengers' negative reports: "Sometimes people just, they don't like how you look, they give you a bad rating."

The third factor that economic analysts credit for the sector's success is that on platforms the value of a service is enhanced when more people use it. As Uber gets more drivers, it attracts consumers because service is faster, which in turn entices more drivers to join. This "network effect" propels growth. I've used the example of Uber because it has advertised its ambitions to be another Amazon, a platform where network effects are substantial.[49] But Uber and most other sharing services are face-to-face and local, which means that network effects fall off fairly quickly.[50] If there are so many drivers that one is always waiting outside my door, rides become exorbitantly expensive because idling time skyrockets. Skepticism about the strength of network effects leads political economists to focus on another explanation for growth, which is the power platforms have over workers and governments.

To understand the political economy of platforms, we need to begin with their prehistory. In the 1980s companies began sending production offshore, to places with low wages, low taxes, and lax environmental standards. Nike was the poster child of global outsourcing, but eventually, the transfer of costs and risks onto workers, taxpayers, and communities became commonplace domestically as well.[51] A crucial switch was from full-time employees for whom the company has many responsibilities, to part-timers, temps, independent contractors, and other "precarious" laborers. Sharing platforms have taken this "fissuring" process to another level.[52] Almost all of them engage providers as independent contractors. Angelo, a courier, thought the system was unfair: "Instead of being an employee, you're an independent contractor now. I understand it with certain companies, [but] not with these big companies, like Uber and Lyft. I don't work for them, but I feel like they're making so much money. Just like these restaurants that have these people working for three dollars an hour as base pay and then tips. It's ridiculous. Like no, your profits are in the millions, hundreds of millions. You can afford to pay an hourly wage." Mitch, who was combining Lyft, Postmates, and DoorDash as he tried to build an audio-engineering business, also considered the whole setup problematic. "Is it fair to me to have to own, pay for, maintain my own car, gas, insurance, parking, cleaning, dealing with the smell of food in my car? . . . Sometimes the smell doesn't go away. And I have to spend all these hours driving around town." Not only do workers provide the tools and pay all the expenses, but independent contractor status also lets the company off the hook for social security contributions, workman's compensation, and unemployment insurance. The companies have also outsourced quality control and human resource functions onto consumers, through the ratings systems.

The other political economy factor is regulation. From the beginning many platforms have evaded, opposed, or outright disobeyed laws and regulations that constrain their activities, especially in the United States. In the case of ride-hailing, breaking the law was crucial to breaking the taxi industry. I'll return to this issue in chapter 6. My point here is that understanding the business model requires recognizing the ways in which successful platforms have been able to wield power over those they transact with and to escape the power of the state.

## Reasonable Hope or Rampant Hype?

Many observers predicted that sharing platforms were a tsunami that would roll over conventional businesses. TaskRabbit founder Leah Busque reported that the company's goal was to "revolutionize the world's labor force."[53] Critic Steven Hill saw them as the "tip of the iceberg" that's remaking the U.S. economy.[54] Perhaps the swift demise of the taxi business contributed to the view that the sector was unstoppable. But the taxi industry was unusual because of its long history of licensing and medallions.[55] So far the evidence suggests that these predictions are exaggerated.[56] Only the big three (Lyft, Uber, and Airbnb) have really scaled—with valuations in mid-2019 of $15 billion, $72 billion, and $31 billion, respectively.[57] Delivery also has a few platforms that are worth more than a billion. But among the other four cases in our research none was remotely close in value.[58] From the list of 105 platforms referenced above, only four made unicorn status ($1 billion valuation); 27 percent are gone, and 18 percent have been acquired.[59]

The most vulnerable segment was P2P goods sharing and renting, the bedrock of the "access" society. Most failed so quickly we weren't even able to research them. SnapGoods, Mootch, ShareSomeSugar, and others shuttered for lack of take-up. Yerdle went into partnership with retailers to encourage recycling. Neighbor-goods morphed into a lifestyle site. Peerby, from famously frugal Amsterdam, has had success there but not in the U.S. Landshare failed, as did Spinlister. Americans' appetite for sharing personal possessions was decidedly tepid. In our national survey only 31 percent wanted to do more of it, with the same number disagreeing.[60]

Failures also litter the landscape in general labor services. Task-Rabbit went through two "pivots" (or transformations of its business model) before being acquired. Zaarly abandoned this market within a year.[61] AgentAnything and HomeJoy both disappeared without a trace.[62] Specialized platforms have had more success. Airbnb has an attractive financial model, partly because it keeps its fees reasonable and provides security through insurance. Its troubles lie with urban residents, who want to control its growth. But even at a smaller size it will be profitable. The economics of ride-hail are rather different, however, and a giant question mark hovers over this sector. Uber has lost nearly $20 billion since 2014, including $5 billion in the third quarter of 2019.[63] Lyft is following a similar path.[64] Is the future likely to bring anything more than these oceans of red ink?

Transportation economist Hubert Horan says no, at least not unless regulators hand Uber global market dominance. In Horan's view, its basic economics don't warrant its outsized valuation or even run-of-the-mill profitability, as it has neither a unique or especially efficient product, strong network effects, nor particularly low costs. He calculated that Uber has been subsidizing each ride to the tune of 41 percent, meaning passengers were paying only 59 percent of the cost of the fare.[65] This is only possible because the company has had nearly unlimited levels of investment capital. In fact, Uber has run through more capital than any start-up in history.[66] Its lack of profitability is why Uber has been squeezing its drivers relentlessly, but that, of course, creates new costs because they must spend to attract and retain drivers.

Daria was a savvy twenty-year-old white woman from a working-class family who'd been a bicycle courier on Favor. She described herself as a "failed opera singer . . . [and] failed software entrepreneur." More than most of our informants, she was skeptical about the hype. "Favor is not a real company. Like they just have a bunch of investment money. Are they making a profit? No way. It's a bubble. It's going to burst. . . . Yeah, I would put a lot of money on Favor is not making money." Daria reasoned that the pricing structure on the app was inefficient, with the wrong mix between delivery fee, tipping, and volume. This led to underpayment of couriers, which wasn't sustainable. As someone who had worked in start-ups, she thought the root of the problem was easy money from investors. "Money from angel investors is just not going to make you a business if you're relying on millions and millions of dollars in funding to do something that we can do with $200," by which she meant couriers buying bikes and organizing the work themselves. "Nothing personal but like it's all just investment and it's all going to go down the toilet."

All along, we were also dubious about the business model in delivery and ride-hail. In the latter the strategy appeared to be a classic power grab—offer below-cost fares to wipe out the competition, create a monopoly, and raise prices. But demand would drop off with higher fares, unless consumers didn't have other options. Public transportation was the main alternative. Is that why rates for Uber Pool were dropped to parity with public systems, which began losing ridership across the country? In its IPO documents, where the company is required to be truthful, Uber did name public transportation as a competitor—thereby giving the lie to its pronouncements to the contrary.[67] (It quickly retracted its admission.)[68] And from the beginning Uber had not only an economic approach (below-cost pricing) but a political one, with intense lobbying and heavyweight investors (Google, JP Morgan, Goldman Sachs, BlackRock, and later, Fidelity, Bezos, and Toyota, among others). But the technology of ride-hail and delivery is replicable, which means that other platforms can compete.[69] In 2019 analysts finally began to raise doubts about the company's path to profitability, and its IPO led to the largest first day dollar loss in history.[70] It is well past the time when Uber should be showing robust revenues relative to costs, raising the possibility that it is less wondrous unicorn than, to quote economist Yves Smith, "a textbook 'bezzle'—John Kenneth Galbraith's coinage for an investment swindle where the losses have yet to be recognized."[71]

## Beyond Capitalism?

In May of 2014 the sharing economy held its "coming out" party in the historic Marines' Memorial Theater in downtown San Francisco. Organized by a new nonprofit called Peers, it brought together a heady mix of platform founders, venture capitalists, nonprofits, consultants, lay enthusiasts, community critics, and a few researchers. Just about everyone was there, with the exception of Uber. Its competitor, Lyft, gave free rides to attendees. Airbnb sent cofounder Nate Blecharczyk and held a reception at its headquarters. Community sharing initiatives were well represented, from people who were running tool libraries to a law collaborative helping to set up cooperatively owned platforms.[72] The cofounders of Peers, Natalie Foster and Douglas Atkin, had stellar progressive resumes.[73] They invited serious critics and groups who weren't naturally inclined to support the sector. Speakers decried the fortunes being made by platform founders and investors and the lack of access for people of color.

While the usual talking points of the idealistic discourse were very much in evidence, the conversation went further. Douglas Atkin told me the plan was that sharing would "replace capitalism."[74] Even venture capitalists joined the system-bashing. An early, prolific investor in the sector, Shervan Pishevar, told a personal story about visiting an Irish village where a lot of sharing was happening. This was leading people to "revert" to where we came from, "thousands of years ago," and led him to an epiphany: "The way the world has been structured is with injustice in the system." It's time to "gain control and give it back to people." Venture Capitalist Brad Burnham talked about how the fortunes being made by platform founders would be eroded and predicted that a true sharing economy wouldn't need financiers. This echoed language I'd heard from other sharing economy founders, such as Charley Wang, who started Josephine, a meal-preparation platform that specialized in helping immigrant women cooks. He described his team as "postcapitalists," whose aim was to move from the ultracommoditized food system to a human, relationship-oriented one. Their for-profit status, he explained, was merely "strategic." It was hard not to get caught up in the enthusiasm. Here we were, in the heart of San Francisco, revisiting the very same issues that had animated the counterculture decades earlier. We were all well-meaning pioneers building a truly human, flat, empowering alternative to the disaster that is global capitalism.

Of course, not everyone bought into the warm and fuzzy. Some even had the bad manners to point out that Peers cofounder Atkin was also global head of community at Airbnb and that the organization was not a grassroots movement of sharing enthusiasts but an "astroturf" effort by the companies financing it. Those happened to be Airbnb, TaskRabbit, Lyft, and the Omidyar Foundation, started by eBay founder Pierre Omidyar, who had recently invested in Couchsurfing as it went for-profit.[75] Was the real agenda one that wasn't on the program at the Marines' Memorial Theater, namely to organize hosts, drivers, consumers, and other participants to fight the regulatory pushback that was beginning in San Francisco and New York?[76] Would Pishevar's touching story have been less convincing if we in the audience knew he was an Uber strategic adviser and major ally of Travis Kalanick?

As it turned out, Peers didn't stick. Within the year Foster was gone, and the organization underwent one of those famous Silicon Valley pivots, disappearing into the ether. But the questions its conversation raised were the same ones that cyberutopians had been discussing decades earlier. Did the technological innovations portend a fundamentally new economic system, as the earlier generation had argued? Was a new world of work on the horizon? Or did genuine transformation require doing away with ownership by VCs and founders? Was the sharing economy capable of delivering on the idealist discourse, much less its postcapitalist rhetoric? Or was this all wishful thinking because platform capitalism would turn out to be even worse than what it was disrupting? To answer these questions, we need to take a closer look at the sector, starting with the experiences of people who were working on the platforms.

# 2   *Earning on the Platforms*

When they launched, the platforms offered a dramatically different way to work. They gave freedoms that few employers do, such as the ability to work when and as much as wanted. They did away with direct supervision. Some platforms let workers set their own wage rates. These are features of jobs that most of our earners and the majority of gig workers desire.[1] For Juan Romero all these factors came into play.

Juan is an enterprising young man who emigrated from Latin America to Florida when he was sixteen. He soon graduated from college, earned an MA in accounting, and settled into full-time employment. Then the 2008 financial crash devastated the Florida economy. It claimed his parents' jobs and their homes and sent his company into a cycle of repeated downsizings. He rightly figured that prospects in Massachusetts were better and secured a good position in his field there. When his brother, who was at MIT, told him about TaskRabbit, he and his wife got active on the site, and it became a big part of their lives. To Juan it was fantastic. TaskRabbit earnings were "walking around money," which allowed them to take weekend trips, buy furniture, and when his wife got pregnant, build their "baby fund." Plus, he explained, they learned the city, met new people, and did interesting and fun things. Juan started with less skilled work, doing deliveries, IKEA assembly, and errands. But he felt the money on those jobs (fifteen dollars to eighteen dollars an hour) was below his educational level, and he hated getting caught in traffic. So he shifted to online tasks such as accounting, virtual assistant work, stenography, and translation. (He knows three languages.) Coming from an entrepreneurial family, he quickly segued into using the platform to start minibusinesses. He subcontracted out the routine parts of accounting tasks to his own virtual assistant (a woman in the Philippines) to maximize his earnings per job. He took translation jobs, hired people to do the work from Odesk (a global, digital labor platform, now called Upwork), and took a large fraction of the fee for himself (between 30 and 50 percent). While he had a few small criticisms of the platform, and derided himself for getting "too greedy" at one point, his overall experience was great. He considered the money "amazing," especially during the six months they were saving for the baby. "I think it's kind of hard to beat the I'm-my-own-boss feeling. That's sort of what it was. I mean, it gave you a sense of empowerment that you can make as much money as you want to make because you will get only what you put in." He did admit that "you can get pretty obsessed with this. . . . Instead of laying around the house, you feel guilty if you're not working." But Juan considered the platform the "ultimate" capitalist tool, in the best possible way. No longer active when we did a follow-up interview, Juan explained that TaskRabbit wasn't available in Florida, where he and his wife had returned to be near his parents after the baby arrived. But he retained some of the accounting clients he met on the platform and wished he still had the opportunities it offered.

If you're at all familiar with debates about the treatment of workers on platforms, Juan's experience may seem unusual, even suspect. Negative accounts of platform earners—detailing repeated wage cuts, mistreatment, and control by algorithm—have become commonplace. But the characterization of workers as "Uberworked and

Underpaid,"[2] to borrow Trebor Scholz's evocative title, is only one story of platform work. And in our research it was by no means the most common. To be sure, we found informants who were exploited, miserable, and living hand-to-mouth. They had plenty of complaints about the platforms. But in contrast to the polarized debate between the companies ("We offer flexibility, great earnings and the chance to be your own boss!") and their critics ("Platforms are the next phase in the degradation of labor!"), we discovered something else.[3]

In accounts of platform jobs, workers' experiences are typically considered homogeneous—either good or bad. We found this somewhat puzzling because we were seeing a mixed picture. Some, like Juan, were happy and making plenty of money. Others were struggling and unhappy. What was especially curious was that this was true even on the same platform. As we started to analyze why an identical setup yielded varied outcomes, we developed an alternative understanding of platform work.

Our finding runs counter to a common, albeit tacit, assumption in most labor scholarship—that when people have the same job at the same workplace, they will have similar experiences. Everyone has to follow common rules, faces a uniform pay structure, and operates in the same market. This assumption made sense in the postwar labor regime because employers exercised a great deal of direct control over employees. But does it still? Surprisingly, given all the rhetoric about the disruptiveness of platform technology, this upending of the labor experience has been mostly ignored. Platforms give workers choices over aspects of the job that conventional employers typically don't. That freedom is the lynchpin for understanding what's unique about platform labor.

In the pages that follow I'll delve into our findings, which cover earners on seven platforms. The fact that we had so many platforms is unusual among research projects and was a big part of how we discovered what we did. I've already noted that workers' experiences are not uniform, with variation in pay rates, job satisfaction, and how they do the work. As we saw these differences playing out at individual companies, we realized that they are explained by how dependent the worker is on income from the platform to pay basic living expenses. The two dominant approaches to platform work—algorithmic management and the precariousness of independent contracting—have largely failed to account for this diversity of outcomes and its significance. That means they have also missed the underlying conditions which have led to so much diversity, which we call the "retreat from control." In contrast to conventional employers, platforms allow workers to choose their schedules and number of hours worked, and do not directly supervise the labor process. That accounts for the "empowerment" many of our respondents describe. Some platforms do try to gain back some of that control, which we'll explain. But for the most part, in comparison to ordinary employers, they cede important decisions to earners.

We have other findings. One is that there's a hierarchy of companies in terms of pay and working conditions, including the degree of freedom workers do have. Another is that conditions are deteriorating for workers on some platforms, as the number of earners grows and the companies cut rates. Thus, there is variation across people, platforms, and time. But before turning to these findings, I provide some details on the sharing workforce, our sample, and the logistics of the platforms.

## The Sharing Workforce

Researchers still don't have a firm estimate of the size of the platform workforce, its rate of growth, or its demographic composition. A long-awaited effort by the Bureau of Labor Statistics to measure the broader "contingent" workforce excluded most platform earners.[4] Survey estimates of the fraction of individuals participating in online or digitally-enabled "gig labor" vary from an estimate of 3 percent earning in the previous month (from a recent Federal Reserve study) to 8 percent participating in the last year.[5] There's also debate about how fast the platform labor force is increasing, with data from bank accounts showing a doubling since 2014. One uncontested finding is the extraordinary increase in drivers.[6] Another feature of platform participation is that 60 to 70 percent of households earn for only a few months a year.[7] As a result, among participating households earnings constitute only 20 percent of total take-home income.[8] Unfortunately, these studies don't include much demographic detail. The Federal Reserve study reported that younger workers are much more likely to do gig work, which is a consistent finding across all studies. We also know that drivers are disproportionately men and care workers are predominantly women. But beyond that we can't say too much, as existing studies have conflicting findings on gender, race, and educational attainment.

As a reminder, we studied lodging, car rental, errands, delivery, and ride-hailing platforms. Our sample doesn't replicate the sector as a whole, and we don't have equal numbers of participants in each of our cases. (We have many more Airbnb hosts and taskers than drivers, for example.) We did initially use methods to ensure a random selection of respondents; however, in some cases we needed to alter our recruitment.[9] Our methods are discussed in Appendix A. In Appendix B we provide summary tables of the demographic makeup of our respondents. Among our 129 earners, 33 percent are women and 66 percent men.[10] They're 59 percent white, 10 percent Asian, 14 percent black, and 10.5 percent Latinx. Race varies a lot by platform, with 69 percent of Airbnb hosts being white, in contrast to 31 percent of Uber and Lyft drivers. Our average age is twenty-nine, although that's partly an artifact of our sampling strategy—when we began participants were almost all young, so we restricted our respondents to the eighteen-to-thirty-four age range. For comparability over time, we mainly kept to that strategy.[11]

The most striking aspect of our sample is its high education levels. That's true of the sector nationally, but we're also in a highly educated part of the country. Overall, 47.6 percent of our earners have college degrees, and 25.8 percent have a postgraduate degree. Only 7.3 percent have only a high school education or less, and many of those who have only some college are current students who will go on to earn degrees. An even more striking characteristic is parental education levels. The fraction with mothers or fathers with a college or a graduate degree is 60 percent and 62 percent, respectively. This high educational attainment is due to a combination of factors. These include a true reflection of the sharing labor force, the fact that we started interviewing in 2013 before the sector expanded, and the small representation of drivers in our sample.

## Platform Basics

A common feature of all the platforms we studied was "ease of entry," meaning barriers to participation are low and it's relatively simple to get started. "List your car today, start earning tomorrow," Turo promises.[12] This ease differentiates platform work from many jobs, where educational or professional credentials are needed or the process involves submitting detailed information and in-person interviews. Many of our interviewees noted how easy it was to get started. When Tyler joined TaskRabbit, the process, including an automated video interview, took just twenty minutes. He was activated in a day. Ben explained that "for TaskRabbit it was just . . . email and fill out a form online, send it in and you go through a little background check and literally for me, it was maybe five days later, four days later maybe, set to go, easy as pie." Daria also marveled at how simple it was. "I don't have a bike but I called them up that day and they were like, so do you know the area? Do you have a bicycle? Like no to both. . . . I'll come and see you on Sunday. And that worked out."

Signup is easy to access, enrollment is remote, and the routine is familiar to people with some digital experience.

It's a bit different on each site, and some require access to (although not necessarily ownership of) a rentable asset. On Airbnb, hosts upload pictures of their properties, set house rules, and write a bit about themselves. Profiles are generally linked to Facebook accounts.[13] Turo has a similar setup. On TaskRabbit and the delivery platforms we studied, there's now a short "onboarding" session before being activated. These were unremarkable for most of the people we interviewed, although Mitch did express his distaste for the Postmates session. He found the organizer "not actively condescending, but, we were the peons. . . . [She was] treating us like rats that will follow the money around."

At the time we did our research, people were not prevented from participating on Postmates because of less serious criminal offenses, unlike with some jobs, where any record is disqualifying.[14] On ride-hail platforms drivers have to provide the specifics of their cars and must pass background checks, the extensiveness of which varies over time and by location. In some municipalities, such as New York City and some California locations, they're also required to get city licenses. The signup process has been a flashpoint for controversy because lax background checks have been linked to driver malfeasance and criminality. Uber and Lyft left Austin, Texas, after the city required fingerprinting, only to return after successfully lobbying at the statehouse for a law that effectively overruled Austin's regulations.[15]

There's also ease of exit, although this is something that hasn't been studied much. In a few of our interviews we had people who were deactivated by a platform because they had not logged on frequently enough. Earners can also be shut off for poor ratings or violations of policy. One of our drivers told us he was deactivated because he had the bad luck of trying to get an Uber executive (unidentified to him) to switch to Lyft. Apparently that was a violation of terms that led him to be banned for life from Uber. In contrast to companies with exit interviews, paperwork, and post-employment processes, platforms can cut people off almost literally with the push of a button.[16]

As discussed earlier, apps also include prompts that ask consumers to rate and comment on providers. For the companies this outsourcing via crowdsourcing eliminates costly performance evaluations and provides a mechanism for disciplining workers. Some providers, especially drivers, complain about unfairness on the part of customers and companies' unwillingness to hold them to account. How large the ratings loom varies by platform and person.

Another dimension of the platforms that has been widely discussed is how earners are classified in terms of employment status under the law. While a few platforms hire people as full-fledged workers, with all the rights and benefits of employment, most, including all those we studied, classify providers as "independent contractors."[17] This difference is casually referred to as W-2 versus 1099 work, in a nod to the IRS forms the two types of earners fill out.[18] Questions about "misclassification" (whether "independent contractor" is the correct employment status) have been at the center of controversies about platform labor, both in the academic literature and in the courts. When companies opt for the 1099 route, it means that workers are entitled to much more freedom about when and how they work. Whether they actually have that freedom is a major point of disagreement. For most of the companies their business model is premised on avoiding the costs of employment and shifting risk onto the provider. A 2018 California case involving the company Dynamex led to an updated, more restrictive set of criteria for independent contractors that created momentum for reclassification.[19] In September 2019 the California Legislature passed #AB5, which explicitly made many gig workers employees. Uber promptly announced it would fail to comply with the legislation.[20] It's an ongoing drama.

Platform earners are not only independent in a legal sense; they also typically do their work independently of other workers.[21] Their main interactions are with customers, in cars or homes. But in some cases even interactions with customers are minimized or absent. Some tasks are done online, or they may take place in homes when customers are out. On the rental platforms remote access has become common, so renters and owners may never meet face-to-face. Couriers generally have only fleeting interactions with the staff at the businesses they pick up from and the people they deliver to. In contrast to the centralized offices and factories of the twentieth century, platform work is much more solitary. Few of our informants complained about it, and there isn't much research on it, but it's an important dimension of the experience. Of course, this isn't to say the job is devoid of social content. We've met people who coordinate their work schedules with friends. People recruit others within their networks to join platforms. In ride-hail and delivery, there are meeting places, online forums, and ongoing attempts to connect and, increasingly, organize workers.[22]

Ease of entry and exit, crowdsourced ratings and reputational data, 1099 status, and social isolation are some of the most important common features of work on platforms. What about differences? There are obvious things like the kinds of work being performed, variations in company policies, and the wide range of wages. But what we discovered is that in many ways the most important differences are about situations for providers outside the platforms, in the other parts of their lives.

## Earning for Extras

In our data Juan stands out for his specialized skills and entrepreneurial orientation on the platform.[23] What's not unusual about Juan is his satisfaction with the experience and the money. Our analysis suggests this is because he's a supplemental earner using the platform to augment income from a regular job. He doesn't need his TaskRabbit money to pay his rent or to purchase food and other basics. Those are covered. As he described it, prebaby, TaskRabbit money was for "walking around."

We call people like Juan "supplemental earners" because they are not dependent on the platform. That turns out to make all the difference. Supplemental earners net higher hourly wages and carve out autonomy in how they do the job. They are less worried about their ratings and deactivation, and they protect themselves more from risks, whether financial, physical, or emotional. They are generally a satisfied lot, far more so than dependent earners.[24] The promise to remake work under capitalism is mostly coming true for them.

In our sample of earners on for-profit platforms, 34 percent fall into the supplemental earner category. (See Appendix B for a breakdown by platform.)[25] At the other end of the spectrum, 22.5 percent are what we term "platform dependent." These people need their platform earnings to pay for rent, groceries, and other necessities of life. The remaining 43 percent are in between—using the platform to cover some of their monthly expenses but having other sources of income and support. While there's strong overlap, our categorization is not equivalent to the full-time/part-time distinction. Part-timers can be dependent on the income for a significant fraction of their expenses; supplemental earners can work long hours.

Dependency varies by platform. In our sample only one Airbnb and no Turo earners are in the dependent category, in comparison to 71 percent of drivers. Nearly all multiplatform surveys find, as we do, that supplemental or partially dependent earners predominate. The 2018 Federal Reserve study found that for 37 percent of online earners the money was used to "supplement their regular incomes." Only 18 percent relied on it as a "primary source of income."[26] Pew found that 42 percent of its respondents could "live comfortably" without the income, and only 29 percent needed it for meeting "basic needs."[27] Two European Union studies, one of "micro-workers," the other of online and offline earners, also find a similar fraction of dependent workers, defined as receiving more than 50 percent of their income from the platform.[28] The microworker study also has a finding that replicates ours: "platform-dependent" workers are worse off than the other two groups, with the lowest earnings and least satisfaction.

Many TaskRabbits who use the platform as an add-on to other income love the whole experience. Charlie was in school during the recession, earning an MA in journalism, a field with low earnings and few full-time jobs. So when he graduated, he was primed for the reality of not getting a regular position. He'd done casual errands through a university site already and continued that through TaskRabbit, specializing in moving jobs. "It's a great way to make some side money. And I also like the fact that probably about 95 percent of the jobs have been with really understanding people. And I also like the thrill of doing something new, sort of, every time. And also getting to know my way around Boston." Charlie loves the idea that he's helping people. He has another job that pays "the majority of the bills" and gives him health insurance. So he puts as much of his TaskRabbit income as he can into his rainy-day fund. His financial situation allows him to avoid tasks he finds "tedious." He's learned how to pick and choose to find gigs that will yield decent money without hassles. While he is still interested in a full-time job in his chosen field, the platform has been a great short-term alternative. Tyler, a music student, had a similar experience of graduating into the recession. He finds the variety of tasks "exciting," especially compared to his part-time chain restaurant job with its scripted interactions with customers. On TaskRabbit "you do build relationships with people, and I think that's one of the most rewarding parts of the job."

Helen also loves the platform as a complement to her regular job. An MIT science graduate, she works in a local laboratory doing research. She loves to organize, clean, and check things off a to-do list, so TaskRabbit is perfect for her tastes. She also likes that she gets to meet people, because her lab is small and her main interactions are with mice. And because Helen gets bored outside of work, it gives her something to do in her spare time that allows her to be "productive," a term she uses a lot. She also finds the work, which is rarely intellectually taxing, stress-relieving. She's using her earnings to save for graduate school and for "adventures," such as travel and music festivals. "I get really restless if I sit in my room for more than a day." TaskRabbit has been a great solution for that.

TaskRabbits often enjoy the work. While many of the posted tasks are routine, there are also more interesting and quirkier jobs. These include dressing up to play characters at parties (one respondent loved the chance to play a pirate) or testing new iPhone apps. Tyler arrived at someone's house "for a cleaning task, quote unquote, and she handed me a sledgehammer and said, 'Knock down this wall and bag it up for me.' . . . It's really been interesting." Tanwen, a highly educated daughter of two Harvard researchers, recounts doing virtual tourism (by Faceting a client around Faneuil Hall), writing letters of recommendation, and even composing breakup texts to send to a customer's boyfriend.

Satisfaction with the money and the tasks, scheduling flexibility, social interactions, and being able to help people are mentioned by many of the people we interviewed. One person who feels like a failure at her job as a substitute teacher says TaskRabbit allows her to feel successful and enhances her self-esteem. Others point out its virtues in comparison to lousy part-time jobs, such as low-paid retail or catering, where wages aren't great, stress is high, and bosses can be demanding. They love that for the most part they control their work process.

Of course, there are frustrations and downsides. When we ask about worst experiences, there is usually an example of a job that took more time than expected or a client who wasn't particularly nice. And there are identity issues. For the most part, TaskRabbits are highly educated, and the work they do is mainly manual. This can cause status conflicts, which we discuss in the next chapter. "I don't want to be a servant," says one easily offended respondent. But overall, this is a happy group.

So far I've focused on the high satisfaction levels of TaskRabbits. We have similar findings from other platforms when the income is a supplement. A particularly enthusiastic interviewee was Suhani, who had recently arrived in the country from South Asia and had no work permit. She was active on many platforms and therefore not dependent on any particular one. Plus, her husband had a full-time job. At the time of our first interview Suhani was an Airbnb host, a ride-hail driver on multiple apps, and had listed her car on Turo and her bicycle on Spinlister. She seemed to love almost everything about the platforms. The money was great, and she preferred short-term guests to permanent roommates. "We just love to serve. . . . You will be met with random acts of kindness." Platform earnings allowed her to buy a house, which she and her husband were renting out as much as possible. Like many of the other Airbnb hosts we interviewed, she emphasized the value of the relationships. Guests "bring us gifts. . . . It's a lot of value people bring into your lives, right?" The only downside, she explained, was that "once the people go, you don't have a chance to keep in touch unless you really try."

Many of our other Airbnb hosts also waxed enthusiastic about the social aspects. Boston attracts foreign travelers, who are interesting because they are "exotic," but "comfortably" so, to use the title of one of Isak Ladegaard's papers.[29] They are different enough to provide novel social opportunities, but not so different that they are threatening. A big reason is that these hosts and guests frequently come from similar well-off social classes, and that familiarity is reassuring.

Another reason Airbnb hosts are so satisfied is that the effort-to-earnings ratio is high. The prices they can charge are good, and the time commitment is relatively small. Respondents say that the cleaning up is manageable, and they can minimize it by requiring longer stays or hiring cleaners. We asked about worst experiences, and with one exception, which happened after our first interview, none were particularly bad. (The exception involved someone whose condo board fined him $10,000 for illegally hosting. This happened only after he'd gotten into a conflict with the board on another issue.) We had respondents who were making tens of thousands of dollars, although those were typically people who rented out their entire place and bunked elsewhere. But in Boston, even those who offered only a spare room could get seventy dollars a night, sometimes more. With one exception, none of our Airbnb hosts was dependent on these earnings. They went for extras, to build savings or pay down debt, or in the case of "partially dependent" hosts, to defray some expenses. (The host who was fined by his condo board had used the earnings to finance a pricey wedding.) If you're wondering about how our account squares with all the bad press Airbnb has gotten, the explanation lies in the contrast between people who use the platform (hosts and guests) and those who don't. For the former there are mostly just benefits. The costs are paid by nonparticipating urban residents, as properties come to be run as commercial lodging rather than shared space in occupants' homes.

Informants who were renting out their cars on Turo for extra cash were similarly positive. The money is much less than on Airbnb and the interactions with the customers fairly minimal. But it's also low-effort. For Bill—a thirty-year-old, single, white political consultant—it has been "an absolutely fantastic experience. It's not like I'm hard up for the cash, but I like to have my car to be able to pay for itself." He books as often as he can to make his car payment and insurance. "And the people I've met have been really great." His favorite experience was helping an "African American woman pastor" whose vehicle broke down and needed the car immediately to get to a service a couple of hours away. She showed up in "full regalia; . . . that was a nice thing." Bill was pleased that he could come to her rescue and at half the cost of a conventional car rental.

Natasha was a thirty-one-year-old married consultant with a couple of Ivy League degrees and an annual income of more than $100,000 when she joined Turo. She and her husband only used their car for errands, so they figured "let's put an asset of ours to use and earn money from it." They were getting "a nice extra chunk of change," which was generally about half their car payment. The other motive was "the idea that we're redistributing wealth. We're spreading wealth with our neighbors and sharing in that way. Less people need to own cars. And I believe in that from a philosophical place. The money alone wouldn't have been enough to do it, and the [sharing] wouldn't have been enough to do it but it was a combination." Other Turo participants also mentioned the ecological benefits of the setup. For Anand, Turo led to his purchase of a Honda Insight, a super-efficient hybrid, for his long-distance trips and to introduce others to the environmental benefits of hybrids. "I bought this car specifically to share," he explained.

On the delivery and ride-hail platforms the hourly earnings are lower. But supplemental workers, or those who are only slightly dependent, are also quite positive. Andy calls driving the "perfect second job." He explains that he originally "took up Uber as a side thing to basically pay for a backpacking trip that I did last year, going all throughout the Caucasus and down into Lebanon and then over to Israel." Danny has another job for about thirty-five hours a week and drives for "gas and car insurance money . . . as well as for like special occasions usually. Like Christmas I'll double down; I'll work harder on Uber, especially holidays when I need more money for someone's birthday generally. . . . I'll hustle and make a lot of money and then go back to focusing on my main job."

For some, platform activity "kills two birds with one stone." Many couriers use their bicycles, so they're getting exercise while they're earning. For drivers, an added benefit might be picking up riders on their way to work, thereby getting their tolls paid and covering vehicle expenses that they would incur in any case. For many, meeting people is the bonus. Samuel is an accountant with a full-time job who decided to start driving because he didn't have any savings, had student loans and credit card debt, and couldn't rely on his family if he ran into trouble. "The only thing my family can help with is probably giving me a plate of food if I need it." The money enabled him to pay off his credit cards and buy some furniture for a condo he'd just purchased. He also appreciates the sociability, recounting one rider who was Irish. "I was talking about how I know people from Ireland and I love their accent and the Irish and all that kind of good stuff so it was a good experience from there . . . just the interaction with him . . . even though they say don't talk to strangers. I mean this guy was a stranger to me and I was a stranger to him so we started chatting." For Andy driving is great because it relaxes him, and he loves the sociability: "I get to meet people my own age, joke around with people my own age, meet people from all over the world. . . . I also do a lot better when I'm in motion, too." At one point, when he was between jobs, he drove full-time. "It actually became quite fun as long as it's nothing too crazy." Finally, for some the draw is the chance to use free time productively rather than sitting around playing video games or being bored.

There are also particular ways that not being dependent on the income lead to better outcomes. One is that being a supplemental earner can yield higher wages, because workers can discriminate among jobs or when they work. One person jacks up his rate for tasks he hates, like waiting in line when new iPhones come out, for which he charges $150 an hour. Because his ratings are so good, he gets those assignments anyway. Ernest, a particularly astute TaskRabbit, explained it this way: "Okay, some people have full-time jobs when they do this. I know a guy, for instance. He charges forty-five dollars an hour, but he doesn't care because he has another full-time income. So he's, like, you want me to heavy lift for you? I don't care if you choose me or not, but if you choose me . . . He has leverage . . . because he has another full-time job." Ernest himself did not have much leverage, as he was dependent on his earnings when we spoke, explaining that "I'll lower my price to create volume."

Aaron, a TaskRabbit who had an in-between "partially dependent" status, explained his pricing strategy. He started off by underbidding, at a time when he wasn't dependent on his TaskRabbit earnings. Once he had accrued enough tasks and positive reviews, "I kind of learned what people who were good were charging so I was able to up my rates and then up them even more. . . . The power of setting your own rates for TaskRabbit is great because especially when it comes to the summer, I'll get hired just because I have a lot of tasks into my notebook, 90 percent positive ratings. So I'll get hired for stuff at a much higher rate than I would, if I worked for a movie company." (He had come from Hollywood.) "I make probably four times what I was making per hour, maybe five times." Later in the interview, he returned to the theme of how much he liked the freedom to set his own price. "I've learned how to really push, really push up my rates, because I'll always end up getting jobs." He also mentioned the side benefit of getting hand-me-downs when he was hired to take things to Goodwill. "I've probably gotten $400–500 in free clothing."

Other strategies include opting for tasks that workers know will take less than the posted times, which boosts the effective hourly rate. Another practice is avoiding any task that has a hint of problem about it, whether it's because the customer might be running a scam (as sometimes happens), or the task is underpriced for the time it will take, or there might be safety issues. Supplemental earners on all the platforms can be more selective and reject exchanges that are lower-paid, undesirable, or even slightly sketchy. Examples include avoiding nighttime work when the likelihood of physical threat is higher, turning down jobs that require going alone into men's homes to avoid harassment (as some of our women informants do), or rejecting customers who appear questionable in any way.

We also found that supplemental workers are better able to get the kind of scheduling flexibility that the platforms advertise. This issue is most acute in ride-hail and delivery where demand is highly variable over the day. For couriers there are peaks at mealtimes. For drivers there's a midday lull, after the morning commute and before the evening rush hour. Supplemental workers have the ability to work when demand is there or when they have free time. They are not forced to be available at all times of day in order to earn enough to live. This is another way they can boost hourly earnings—by working when there's money to be made.

Gideon, a recent college graduate, and actor and dancer whose career was going relatively well, relied on platform work to supplement his theatrical earnings. He worked about twenty hours a week on Lyft and TaskRabbit and has also put in time on Instacart, which he liked less because the work was "isolated and lonely." Earlier, he'd worked in food service and at Starbucks, which he also didn't like: "It was really taking over my life so, I was living to work versus working to live. TaskRabbit feels like I'm working to live." For Gideon, scheduling flexibility was paramount and app-based work allowed him to go on auditions and to rehearsals. "These other jobs [TaskRabbit, Lyft] are keeping me out of a slave trade service, and it's giving me that control to really make the work that I want to work and it's twenty hours at jobs that pay more than most part-time jobs do."

## Dependent Earners

For dependent earners the picture is different. The horror stories coming from journalists and ethnographers about ride-hail especially, but also other platforms, are now well known. Many of these describe conditions for dependent workers. Alexandrea Ravenelle,[30] who did extensive interviewing with seventy-eight platform workers in New York City, described people desperate to earn and forced to endure harassment, unsafe conditions, and scams. Many researchers who have been studying Uber paint a similarly bleak picture.[31] It's the twenty-first-century equivalent of older labor systems such as sweatshops, putting-out, and debt peonage. Platform jobs take their place alongside service work, truck driving, and labor-intensive manufacturing that are being degraded through neoliberal policies and global competition for work.

We, too, have stories of desperation, although on average our respondents aren't as bad off as the foregoing picture suggests. That's likely because Boston is a less-harsh city than others that have been studied, such as New York. In Boston wages tend to be high, unemployment is low, and the social welfare infrastructure is relatively good.[32] In addition our driver sample is small, so we have fewer worst-case examples. But our findings for dependent workers do align with others' pessimistic accounts in an important way. With some exceptions our data suggest that being dependent on a platform for expenses is not a viable way to make a living. Total earnings are frequently below the poverty line, even when hourly wages are good. Dependents lose autonomy and scheduling flexibility. They also worry more about deactivation, so fear of ratings undermines independence. Dependent earners are less able to avoid situations of jeopardy. They lack benefits, unemployment insurance, and workers' compensation, so insecurity is pervasive. Overall, they are less satisfied than supplemental earners.

Among our TaskRabbits, the worst off were a couple of guys who had lost lucrative jobs—one in software, the other at a hospital. The latter, Josh, was thirty-two years old, white, and had some college education. He was hustling to be a software entrepreneur but was earning most of his money on the platform. He'd also been struggling with homelessness. He explained that after he was laid off, he sold all his stuff and joined a coworking space. "A lesser person would have not stuck it out. . . . I slept in my office for six months. It's anonymous [so] I don't mind telling you." He would get up early before anyone arrived, and go for a run, to maintain the fiction that he was just coming in from exercising and needed a shower. But, he explained, it's "absolutely mentally exhausting to keep up all these projects and this farce about my living situation." Josh felt that TaskRabbit is "actually really a race to the bottom." He recounted one of his clients telling him, "It's almost exploitative the things she can get people to do for ten dollars." Josh had big plans for his future. He was going to learn the software program Ruby on Rails, which he was counting on to allow him to "walk right into a minimum $80,000 a year job. Which solves all of my problems." His optimism for the future belied the riskiness of the life he had been living: "It's like I'm going to die because I'm not going to buy food, or I'm going to freeze to death in the wintertime. . . . I made it work though." It's true he wasn't dead, but after his experiences as a gig worker he'd come to a sad opinion: "The real-world sucks."

Rich had a similar take on platform work. For him Task Rabbit was a serious comedown. He was better off than Josh, as he had a home and a wife with a job. But after he was let go from his $250,000 tech position, he found himself hustling on Craigslist and TaskRabbit, earning below the poverty line. He had good manual skills and mainly bid for tasks that required them. But he would sometimes end up with jobs that paid only ten dollars an hour. Those were extremely frustrating and made him feel he'd be better off working at McDonald's. Perhaps not surprisingly, an internal slide deck from Uber seen by the *New York Times* showed that other than Lyft, the company considered McDonald's to be their primary competitor for labor.[33] Isabelle, another dependent Task Rabbit also didn't earn above a poverty income, despite good ratings and lots of experience. The issue with TaskRabbit was that while hourly wages are high, there isn't enough demand to support a good full-time income. In these three cases earnings weren't sufficient to afford rent. Josh had been homeless, Rich had his wife's support, and Isabelle lived with her parents.

Uncertainty about whether jobs will be available was an added stressor. Aaron was generally upbeat about his work on TaskRabbit, in part because he was also managing an Airbnb for a friend, from which he earned quite a bit. But three-quarters of the tasks he did were same-day assigns: "From the way the markets work . . . I know something will come up tomorrow. I don't [know] how many. I don't know if I'll do one job or two jobs. So that's kind of what it is and there have been days when I've been scared and frustrated over am I going to be able to get this job or that job. . . . For example, last week there were one or two days where there weren't as many jobs and that happens from time to time." With independent contracting the risk of inadequate demand is all borne by the earner. With employment the company absorbs more short-term dips in business.

Precarity and financial worry is also a theme among couriers. Abigail, the twenty-eight-year-old multiplatform worker we met in the introduction, speculated about how demand on Postmates, where she had a lot of deliveries from college students, might just suddenly disappear. "I feel like something else could come out, and they could have a special where kids like get free burritos or something and all of the sudden no one uses Postmates for like a week. I don't know, it's really fickle probably." Abigail was extremely averse to a nine-to-five job or even any kind of set work schedule because she loved traveling and had family obligations. So she stayed on the apps despite the financial insecurity: "It's a sacrifice I'm willing to make to not have to make a commitment to working hours and days that I don't want to work or working for someone for a certain number of months if I want to travel." But traveling also took a toll. Once she was going away for a few days at the end of the month and had to work for three days straight to make her rent. "I was just so tired." Or sometimes she really has to hustle even when she's in town: "Oh sh*t, I need more money at the end of the month and then just work for twenty-four hours straight if you're a bad planner like I am."

Daria, however, the "failed opera singer . . . [and] failed software entrepreneur," couldn't make it work, despite loving the bicycle riding. Like many of the people we interviewed, she wasn't interested in a nine-to-five job. But she did need more money than she could earn at her convenience-store job. "So I was single-handedly at nineteen, paying exorbitant rent on a downtown apartment and supporting a twenty-nine-year-old diabetic [her ex-boyfriend] on a convenience income so yeah . . . trying to find anything that I could fit into my schedule." To make extra money, Daria joined Favor. For a while she worked both jobs and was putting in ninety-hour weeks. ("Fun times.") She shifted exclusively to Favor, partly because she disliked cleaning the kitchen at the convenience store. Then tax season rolled around. "I was like oh . . . this isn't mine to keep really." Her pay didn't exceed the company's then ten-dollar-an-hour guarantee, so she ended up quitting after a few months, as many platform earners do, because the money wasn't enough to live on. She was lucky to find a real job doing bicycle delivery that paid twice as much.

Mitch's situation also showed the limits of supporting oneself on the apps. He was hustling on multiple platforms and was pleased about how things were going. "Honestly, even with Postmates, trying to do it every day I found I have a surprising amount of money. I'm not swimming in debt anymore and I'm accruing a little bit." But then he acknowledged the limits of the strategy. "But you know, I don't really pay rent right now. I'm living at home. I have a girlfriend—we split costs on food, which helps a lot."

The differences between supplemental and dependent earning are illustrated by the experience of Kendrick, a ride-hail driver who made that shift. Although he had only a high school education,

Kendrick had a lot of skills, including carpentry and auto mechanics. When he started driving, he had a regular, full-time job doing satellite TV installation. "So when Uber came around . . . it was the greatest part time job I ever held, and I loved doing it. . . . As you know, you work your own hours. No one forces you to go out there. So I think it was great. . . . It didn't matter whether I made a dollar or I made two hundred dollars. It was part-time, extra money in the pocket." His installation job was "dead-end," and he wanted to earn more, so he decided that he'd try doing Uber full-time. Now he "has a different view on the ride-sharing business," citing "excessive" wear and tear and maintenance on his vehicle (he had to buy a new one), decreases in pay, (lower-paid) Uber Pool passengers, and back pain from sitting in the car too long. (H.C. Robinson has found that part-time drivers failed to recognize the costs of maintaining their vehicles, in contrast to full-timers.)[34]

Kendrick had hoped that full-time driving would give him more time for his family but discovered that when they are available, he has to be on the app. And "for a driver to really make it out there, you know, he has to work a minimum of twelve hours plus. To really see a livable wage coming in." He's working seven days a week and needs everything he earns to pay basic expenses, which means he hasn't been able to set anything aside for the tax bill at the end of the year. He foresees this as his "downfall." He and his wife are subletting their living room on Airbnb in anticipation of Tax Day. But "it's scary, and I am definitely wanting to get out of the business. . . . I don't want to do it full time anymore . . . because I just know . . . I'm going to put myself in a big hole."

As Kendrick explained, dependency reduces the freedom to choose one's schedule. Danny, a partially dependent driver, echoes a sentiment we heard from a number of our respondents. When asked about scheduling freedom, he responds: "It's a play on words. . . . Yes, of course I can work whenever I want. I can put the app on and shut it off whenever I feel like it, but I'm dictated by the market. . . . [If] I want to make money, then I have to play by their rules. . . . We're talking like days when you can make $50 or $200 based on what time you work. That's not a freedom to pick when your shift is. . . . That puts you on a schedule. . . . So to answer your question, no. It's just you want to make money or you don't."

Dependent workers are also more concerned about ratings and the threat of deactivation. A number of our respondents described incidents in which they were shut off. Some were able to reactivate, but others weren't, so they moved onto competitor platforms or to other activities. And while all earners are potentially subject to losing their accounts, dependency status can make all the difference. Ernest, the tasker we heard from above, was a thirty-year-old college graduate. He also drove for Uber and Lyft and managed some apartments on Airbnb while he was building a company in the music production business. He prefers platform work because it is less mentally taxing than freelancing for music production. He explained the jeopardy of deactivation and how it differs from ordinary jobs. And he was forceful about not working full-time for Uber or similar platforms. "I would never rely on any of these [platforms]. And I say that because they're so volatile. You get three bad responses from somebody—and it may not even be completely correct—they'll suspend you from the platform." By contrast, "a full-time job would never . . . just kick you off. . . . But these apps, you do something, a couple things wrong, they'll suspend you quick. So if that's your full-time income, and you don't even get to talk to anybody, there's no sitting and meeting. . . . If you had your boss and something went wrong . . . they'd say, . . . 'I need to hear your side of this before I let you go.' Not with this. Not with this. You'll get an email. Suspended. You got to wait seven days."

Isabelle's experiences on TaskRabbit also shed light on how ratings fear can reduce earnings in ways that are especially disadvantageous for dependent earners. She recounted a cleaning job in a luxury apartment for a woman who had underestimated the size of the task. Isabelle gave the kitchen a quick once-over as she calculated the mess in the other rooms and the time allotted for the job. Meanwhile, she cut her hand doing the dishes. The client minimized the injury and gave her a Band-Aid. But when Isabelle moved on to the bathroom, the client was angry about the state of the kitchen counters and asked her to leave. Isabelle immediately downgraded the original fifty-dollar job to ten dollars, thinking that was fair. So when she received a bad review, she called the company and explained the situation. The only recourse they gave her was to cancel out the job altogether, which she did to avoid the jeopardy of the review. In the end Isabelle not only earned no money for the work, but she was responsible for the cost of the hospital visit to treat what turned out to be a significant laceration.

Phuong is a courier who exemplified many of the downsides of dependency status: low earnings, safety concerns, and status insults. Phuong was using Favor to support himself while he completed his B.A., earning less than $18,000. He came from a low-income Vietnamese immigrant family and was an outstanding student, having placed into one of the city's most competitive schools at an unusually early age. He'd been working in a restaurant, but his commuting costs were high, and he loved to bike, so he quit the restaurant job and started on the app. He estimated he was earning thirteen dollars to fifteen dollars an hour, although that didn't account for the tax bill he worried he'd be facing at the end of the year. Status issues came up early in the conversation. Favor plays on the luxury image, as its logo is a bow tie, and its T-shirts have a tuxedo image on the front. "Going up to these places [high-rises] makes me so uncomfortable. The first time I went through one of these luxury houses I went to the concierge and I was like I have a delivery. He was like go through the service entrance. You mean like a poor door or something like that? They had a poor door." (A poor door isn't an old-style service entrance; it's a separate, inferior door for affordable housing tenants in luxury buildings.) Phuong had been a community organizer and is highly attuned to gentrification and growing inequality. "So when I'm thrown into this rich world where I'm taking from the rich, it feels okay, but at the same time it's like I'm losing the idea of trying to fix morals or something like that. It's very demeaning."

Phuong's need to earn tips also felt humiliating. One of the things he liked about his restaurant job was that he was back of house and didn't need to be "very inauthentic to myself" to please the customer. But his reliance on tips on Favor meant he'd lost that freedom: "I always take off my helmet. I don't know why. I fix my hair and make myself presentable. . . . They mentioned that in the orientation, you should have a good picture, with a good shirt, be personable [with customers]. I was like 'that's nice.' But when I *do* do that, and the interaction ends there, it feels like I was on the cheap side of a relationship. . . . They tried to instill 'the harder you try, the better tip you get,' and it really ingrained in me that, how much I need to put in there to get the tip."

While Phuong was able to schedule the work around his classes and homework, his goal was to take shifts that offered the biggest guarantee he could get, thereby reducing his choice of hours. (At the time, Favor offered a wage guarantee if the courier committed to a four-hour block.) The nature of the job also meant he was taking frightening safety risks—"you're kind of anxious on the road all the time. You don't want to get hit." "I can be reckless," he explains, a common refrain from couriers for whom speed is essential to earnings. And the work can be "exhausting" at times, even for someone who loves to bike. Asked how he thought Favor aligned with his long-term goal of being a community educator or a teacher, he replied: "I don't think it's helping me get there. I think it's helping me survive." While he appreciated the opportunity and flexibility of Favor, he saw the platform as "another tool for keeping poor people poor."

While Phuong is right that for many, platform work was "keeping poor people poor," our data suggest those are largely dependent workers. The experiences of supplementals are different, as they are able to boost earnings to finance discretionary spending or savings. Situations outside the platform make all the difference. Recognizing this basic reality led us to reevaluate the two dominant theories scholars have used to understand what's going on with platforms—algorithmic control and policies of precarity.

## The Algorithmic Manager

Algorithms have become a pervasive feature of modern life.[35] They drive search results on Google, predict outcomes in the criminal justice system, and determine access to healthcare and social services. In workplaces, "people analytics" are being used for hiring, performance evaluation, and surveillance.[36] But while algorithms are capable of yielding good outcomes, they are also problematic "black boxes," as Frank Pasquale and others have argued,[37] that are known to produce racially biased outcomes and inaccurate results. It's also becoming clear that they can help their owners wield power over labor. Scholars in this camp[38] contend that what's unique about platforms is that they employ software to control workers, a view summed up in the title to a widely cited article: "When Your Boss Is an Algorithm."[39] The claim is that previous models of labor control, such as face-to-face supervision by human managers (so-called direct control) and rules-based organization (bureaucratic control), have been made obsolete by Artificial Intelligence, the new remote supervisor.[40] Some even call it "algorithmic despotism."[41]

There's no question that algorithms are important for platform work. This is especially true of driving and delivery. In ride-hail the software does the work of pairing riders and drivers, pricing, and giving workers behavioral "nudges"—or even shoves.[42] On other apps the matching algorithm decides which workers or product listings to show to customers and in which order. Platform companies are using AI, or artificial intelligence, to do many functions that were previously done by management, such as performance evaluation, employment support, and even the initial sign-up. Algorithms are frequently a source of frustration for workers, owing to lack of transparency and asymmetric information.[43] In ride-hail and delivery, platforms switched to "blinding" job destinations,[44] which eliminated a key component of worker choice, supposedly one of the hallmarks of this kind of work. Couriers report not being sure how turning down jobs affects their position in the queue for new ones,[45] and more generally, we found that they were confused about how jobs were allocated. (We were also confused about why our researcher was never able to snag a task after successfully signing up for a platform.)[46] Studies of drivers find they spend considerable effort attempting to learn how the algorithm operates.[47]

But the algorithmic control approach has its limitations. One is a tendency to overstate what's new here. Algorithms are an example of a long-standing system of labor management called "technical control"[48]—situations where machinery dictates the pace and pattern of work. The assembly line is the most famous example. Before its invention, car factories comprised skilled workers who moved around to fixed work stations. Henry Ford inverted the process by immobilizing (and deskilling) labor and installing a moving line, whose speed he controlled.[49] David Noble's classic book *Forces of Production* showed that firms choose new technologies in part on the basis of their ability to control workers.[50]

A second issue is that algorithms, like any system of control, are never all-powerful.[51] After a time the assembly line became the subject of labor disputes. How fast would it go? Who had the right to shut it down? Researchers are discovering that platform workers, especially drivers and couriers, are also finding ways to beat the system.[52]

Will Attwood-Charles's interviews with Postmates and Favor couriers reveal that they subvert company policy in numerous ways.[53] Angelo, a twenty-seven-year-old Favor worker, tells the app he's on a bike when he's in a car, so that he gets orders that are closer together. Will also found that the companies were unable to rely solely on the algorithms to control the workers and had to supplement with calls, texts, and other forms of human contact.[54] Lindsay Cameron, who interviewed Uber drivers (and became one), identifies tactics such as using passenger accounts to get rides or driving away from rides they've accepted, which she terms "feigned acquiescence"—that is, nominal obedience but actual resistance.[55] Aaron Shapiro found "subtle models of resistance" among couriers.[56] H.C. Robinson's Uber driver informants engineered a "fake" driver shortage in order to trigger artificial surge pricing while she was studying them.[57] (The company threatened deactivation.) Julie Chen, who conducted the first major study of Didi, the Chinese ride-hail company, found that 40 percent of the more than eight thousand drivers she surveyed had either installed bots on their phones or purchased multiple phones to game the system, a practice she terms "algorithmic activism."[58]

Visions of total control also unwittingly minimize the human choices behind the software. What's the rating at which a driver will be deactivated? How do acceptance and rejection rates for tasks affect work flow? What parameters did the platform managers instruct coders to use in deciding who's an "elite" tasker? To some extent, algorithms are self-learning entities that change without human intervention. But on labor platforms they are also paired with policy decisions made by real people.

Our findings also suggest that algorithmic control varies with the situation of the worker. Dependent earners are more under its sway, as they worry about their reviews, rejection rates, and communications with the company. By contrast, supplementals are more likely to do things their own way, algorithm be damned.[59] Tamara, one of

Will's respondents, was a married courier with a full-time job and multiple platform activities. She refused to leave her car after dark, in clear violation of Postmates' policy. "If they start saying, oh well you have to get out of the car, no. No, no, no, no, no, no. You come down and get your food." Another of our supplemental couriers, a college student, explained that he refused to use the insulating bags and stickers the company provided. He isn't all that worried about his ratings.

## Why Dependency Status Matters So Much: The Cost of Job Loss

The difference in willingness to defy algorithmic control by dependency status can be explained by some simple economic reasoning. A key principle of game theory (as well as common sense) is that power depends on "outside options"—that is, the available situations if the deal doesn't go through. Those with better alternatives have more power in a negotiation because they are more willing to turn down offers they do not like. Desperation yields bad deals. This insight is at the core of why dependency status matters so much in platform work. Supplementals are more likely to "do it their way" and have an easier time walking away when things aren't to their liking. As Mike, a full-time law student and part-time courier, explained when we asked about the downsides of the work: "I'm not investing blood, sweat, and tears into this. If it gets too hard or I have too much work I'm not going to [use it]." Discussing how he'd react if his rating dipped and the company required him to attend another onboarding meeting he replied: "I probably wouldn't go back."

Supplemental earners have good alternative options, as measured by what colleagues and I have termed the "cost of job loss."[60] This is the difference between income on the job and what can be earned after a termination or resignation. When the cost of job loss is low, workers have more power and control. Where good alternatives are hard to find, workers are more subject to their bosses, whether they are humans or algorithms. Factors that determine the cost of job loss include the state of the labor market, benefits available to the unemployed, and for platform workers, conditions on other apps they can access. Supplemental earners have alternative sources of income, and the money they do earn isn't as essential. By contrast, dependent earners are reliant on the platform. Years ago, Samuel Bowles and I created the first empirical estimate of the cost of job loss for the U.S., and I also calculated one for the U.K. We showed that this measure is able to predict a variety of outcomes: how likely employees are to strike, their ability to get wage increases, and literally how hard they work.[61] On platforms, the market and the worker's own situation do much of the disciplining. For dependent workers that discipline is harsh. For supplementals, it's lax.

## The Perils of Precarity

The other main approach to understanding platform labor focuses on company policies, in particular the decision not to hire workers as employees but as independent contractors. This choice allows platforms to put costs and risks onto workers and to avoid compensating for lost earnings, injury, damage to the workers' property (e.g., car accidents), lack of market demand, or mistreatment by customers. (While some platforms do carry insurance policies, they are typically circumscribed in their coverage.) The independent contractor model is an example of what labor scholars call "precarious work" or work that is "uncertain, unpredictable, and risky from the point of the worker," to use sociologist Arne Kalleberg's definition.[62] First identified as a trend in the 1980s, scholars have been chronicling the increasing tendency of employers to outsource work, convert employees into contractors, take away benefits, and devolve risk. Different terms have been coined to describe this process—the creation of a precariat, fissuring, risk shift, responsibilization[63]—but they all contend that the stable employment regime of the post-World War II period has been eroded, with precarious labor taking its place.

Uberization drives precarity to its limit.[64] While some observers think this new regime gives workers freedom and autonomy,[65] most precarity scholars emphasize income instability and the lack of security. Some have even argued we're on our way back to the world of temporary day labor, with smartphones replacing street corner pickups.[66] Within this tradition the issue that has gotten most attention is misclassification.

As with the algorithmic control approach, there's a lot that is insightful about the focus on precarity. Many drivers and couriers *are* misclassified, and platform employment can be tremendously insecure. But this approach tacitly assumes that the key determinant of outcomes is employment classification. If that's true, workers should have fairly similar experiences, which we find they don't. The policy approach also assumes a continuity between conventional precarious labor and platform work and that not much is fundamentally different about platforms. They're merely the logical endpoint of a decades-long process. As I'll explain shortly, we think platforms have ushered in fundamental changes in the organization of work.

## Platforms as Parasites

The differences we discovered between dependent and supplemental earners reveal another underrecognized feature of platforms. They are what social scientists call "free riders." The classic understanding of a free rider is someone reaping advantage from a common resource without contributing to it. Free riders take but do not give. An obvious case is a person or company who doesn't pay taxes but uses roads, education, or health care that is paid for by the government. With the platforms, it's not just about taxes but also the fact that they are relying on benefits provided by other companies to make their model work. In this way platforms are parasites, organisms that live off other organisms. Our findings suggest that these "other organisms" are conventional employers.

While this characterization may seem awfully critical, our point is an analytic one—it's a parasitic relation because platform work is generally not viable on its own. The workers who are satisfied, earning amounts of money that they are happy with, and who have reasonable autonomy and security are mostly supplemental or only partially dependent earners. Many have full-time employment, with decent pay and benefits. Others rely on the earnings and benefits of their partners. Some have part-time jobs or side businesses. Platform earners are reliant on these other sources of income for satisfaction and security, hence the parasitic relation. By contrast, dependent workers, who don't have other employment or family earnings, are not in sustainable situations. Many earn below the poverty line, with low hourly wages. Or in some cases, as with dependent TaskRabbits, hourly wages are good, but despite hustling all day they are unable to earn a decent living. Added to that is the lack of benefits. This finding casts doubt on the rosy "end of employment" scenarios in which everyone works for a platform and has flexibility, autonomy, and a decent income.

## The Platform Hierarchy

So far I've focused on the distinction between dependent and supplemental workers, emphasizing that even on the same platform, outcomes vary quite a bit. There's also tremendous variation across platforms. While many accounts of this sector treat it as an undifferentiated whole, there's actually a vertical structure, as in the conventional labor market where jobs are ordered by earnings and autonomy.

Some analysts have divided the sector into platforms on which earnings are mainly coming from renting out a capital asset (such as a spare room or a vehicle) and those that mobilize labor (ride-hail, delivery, errands).[67] While that distinction can be overstated because all production requires at least some capital and some labor, it does accord with our findings. The "capital" platforms are at the top of the pyramid, with the labor-intensive ones at the bottom, a finding that replicates occupational rankings in the conventional economy. We also find that demographic and socioeconomic differences among earners reflect this ordering. The platform workforce gets whiter and more educated, and it hails from a higher social class background as one moves up the hierarchy, from delivery to home rental.

Airbnb, which requires the highest level of capital, yields the highest earnings, both absolutely and per hour of labor expended. It also offers autonomy, control, and high satisfaction to hosts. On Turo, owners also have high levels of control. While total earnings aren't high, effort is minimal, so income per hour is good. TaskRabbit has more autonomy and better hourly wages than Uber/Lyft or Postmates/Favor, with respondents reporting a floor of twenty dollars to twenty-five dollars an hour. There's debate about hourly wages in ride-hail. Early on they were higher than on delivery platforms, which hover in the fifteen-dollars-per-hour range. But as we'll see in a moment, drivers have been squeezed, and their operating costs are high. Barriers to entry also roughly align with our ranking, with Airbnb having the highest requirement (a rentable space), TaskRabbits generally having at least a college degree, and ride-hail drivers needing a late model car.[68]

Some of our participants who had experience with multiple platforms referenced this hierarchy in their interviews. Ernest started on Uber, but as he saw the wear and tear on his car, he realized that the twenty-five dollars an hour he was grossing was more like fourteen or fifteen after expenses and depreciation. So he joined TaskRabbit, where he said he was "averaging around close to thirty dollars an hour. Easy. At least thirty." He also figured that the lowest possible wage on TaskRabbit was twenty dollars to twenty-five dollars. "I feel like TaskRabbit is the next level. . . . I think Uber is the easiest one to get into." The most disadvantaged workers sometimes articulated how bad it is at the bottom, as courier Abigail did near the end of her interview: "That's in every job where you're in the bottom of the pyramid of capitalism, a wage slaved worker."

## The Downward Trajectory

Conditions for workers have also gotten worse on many platforms, a development quite a few of our interviewees talked about. In 2014, to great media attention, TaskRabbit engineered a pivot, in which it scrapped its bidding system, shifted to algorithmic matching, and raised fees. While there were some aspects of the pivot that workers liked, many of our respondents were unhappy with losing their ability to bid on tasks, the requirement to respond in real time before communicating with the customer and getting details about the job, and the fact that the higher fee became invisible to the client. They also reported suffering consequences when they turned down jobs. While the change likely raised hourly wages, it increased costs for customers, thereby limiting demand. And it concentrated work among "elite" taskers, who have high ratings and place in the top 5 percent of earners. The practice of algorithmically prioritizing high-hours workers has also become common on delivery platforms, where failure to sign up for shifts jeopardizes future opportunity, so that flexibility and autonomy erode.[69] Couriers are also experiencing declining wages. One study reported a drop from twenty dollars an hour to twelve dollars, most likely owing to oversupply of workers.[70] In May of 2019 Postmates announced changes that eliminated its minimum pay and reduced rates by what some argued could be as much as 30 percent.[71] It's especially notable that these degradations are occurring in a labor market that has tightened and in which conventional employers are raising wages. This augurs ill for a future of decent platform work.

The deterioration has been most pronounced on ride-hail apps. Driver Danny offered an astute, and poignant analysis: "It used to be much more profitable. When I first started Uber and Lyft, you could really make a killing, and it actually would cover depreciation and the miles and you could actually come out ahead. But now with Uber lowering the rates, it's much harder. Also the oversaturation; there's so many drivers, so much competition, and I notice it's much more difficult to get rides than it used to be." Danny explained how the cut in fares was affecting his earnings. "It used to be twenty hours could get you $800; now that same might get you maybe $400, so it's really been cut in half from the way it used to be. . . . The rates were $2.75 a mile; . . . now, it's $1.25 a mile." (Drivers report that per-mile rates are even lower now.) When we asked what he felt the future held, Danny was pessimistic. "I feel Uber is kind of letting us go. . . . Basically they're going to lower the rates until we break." Drivers' complaints are borne out in company data. Between 2014 and 2016 Uber reduced drivers' share of total revenue from 83 percent to 68 percent.[72] Then, facing increased competition from Lyft, on account of boycotts, bad press, and driver exit, Uber raised its payments to drivers to 77 percent in 2018. Meanwhile, Lyft took the opportunity presented by Uber's squeeze to increase its take, reducing drivers' share from 82 percent to 73 percent between 2016 and 2018, excluding additional reductions in incentives.[73]

In 2019, as the ride-hail companies prepared for their IPOs, they were forced to provide some transparency in their SEC filings. Uber admitted that "as we aim to reduce driver incentives to improve our financial performance, we expect driver dissatisfaction will generally increase."[74] It didn't take long. Weeks later, drivers went on strike in multiple cities.[75] City-specific studies revealed wretched conditions, and driver practices such as eating and sleeping in their cars. A UCLA study found a shift toward older, nonnative earners who were likely supporting family members and had longer tenure on the platform.[76] Of their sample, 47 percent worked exclusively as ride-hail drivers, and for 66 percent this was their main source of income. Drivers were also becoming more financially dependent, as leasing and purchasing of vehicles specifically for this work has become more common. Katie Wells's study of Uber drivers in Washington, D.C., found that a third had taken on debt to work for Uber and that most of them were unable to figure out how much they were actually earning.[77] We also found some evidence of this. Courier Mitch didn't have an answer when Will asked him about his hourly earnings. "I really haven't done a calculation to see how much I've made per hour." So he tried to figure out his Postmates rate on the fly, and the answer wasn't pretty. "I just checked last night. I've made, like, $500, $505 in the past three or four weeks working four to six hours. So if we say 4×5 is 20, times 4 is 80, so 80 hours, $500, $6.25."

A national study by the Economic Policy Institute found that Uber drivers earned only $11.77 an hour and even less when mandatory social security contributions are taken out.[78] This is below minimum wage in many places. The JPMorgan Chase data are perhaps the most vivid indicator of the collapse of driver earnings. In contrast to a rising trend for all other types of platform workers, as the number of drivers increased, incomes fell. Between 2014 and 2018 drivers suffered a 53 percent collapse of monthly earnings, from $1,469 to $783.[79]

## A New Labor Regime? Retreat from Control

If algorithmic control is overstated, and precarity has been around for decades, is there anything new about platform work? Our findings lead us to focus on what the companies *aren't* controlling rather than what they are.[80] What's novel is employers' retreat from managing the labor process and their willingness to permit wide variation in hours of work, how people perform the job, education levels, and dependency status. (To be clear—the comparison we are making is to employees, not genuine independent contractors, who have historically enjoyed high levels of autonomy. For that group platform work may result in more employer control.)[81]

The lack of direct supervision over the work process is reminiscent of the prefactory era of the home-based "putting-out" system in many manufactures, including textiles, shoes, and apparel. In this way platforms are unlike conventional workplaces, where the employees who do a particular job tend to be subject to common scheduling policies, must follow a prescribed work process, and exhibit similar educational attainment and economic situations, as a result of steering by Human Relations departments. By contrast, platforms don't require a uniform type of worker. They accept nearly all comers. Thus, one consequence of the retreat from direct control is a more heterogeneous workforce. We've already focused on differences in levels of dependency and how that affects experiences. There are also other ways in which heterogeneity manifests.

One difference is that platform earners have more individual control over scheduling and the performance of the work. Airbnb hosts can choose when to make their properties available, the amenities they offer guests, how much socializing they do with them, the degree to which they pack away belongings, and many other aspects of the experience. TaskRabbits are often free to do tasks as they prefer, although in some cases clients are more directive. Ride-hail arguably offers the least amount of freedom. But even there, soft control via nudges affords workers discretion.[82] Cameron finds that drivers have "contingent autonomy."[83] Alex Wood and colleagues, who studied microtasking, describe "autonomy in the shadow of algorithmic management."[84] While we find more worker sovereignty on the more lucrative platforms, the sector as a whole differs from conventional workplaces in this regard.

Earners are also able to pursue divergent economic strategies without platform interference. This hasn't been written about, but it stood out in our data. In our first round of interviewing we looked at three platforms—Airbnb, Turo, and TaskRabbit—and found that while all of our respondents wanted to earn money, they followed different behavioral models.[85] One group fell into what is known as *homo economicus,* or "economic men [*sic*]," and acted as the mainstream models predict they will. They wanted to maximize their incomes and were highly rational about doing so. They analyzed the market, put thought into pricing strategy, and calculated expenses, time, and revenues carefully. Anand, from Turo, exemplifies this approach. "So any cash that comes in I keep track of in a spreadsheet. I keep track of all my expenses associated with the car and all the rental income so that I can, in the end, calculate the return on investment. Unfortunately, it's really hard to keep track of the labor because it's so distributed—like responding to people's messages, or buying stuff for the car, maintaining it—it's really hard to keep track of how many hours I spend on it. But I can have a general sense of that and eventually figure out what my implied labor rate is."

The second, and largest group, had strong social motives. In addition to earning, they valued other aspects of their platform experience. Sociability was the most commonly mentioned benefit, but other pluses included environmental impact or efficient use of resources. For some there were negative motivations, such as avoiding status insults. What was common to these people was that they didn't make decisions purely to maximize their incomes. Some used ethical criteria to set prices. One Airbnb host explained that she wasn't comfortable earning more on her spare room than she was paying her landlord for the space. Others turned down jobs they felt were beneath them or that they thought people should be doing on their own. Aaron Shapiro found that couriers invoked a "moral economy," which led them to deviate from economic rationality, a finding similar to ours.[86] The third, smallest group, were financial *satisficers*, to use Herbert Simon's classic term for people who don't maximize but are content with finding an acceptable outcome. They typically needed money and just tried to earn some. They didn't put too much thought into how to price and didn't care much about social benefits. Abigail fits neatly into this category: "I think about how much I need to be making a week on average or a month on average to be able to pay my rent and my gas and feed myself. I just sort of work until I've made that." Economist Michael Sheldon's study of Uber drivers found that while many started in this satisficing group, over time they shifted to maximizing behavior.[87]

Another feature of the relinquishment of control that has not been adequately recognized is the extent to which earnings come to depend on individual strategic capacities. In contrast to contexts in which management figures out the most productive way to organize production and directs its employees to follow it, on platforms more of that responsibility falls on the worker. Danny, the ride-hail driver quoted above, explained: "I have to be a lot more savvy in how I pick my areas, pick my clientele and know where to get certain passengers. Whereas before I would just turn it on and boom, I'd get someone." Danny is capable of mastering the market. Others struggle. Without the equalizing forces of unions or company wage setting, we believe this regime exaggerates earnings variation among individuals doing the same work, yields more winner-take-all outcomes, and leaves less adept, but hardworking, earners with little to show for their labor.

The "retreat from control" represented by platform work is the opposite of what some observers, such as those who invoke algorithmic control, believe has been occurring in the world of work. It also runs counter to George Ritzer's idea of "McDonaldization,"[88] which holds that standardization and centralized control are overtaking all aspects of production and, indeed, society. By contrast, our approach suggests that platforms have led to widening variation in situations and outcomes, as well as a shift to market discipline and autonomy rather than direct employer control.

Of course, it's possible that the current situation will prove infeasible for platform companies. The history of work under capitalism is a story of employers' attempts to control labor, and it shows that failure to do so undermines profitability. The downward trajectory looks suspiciously like a path toward more control, as platforms attempt to get a more committed, disciplined labor force, which they induce to work more hours. Continued momentum in this direction may result in more platform earners turning into de facto employees, whatever their legal status. But there are also forces that may push in the opposite direction, such as the improved position of earners in the larger labor market, platform worker organizing, and increased regulatory activity.

I ended the previous chapter with questions about the nature of the sharing economy. Does it represent a new paradigm, based on a liberatory technology? Can platforms free earners from the strictures of centralized control while providing decent incomes? Is sharing a step forward into a postcapitalist world that offers a sustainable new way to organize livelihoods? We took a deep dive into workers' experiences to help answer these questions.

As we have seen, by doing away with many aspects of labor control, platforms *can* provide meaningful work, freedom, and autonomy. At their best they combine these features with good wages. We've called this the "retreat from control." Its success raises an important question: now that algorithms can do so much, can workers get along without bosses? More workers are contemplating that possibility, as investors' "growth at all costs" mentality has triggered a downward spiral of wage cuts and attempts to claw back control. At the same time, our findings for dependent workers suggest that even under the best circumstances, sharing platforms haven't proven to be capable of providing good full-time incomes. In part that's because dependent workers are often the most vulnerable and insecure members of the workforce. To figure out how to make the platforms work for everyone, let's step back from the work itself to see how they fit into the larger, unequal environment into which they were launched.

# 3   *Shared, but Unequal*

In 2015 Quirtina Crittenden, an African American business consultant, started the hashtag AirBnBWhileBlack to share her problems
making reservations on the platform.[1] A year later, a Harvard Business School study found that would-be African American guests
were 16 percent more likely to be turned down for rentals than their
white counterparts.[2] When the study hit the media, #AirBnBWhile-
Black went viral. The Harvard findings were compelling because
they cataloged actual rejections from an experiment. The researchers had created profiles of fictitious individuals, identical on all dimensions but race.

A persistent complaint from African American customers was
that Airbnb had been slow to address their experiences of discrimination. A week after the Harvard study was released to the media,
the company responded with a public relations blitz. Airbnb has attempted to portray itself as a socially responsible, progressive alternative to the stodgy hotel industry, and being branded as racist was
not consistent with its image. So the company instituted a nondiscrimination pledge for hosts, changed some features of the platform,
and partnered with civil rights organizations.[3] It has also had to
contend with a few racial discrimination lawsuits.[4] As it happened,
I'd tried to warn the company a few years earlier. Discussing possible

research collaborations, I proposed a study that could identify racial bias. Airbnb didn't take up the offer. I figured it was only a matter of time before this issue would burst into public view.

From the beginning of our research, we'd been worried about the potential for person-to-person discrimination on the platforms. Accommodation laws prohibiting racial refusal don't apply to small hotels and B&Bs. Photos, which are ubiquitous on the sites, enable biases based on skin color and other features of appearance. (As one of our informants offered, if someone doesn't "look a certain way, that's creepy.") But supporters of the apps countered that they reduce discrimination. Therefore, the growth of the sector raised an important question. Are platforms disrupting or reproducing inequalities, particularly those of race, gender, and social class?[5]

## Disruption or Social Reproduction?

From the beginning the companies spun narratives of virtuous disruption against entrenched interests. Technology resulted in more value going to producers and consumers, because it cut out the "middleman." Ride-hail apps were upending the taxi monopoly, which unfairly benefited from barriers to entry. Airbnb was "combating" the squeeze on the middle class with a new source of income that allowed people to retain ownership of their homes, finance health insurance, or buy food.[6] Disruptionists touted the superiority of platforms over the "legacy"—that is, conventional economy—on grounds of inclusiveness. According to economist Arun Sundararajan this "democratization of opportunity . . . is already turning the tables, even if slightly," on the growth in extreme inequality, by making income-earning "capital" (i.e., rentable assets) available to everyone.[7] He offered a study of Getaround, a P2P car rental platform, to prove the point.[8]

A common argument was that lower-income households will benefit disproportionately from platforms. If that is true, one reason is "ease of entry." As we have noted, platforms are simple to sign up for, have relatively few screens to exclude people, and often require little capital. And for a number of our respondents, getting started *was* just an internet search away. Allegra was a freelance musician and part-time music teacher who often had trouble paying her bills, especially in the summer, when she wasn't teaching. "I really needed money, and I think I was Googling about ways to make money and some website or other mentioned you could rent out your car, so I signed up. . . . And then I just started renting it to everybody." On Airbnb, even if you don't own your home, you can be a host.

Given the persistence of significant racial inequality—black households earned only 62 percent of what white ones did in 2017[9]—another disruptionist prediction is that racially disadvantaged groups have more to gain in these newer, less discriminatory markets. They will therefore have higher participation. Platforms are also expected to reduce what economists call "statistical discrimination." That's when the absence of information about an individual in a group leads discriminators to rely on negative stereotypes and penalize all members of that group.[10] Since ratings and reviews provide accurate accounts of the trustworthiness, qualifications, and competence of individual providers, some researchers think they will eliminate this stereotype-based bias.

The opposing school of thought studies how existing inequalities are reproduced in these new settings. #AirBnBWhileBlack is a vivid example of the person-to-person racial discrimination that can flourish on a platform. There are no laws outlawing this type of behavior because the "Mrs. Murphy" exemption to the Civil Rights Act of 1968 excludes landlords who rent out fewer than five rooms in their homes.[11] Therefore, many Airbnb hosts are legally free to discriminate by race, in contrast to hotels. The platforms claim they have no institutional responsibility, on the grounds that they merely facilitate transactions among independent parties. The courts have not yet challenged that view. Only reputational pressure remains, and it hasn't been very powerful. Without requirements for platforms to release their data, there isn't even transparency about what is occurring on these sites. These institutional characteristics lead analysts in the "social reproductionist" camp to expect that platforms will be sites of discrimination and inequity rather than disruptors of it. As Tawana, the African American blogger, warned: "I think it's important to remember how our real-life interactions with one another bleed over into how we handle each other and mishandle each other using technology."

A second reproductionist argument is that existing inequalities skew participation and outcomes. Disruptionists assume that people can overcome their economic disadvantage by accessing credit (including via crowd-financing), purchasing assets, and becoming earners. In reality it's not so simple. Consider the situation faced by a low-income individual with poor credit who wants to earn on Getaround, the site Sundararajan studied. They will need to borrow for a newish car, and the monthly payment will probably exceed $500. The hourly rental rate is only five to eight dollars, the company takes 40 percent in commission, and there's a chance of low customer demand. The risk-reward ratio looks awfully shaky.[12] Perhaps that's why most owners on the car rental platform we studied were financially secure. (Allegras were in the minority.) In the real world, access to finance remains constrained by class and race, and the distribution of physical capital and skills matters for success on the platforms. We have studied this "structural inequality" and find that it affects outcomes. Platforms facilitate the entry of individuals, but not necessarily those who are socioeconomically disadvantaged.[13]

Finally, there's the question of who reaps the economic value created by the new technologies. Rather than assume it automatically flows to earners and consumers (as in the idealist discourse), we need to consider the hierarchy of platforms and the power they can wield.

Those with higher proportions of supplemental earners tend to be less predatory—taking a reasonable fee from each transaction, without attempting to soak the earners. Etsy, a crafts marketplace, takes 5 percent.[14] Airbnb takes about 15 percent. This makes sense because supplemental earners have more ability to walk away. Contrast these rates to the 30 percent TaskRabbit instituted on first-time trades, or the 25 percent to 50 percent that Uber takes, depending on the size of the booking fee.[15] (The 40 percent taken by Getaround is an exception, but it includes costly auto insurance.) By offering high returns for well-off people with capital on a platform like Airbnb, but low hourly rates on the labor-intensive ride-hail and delivery apps, the platform sector looks to be reproducing, rather than eliminating, existing inequality. To see why we think so, let's go beyond theory to the empirical research.

## Evidence of Person-to-Person Discrimination

There are now a number of studies that investigate biased behavior on sharing platforms, looking at both buyers and sellers. In all of them researchers find evidence of discrimination. A second Airbnb experiment similar to the Harvard study found even higher levels of refusal of African American guests: they were 19 percent more likely to be rejected when they attempted to book rooms than were whites.[16] There's also evidence of discrimination in the other direction— against hosts of color. Using data scraped from the Airbnb website, two of the Harvard researchers found that black hosts earned 12 percent less for their listings than nonblack hosts, controlling for quality and other determinants of price.[17] As we'll see in a moment, our research yields a similar finding. Another Airbnb study that also included Europe, and looked at both blacks and Muslims, found that hosts in both groups netted lower room rates.[18]

Interpersonal discrimination has also been found on labor platforms. Analysis of scraped data from TaskRabbit found that the platform algorithm is less likely to recommend black taskers.[19] A survey-based study of TaskRabbit in Chicago found that residents of lower income neighborhoods of color were underrepresented as earners.[20] (The median income of Chicago taskers was twice the poverty line.) A field experiment on ride-hailing apps found that black users experienced longer wait times and twice as many cancellations and that women's rides were longer (and more expensive) than men's.[21] While ride-hailing is acknowledged to be less discriminatory than taxi service,[22] for which there is a long history of racist refusal of individual passengers and unwillingness to take fares to certain areas, it has not completely eliminated this bias. The first study of gender differences among Uber drivers found that women are earning 7 percent less than men.[23] Contrary to disruptionist predictions that the gig economy will favor women because it offers flexibility, the economist authors of this paper suggest there's little reason to believe this gender gap will close. Another type of discrimination is by disability.[24] Even with some recent adaptations, ride-hail vehicles are still less accessible than taxis. Airbnb listings don't have to comply with disability regulations. This inequity is growing as the platforms scale.

In our interviews respondents usually avoided the topic of race. But it did occasionally come up. Airbnb host Mark, whom we met in chapter 1, recounted a disturbing incident with other tenants in his luxury building that "really got at my core." Mark had rented to a family he described as "of a minority race," who were in town when their son or daughter (he wasn't sure which) was running the Boston Marathon. Earlier, Mark had confided in some of his friends in the building that he was hosting on Airbnb. One of them saw the family in the lobby, assumed they were his guests, and made a complaint about them to the front desk attendant. Mark explained that everyone in the building is white or Asian, plus a few Saudis, so his renters "probably stood out a little bit." Later, he confronted his friend about it, asking what her objection was. Soon afterward, the friend and her (lawyer) husband asked him to stop the hosting. He described their attitude: "'We live in this building and we're entitled' . . .—they used the word—'we're entitled to exclusivity. . . . We bought here because it's very secure. And you're letting in people that could murder my daughter, rape my daughter.'" Mark explained that "that argument offended so many of my senses." But he did slow down his hosting.

Mark's story reveals not only interpersonal racism but the context for the findings we report below—the privileged position of whites in the housing market. Alexandrea Ravenelle reports that some of her hosts "admit to discriminating on the basis of race."[25] We also had a few discuss bad experiences where the focus was on the race of the guest. Many Airbnb hosts recount the ways in which they screen potential guests. Lily explained that "I only accept people that would look like they were our friends," ostensibly as a way of concealing the fact of her hosting from other tenants and her landlord. She explicitly referenced exclusions by age, rather than race and class, but we were left to wonder about those. Other hosts report that they look for evidence of jobs, property ownership, and other markers of race and class before accepting would-be guests.

Tawana, who is African American, talked explicitly about her experience of racial refusal on Turo. She was back at home in Chicago over the winter holidays and had stayed downtown away from family to get some "peace and quiet . . . And I really needed to borrow someone's car to go through the northern suburbs. It was Christmas, not a lot was available." Tawana was declined six times, at which point she gave up. Recounting the incident, she explained that she's always careful about sending a personalized, "tailored message" when trying to rent. "I operate with the assumption that I'm not beyond the reach of discriminatory practices," and a racial turndown is "always in my mind." She fills out the entire online profile and includes positive things like her volunteering activity. This is an example, she explains, of how "folks of color, but specifically black folks, use technology to render themselves legitimate and trustworthy." She muses that she'll never know why she was repeatedly rejected that particular time but does offer: "So yes, I'm pretty sure it's happened, but nobody's ever been, like, 'I don't rent to dark people, but my friend does and I'll give you her number.'"

Qualitative researchers have also found racist dynamics on ride-hail platforms. Alex Rosenblat reports that immigrant drivers often conceal their countries of origin for fear of encountering xenophobic attitudes. She described an incident in which an unhappy passenger went off on a driver with racial slurs.[26] A poignant case in our sample was Karim, the Uber driver we met briefly in chapter 1. Karim was teetering on the edge financially, after a disability made it difficult for him to remain in hotel hospitality, the field he'd been trained for. After more than two thousand rides for Uber, he received a two-day hold and notice of an investigation, after which he was deactivated. He said passengers complained that he discussed religion and was trying to be friendly. One said his car was dirty, although it was only two weeks old. "Someone could lose job because someone just racist. You know, sometimes I have Hebrew music. Sometimes people don't understand why this Hebrew, think I'm terrorist . . . completely lose my job . . . Maybe the only job this I can do." Karim felt passengers have too much power. When we interviewed him, he was still working for Lyft but worried about his lack of security on the platform, even after driving for more than a year.

An important question in the literature is the extent to which statistical discrimination can be eliminated through the public reputation systems. There is growing evidence that ratings and reviews can reduce unfair outcomes. The second Airbnb field experiment noted above (which yielded the higher rejection rate for African Americans) was able to equalize rejections across race when at least one review was present for would-be guests.[27] Studies using scraped data find that reviews reduce racial differences in prices.[28] And a study using an online game played by thousands of Airbnb users found that the presence of reputational data increased trust among dissimilar kinds of people.[29] Analyses of eBay transactions find reduced racial discrimination for highly rated sellers.[30] These findings suggest that ratings may be at least a partial cure for discrimination. But what if the ratings themselves are biased? Can the public reputation systems really eliminate discrimination? Our research helps answer these questions.

## Our Airbnb Study: The Reproduction of Structural Disadvantage

After Airbnb declined our offer to study racial discrimination using its data, we decided to collect our own. Mehmet Cansoy took the lead and scraped Airbnb data from 104 metropolitan areas across the country, eventually yielding about two hundred thousand listings.[31] We also purchased data from a company that was doing something similar. Here I'll focus on findings from 335,000 listings in the ten biggest Airbnb markets, for which we've done extensive analysis. In contrast to the studies I've discussed so far, ours differs in that we don't link the property listings back to individual hosts. That is partly for privacy reasons, partly because the racial coding methods used by researchers aren't yet perfect, and partly because we wanted to explore neighborhood-based inequality. Our findings help to explain the context for Mark's experience—white privilege in the housing market.

We discovered that there are clear limits to the power of the public reputation systems to combat inequality. The first difficulty for hosts is getting a booking and hence a rating. While there's only slight difference across neighborhoods in the likelihood of never being booked, there is divergence in the length of time to get a booking. It takes three days longer for a first booking in a neighborhood with

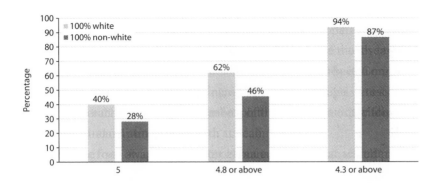

FIGURE 1. Predicted Probabilities of Airbnb Ratings by Race of Neighborhood.

more than 90 percent residents of color than it does in a neighbor-hood with fewer than 10 percent residents of color.

We also found that ratings are systematically lower for hosts who live in neighborhoods with more nonwhites. Around 29 percent of our sample has a perfect five-star rating, which many guests look for when making a booking. Our analysis predicts that an average Air-bnb listing has a 40 percent probability of receiving this rating if it is located in an all-white area, but the probability falls to 28 percent if the listing is located in an all-nonwhite neighborhood.[32] The same likelihoods for the rating of 4.8 or above are 62 percent and 46 per-cent, respectively. Even when we lower the cutoff point to 4.3 stars, racial inequality remains. A listing located in an all-white area is 94 percent likely to get a rating at that level or above while a listing in an all-nonwhite area is only 87 percent likely to achieve that level (see fig. 1). Our data also replicate the well-known result that ratings tend to cluster at the top.[33] This puts hosts who live in "neighborhoods of color" at a serious disadvantage, given guests' preferences for high ratings and the platform's requirement of at least 80 percent five-star ratings to be eligible for the "superhost" designation.

The TaskRabbit study cited above has findings similar to ours.[34] Using scraped data from all TaskRabbit cities, researchers found that

African Americans had fewer reviews, and when they did get them, they came with lower ratings. The disparity was particularly large for African American men. Women also received fewer reviews than men. These are the first studies we know of on this topic, and both suggest that the online environment is reproducing "real-world" discrimination. This problem of racist bias from customers is the subject of a complaint filed in 2016 with the Equal Employment Opportunity Commission on behalf of an Asian driver.[35] Because EEOC filings are not public, we don't know how this one is being (or has been) handled. But it's increasingly clear that companies' use of ratings for deactivation decisions or in prioritizing people for opportunities can reproduce racially unfair outcomes.[36]

Our study was designed to get beyond person-to-person discrimination in order to test for structural inequality. This refers to institutionalized features of an economy or society rather than just the biases of individuals. Structural inequalities include things like persistent disparities in incarceration rates, educational attainment, or employment opportunities. We were interested in how residential segregation in urban areas affects outcomes on Airbnb. We knew that U.S. cities are highly segregated by race. Residents of color have been historically confined to less desirable neighborhoods and have been subjected to discriminatory zoning practices.[37] They have also been victims of "redlining"—banks' unwillingness to give mortgages in certain areas. Originally these were African American, Jewish, and Catholic neighborhoods. More recently African American and Latinx populations have been subjected to this now-illegal practice.[38] As a result, members of these groups are much more likely to live in areas of concentrated poverty, which have fewer amenities and higher crime rates. They also have lower rates of homeownership than whites.[39] We reasoned that this would yield unequal outcomes on the platform. To figure out how living in a certain neighborhood matters, we conducted a two-tiered statistical analysis that controls for where people live.[40] This allows us to see whether the structure of the housing market affects platform experiences. We measured four variables: how likely people were to list their homes on Airbnb, the prices they received, how often they were able to find renters, and their annual revenues. Let's start with participation.

Disruptionists predict that more disadvantaged people—in this case, by race—will be more likely to get active on platforms. We also thought that would be true. Facing discrimination in the legacy economy, disadvantaged individuals would be particularly attracted to this potentially fairer opportunity. So we measured the probability of listing a property, given the racial composition of the neighborhood. On the face of it we found something unexpected: neighborhoods of color had fewer, not more, listings. But this is because race is correlated with factors that reduce the likelihood of listing, such as income and especially education. (Nonwhites have lower incomes and educational levels.) Once we controlled for those, as well as a number of other variables, we found what we'd expected. People who live in neighborhoods with higher numbers of nonwhites are more likely to list their properties. Comparing an all-nonwhite to an all-white neighborhood, we found an average of ten listings versus seven. It does seem that those who are facing disadvantage are looking to platforms for an even playing field. But do they find one?

Our results for prices, bookings, and revenues suggest not. We found that in neighborhoods with higher fractions of residents of color, prices are lower, bookings are fewer, and annual revenues are smaller. On average, without accounting for other factors, we show that a listing in a neighborhood that's all nonwhite earns seventy dollars less per night than a listing in an all-white area. It will also get fewer bookings. In a year those differences amount to $324. Once we control for the other factors at play, such as income, homeownership, education, and housing values, the nightly difference is $13 and the annual revenue disparity falls to $249 (see the accompanying box).

Predicted Nightly Price of an Airbnb Listing in an All-White and an All-Nonwhite Neighborhood

|  | All White | All Nonwhite | Difference |
|---|---|---|---|
| Nightly price | $218 | $145 | $73 |
| Nightly price with controls | $187 | $174 | $13 |
| Annual revenue | $1,204 | $880 | $324 |
| Annual revenue with controls | $1,168 | $919 | $249 |

*Note:* The reported values are for an entire unit listing that is not instantly bookable. All other variables at the listing level or the neighborhood level are assumed to be at the population mean.

But remember that those "control" variables are also unequally distributed by race. They allow social scientists to parse out the effects of these different factors, but for the individuals involved, lower income, education, and homeownership rates are an integral part of the experience of being African American or Latinx.

Overall, our findings show that privilege is being reproduced on the platform. Hosts who live in whiter areas get higher prices and more bookings. At the same time, higher rates of participation support the idea that online opportunities may be disrupting inequality. But there's an important limitation of our method that needs to be considered before we come to this conclusion. It's that we don't know exactly who our hosts are, and we don't know their racial (or class) status. Within a neighborhood of color it may not be the residents of color who are primarily benefiting. In fact, there's a specific kind of neighborhood that is popular on the platform, where this may be especially true: a gentrifying one.[41] Gentrifying neighborhoods are typically getting whiter, richer, and hipper. They start out heavily nonwhite, with low real estate prices. Over time their racial and class composition changes, as upscale retail moves in, amenities improve, and they gain a reputation as a desirable place to live. During this process the composition of the neighborhood is mixed, housing both long-term, poorer residents of color and whiter newcomers. With our method we can't tell which group the Airbnb hosts belong to, although we are pretty sure that they are more likely to be the latter. One study for New York City did ask this question and found that in areas where African Americans were the biggest racial group, nearly 75 percent of Airbnb hosts were white.[42] This suggests that our results may be significantly understating racial differences in outcomes on the platform.

## Reproducing Social Class Inequalities

Since the Occupy protests of 2011, the public conversation about economic inequality has focused on the concentration of income and wealth at the top of the distribution. In 2017 the three richest Americans (Warren Buffett, Jeff Bezos, and Bill Gates) had more wealth than the bottom half of the population. The top four hundred from *Forbes*'s list of the richest Americans have nearly as much as two-thirds of the population.[43] In addition, the share of the top 1 percent has grown substantially, and their assets now exceed those of the entire bottom 95 percent.[44] This is the highest level of wealth inequality in a half century. Income has followed a similar trend. Between 1993 and 2017 the top 1 percent of households roughly doubled their incomes, taking home more than half of all the gains in income, compared to a mere 15.5 percent increase for the bottom 99 percent.[45] The first decade of the sharing economy has conformed to these patterns, with fantastic wealth accumulation for founders, some of whom are now among the billionaire class. In early 2019, Uber founder Travis Kalanick was worth just under $6 billion, and the three cofounders of Airbnb were in the $3.7 to $3.8 billion range.[46]

The 1 percent theme did come up occasionally in our data, as earners talked about the customers. An insidious aspect of labor platforms is that they are essentially recreating a servant economy. Couriers talked about frequency of delivery to wealthy people in high-rises. When we asked about the customers, Don offered that they were "anywhere from the college student that's hungover, doesn't want to go out, to those 1-percenters that have you pick up a single doughnut, and the delivery charge is three times as much as the doughnut."

The amassing of outsized fortunes and the growth of a servant class are obvious ways the sharing economy is intensifying inequality. But our research also led us to other, more subtle ways in which sharing platforms are contributing to cleavages among the population. These are mostly taking place not between the 1 percent and the 99 percent but among the bottom 80 percent.[47] While we haven't quantified them, our interview data suggest two dynamics: a "crowding out" effect in which college-educated people are doing forms of labor that were previously done by those with lower educational attainment, and a "supplemental earner" effect in which people with full-time jobs are taking on additional work. Both direct income upward within the bottom 80 percent, which likely results in more inequality.

## Manual Labor with a Bachelor's Degree

A striking aspect of our data is that our respondents are almost all highly educated, yet they were taking on jobs traditionally done by people with much lower levels of formal schooling. We wondered how these earners felt about performing tasks that are generally not done for pay by people of their social class, particularly when it is "dirty work" such as cleaning. And we thought about how it might be affecting the livelihoods of those traditional workers.

The bulk of the work done on the platforms we studied is manual labor, pink and blue collar. On Airbnb, hosts spend some time making arrangements with guests, but washing sheets and towels, and cleaning bedrooms and shared spaces are often the most time-consuming chores for hosts. On TaskRabbit, housecleaning is a typical job for many of our women respondents. Moving and handyman work, including furniture assembly, are frequent activities for the men we interviewed. Delivery was also popular on TaskRabbit, and of course, it's the only task on Postmates and Favor. Driving is the most prevalent service overall in the platform sector, given the large size of Uber and Lyft. As TaskRabbit Josh explained about the work: "It's manual labor in person."

In the conventional economy nearly all these occupations are dominated by people without formal higher education. According to 2017 data from the Bureau of Labor Statistics,[48] 76 percent of maids and housecleaners had either a high school degree or less, in roughly equal proportions. Only 5 percent had a bachelor's or more. Sixty-three percent of movers are in the high school or less category; 6.5 percent have a bachelor's degree, and zero percent have master's or postgraduate credentials. Among delivery workers, just under half (48 percent) are in the high school or less category; 6.5 percent have a bachelor's or a higher degree. In the taxi driver and chauffeurs category, high school or less characterizes 46 percent of the labor force and 20 percent have a bachelor's or above. (That's in part because by 2017, higher educated ride-hail drivers were already a significant fraction of this occupation. In 2015 Uber reported that nearly half of its drivers held college degrees.)[49] Back in 1970, only 1 percent of taxi drivers had a college degree.[50]

Now contrast these statistics to those of the platform earners we discussed in the last chapter. Just 7 percent of our sample has a high school degree or less, and 73 percent have a college or graduate degree. Our informants come from a wide range of occupations. They are aspiring entrepreneurs, artists and creative workers, management consultants, software developers and project managers, medical and scientific researchers, teachers, an accountant, a lawyer, a political operative, a college teacher, and people from corporate management, publishing, and sales. While it's true that middle-class high schoolers and college students have traditionally taken on part-time jobs such as lawn care and babysitting, platform activity represents the incursion of highly educated adults into traditional working-class occupations. A 2018 Airbnb survey found that nearly one in ten of its hosts are teachers.[51]

One consequence of highly educated individuals doing work they are unaccustomed to is that they are not always good at it. Valeria, an immigrant and student who does a lot of cleaning on TaskRabbit, explained that it has been a challenge because she grew up with privilege. "In the beginning I sucked at cleaning. I sucked. People were leaving bad reviews, like, 'Oh, she's okay. She's not awesome.' Because back at home I didn't even make my bed, you know? There was a cleaning person in my home." Aaron, the TaskRabbit we met earlier, has a degree from UCLA and describes himself as coming from an upper-middle-class family. He explained that he didn't like doing cleaning, because it is "monotonous . . . dirty . . . chemicals, all that shit, you know." But in the winter months, when there aren't as many jobs, he opts for it, just to get work. "Say tomorrow in the evening if something comes up and it's cleaning I'm like—Oh, that's cool. I can do that. I've done that plenty of times. But there still is a feeling of apprehension because though I am pretty good at it I'm not very good at it." Zack, another TaskRabbit, explained how his participation on the platform taught him to do things he'd never known about: ironing, raking leaves, cleaning. These were tasks he'd avoided growing up in a middle-class home with a father who owned his own business and a mother who was a professor.

What accounts for the willingness of our informants, many of whom are from the upper middle class or have high-status jobs, to do this kind of historically devalued labor, even when they are not particularly skilled at it? We found a number of factors at play: a destigmatization process, the economic squeeze on the middle class, and the sheer ease of earning for those with valuable assets.

## Destigmatizing Platform Labor: The Experience of TaskRabbits

To understand why we found lawyers cleaning houses and graduate students on driving apps, we need to return to the early days of the platforms. They launched with a clean design, showcasing their cutting-edge technology, often adding cues to signal that they wanted to make the world a better place. Some had upbeat videos that featured good-looking, mostly young folks, with just enough multiracial casting to prove their progressiveness. In the 2011 introductory video for Zaarly (a TaskRabbit wannabe that has since changed its business model),[52] Casey, a perky red-headed woman, sits on her couch as the room fills up with cool Zaarly users liberally fist bumping and high fiving. She meets her photographer neighbor for the first time. The African American DJ he just hired on the platform glides in. Then we're treated to a basketball player, an artist, a horseback rider, and a belly dancer. It's a big happy "community" (Casey's term) in which she responds "to Zaarly postings that allow her to express herself creatively." The message: here's an app where you can be creative and make money.

Phuong, the courier we met in the previous chapter, is critical of the platforms. He zeroed in on one of the most important ways they have been able to attract educated workers: hipness. "It's just disguising old models of for-profit drive mentality in a new, younger, hip kind of way. And people are eating it up, because it looks fun and hip. It's innovative. It's new. It's Steve Jobs and I think it is hiding old school models of exploitation." By featuring attractive young people enacting a new economic model on their computers and smartphones, platforms were able to reduce the stigma associated with the often mundane service work they were offering. The use of the idealist discourse was also central to the symbolic cleansing of manual work, and our respondents did that in part by invoking community, environmental benefits, efficiency, cultural exchange, and opposition to soulless corporations. They considered themselves architects of an alternative, person-to-person economy. The vibe of hip do-gooderism helped turn cleaning toilets and assembling furniture from something that was "beneath" highly credentialed professionals into a transformative, attractive activity.

Nicki had an MA in a science field, a good full-time job in biotech, and was earning to pay off graduate school loans. She referenced a kind of trendy factor when she talked about one of her favorite Task-Rabbit jobs—testing apps, which she thinks is "cool." Plus, "you get to see—especially with the tech stuff—before it comes out. That's cool. That's a cool benefit." Katie, a lawyer, also referenced "cool" in her decision to join TaskRabbit, which she learned about when she was temping at an online jewelry company, because she couldn't get a job right out of law school and needed income while she was trying to pass the bar.

But cool and hip only goes so far. Both Nicki and Katie discussed the identity conflicts that platform work can raise. Katie found that doing this work after she had already become a lawyer "was very, very humbling. That was actually the one thing that would bother me sometimes doing TaskRabbit. So I put in my profile that I went to law school and everything, because I wanted to look more credible. But people sometimes that would hire me to come over and clean, would almost make comments almost pitying me for having to clean their apartment, having gone to law school, and I hated that. . . . They would be, like, 'Oh, it sucks you have to do this.' Yes, I know it sucks. You don't have to remind me."

Nicki refused to do cleaning jobs, reasoning that she cleaned her own house, so she didn't need to do anyone else's. "I don't want to be a servant." But even avoiding that lowest-status work, she faced identity threats. "It doesn't make me feel bad. . . . I don't feel like I'm demeaning myself. . . . It's fine. I try to pick stuff that's like normal to do." Was it really "fine"? She draws the line at some tasks, particularly those that she considers "lazy or selfish" or that people can easily do themselves: "I saw one that was 'Get me a latte from Starbucks and I'll pay you $8' . . . Like no, get off your butt and get it yourself. Because that's lazy." Her discomfort with the servant role was most acute when she saw a delivery task posted by someone she'd known from her elite private high school. "Wow. Okay, this is strange. Like, this person is the same age as me, and this is like role reversal." When we asked her to elaborate, she explained that when she started, she thought it was "normal" work and that she knew people who were looking into or doing it. But seeing her former classmate on the app was different. "It was weird for me to see this other person in my peer group, on the other side of using that sort of service. You know what I mean, he was sort of, like [an] 'I'm in charge here,' person and because it's sort of that kind of relationship, you're paying someone to do something for you, and so he was in a power position, I guess, and I was not. But I didn't accept the task. I never told him that I saw it."

## Riding the Down Escalator

The financial crash and ensuing downturn was an important spur to early platform participation. Platforms were launching as the Great Recession began and were busy attracting workers during the darkest days, which featured double-digit unemployment, with especially high rates among youth. When we started our interviews with for-profits in 2013, we met a number of providers who had graduated from college when there were no jobs available or who had been laid off. Many were cobbling together multiple gigs, including on platforms. Given their education and training, our interviewees were riding a down escalator in the labor market, taking on work that was lower-paid and lower-status than they would have accepted in ordinary or good times. That's a cascade effect that economists expect during recessions. People with more training and credentials bump down those below them in the hierarchy, who fall into worse jobs or unemployment. This is one of the dynamics that led us to think that higher educated workers were crowding out or replacing those with less formal schooling.

Another issue is how the competition with legacy businesses played out in terms of jobs lost and "jobs" (or gigs) created. To date there are few studies of this question.[53] Ride-hail apps appear to have devastated the traditional taxi industry. In New York City, where we have data, taxi rides per day were halved, from 479,000 in 2010 to 263,000 in 2019, while ride-hail rose from 82,495 in 2015 (the first year of data) to 769,729 in 2019.[54] New York is a city where cabs have traditionally been plentiful and relatively inexpensive, but there are now four times as many trips on ride-hail vehicles as taxis. While eventually many taxi drivers did convert to the platforms, others were unable to because of loans they'd taken out for medallions[55] or because earnings are lower on the apps. Another affected occupation is maids and house cleaners. One paper estimated the impact of Airbnb on hotel revenue in Austin, Texas, and found an 8 to 10 percent drop between 2008 and 2013.[56] This decline likely reduced employment of hotel cleaners. Effects on residential cleaners are harder to estimate because so much of that market is informal.

On the other side of the ledger the platforms have raised consumer demand for rides, accommodation, delivery, and tasks because they offer lower prices and increased convenience. We don't know which effect is larger. But whatever the mix between crowding out and crowding "in," based on the educational attainment levels of legacy versus platform workers, the first decade gave opportunity to the more privileged segments of the broad middle class, seemingly at the expense of members of the working class.

## Enhancing Privilege

In the previous chapter I discussed the phenomenon of supplemental earning by people who already have full-time incomes or jobs. Because the platforms are a novel, socially acceptable way to make money, we think they are contributing to enhanced labor effort for this group rather than just causing a shift from other work these people were already doing. We came to this conclusion on the basis of how people told us they got started on platforms. Dependent and partially dependent earners were more likely to have switched over from other, less appealing jobs. Supplemental earners were less likely to describe that kind of transfer, and more likely to have just hopped into the gig economy. This suggests that the platforms set off a dynamic in which the relatively well-off are getting even better off. Of course, quite a few of our respondents were experiencing financial pressures associated with the squeeze on the middle class. Graduates were using earnings to pay their education debt, which has skyrocketed in recent years.[57] Housing costs have risen sharply in cities around the country, including Boston. That so many teachers are Airbnb hosts is a testament to the marked erosion in teacher pay. Not all supplemental or partially dependent earners are financially secure. For this group, platform earnings have been a way to avoid downward mobility.

But there's a significant group among the supplemental earners for whom participation is less about need and more about opportunity. They might be like Shira, who has a decent salary as a dental hygienist, but the chance to earn thousands on Airbnb was irresistible, so she vacates her apartment frequently to stay with her boyfriend.

Dennis, a married twenty-three-year-old, first referenced the expense of living in Boston, and went on to explain what easy money hosting can be: "Someone sleeps in the bedroom for a couple days, and you got a couple hundred bucks. So, good deal." The social bonus that so many of our hosts mention makes the money even sweeter. A third of our Airbnb hosts have annual household incomes above $75,000, and 9 percent of them earn more than $125,000. Similarly, car owners on Turo who are making more than six figures just don't want to pass up the chance to have someone else's money take care of their monthly car payment. There are fewer six-figure earners on TaskRabbit, ride-hail, and delivery platforms, but they are there. As we noted in chapter 2, the chance to earn while cycling, or to fill hours with something more productive than video games or TV, led financially secure people into platform work. This makes us suspect that supplemental earning enhances the incomes of people in the higher end of the 80 percent or even, in some cases, the ninetieth percentile of the income distribution. It's just a hypothesis at this point and needs to be rigorously tested. But if we're right, the platform economy is not just enriching the 1 percent; it's also contributing to greater inequality within the middle class.

I've now discussed a number of our research findings on for-profit platforms. We've looked at what motivates people to use platforms, the varied experiences of earners, and how the sector is affecting inequalities of race and social class. The idealist discourse made big promises about a new way to work and access to opportunity. Platforms positioned themselves as an innovative economic form that would change the world for the better. We've seen that for the most part these promises haven't been fulfilled, at least not for everyone. In the next chapter I'll address remaining aspects of the rhetoric, including how platforms are doing on other economic measures, their ability to enhance social connection, and how they're really affecting carbon and eco-footprints.

# 4 "The Shared Economy Is a Lie"

## Summing Up the First Decade

In 2014, in a bid to win residents' support for overturning a law that prohibited short-term rentals, Airbnb mounted a major advertising campaign.[1] Subway ads trumpeted the message that "New Yorkers Agree: Airbnb is great for New York City." In smaller type the ad noted that the platform provides supplemental income for thousands of New Yorkers, helps local businesses in neighborhoods, and "strengthens our communities." "Join the movement," the company urged. Some versions featured pictures of ordinary people talking about how Airbnb had changed their lives for the better. By day's end, however, the ads were conveying a very different message. "The dumbest person in your building is passing out a set of keys to your front door!" "Airbnb accepts NO liability."[2] Some crossed out "Airbnb" and substituted "New York" (is great). Our team found a hack that summed up what many have come to believe about the sector: "The Shared Economy is a Lie."

The graffitists were on to something. Over the next three to four years, Airbnb activity would have a profound impact on the city, driving up rents and removing long-term housing from the market. Nightly stays typically earn much more than what landlords can get from yearly (or even month-to-month) leases. With that kind of money to be made, landlords began converting their properties into Airbnbs, or illegal, invisible "ghost" hotels.[3]

Early on, Shira, the dental hygienist and absent Airbnb host, clued us in to the process. Her mother's fiancé owned a number of properties in Boston's North End, the old Italian neighborhood and popular tourist destination. "And what happened was, he found out his—I think it was his three-unit building in the North End—this guy was doing Airbnb. So the guy was only paying him—say it was a thousand dollars a month for rent—here he was getting, like, four or five thousand a month. . . . So, as a landlord, he got wind of this and was, 'Hey, what are you doing, blah blah blah?' So now he cuts him a percentage of it so he can continue." The guy is "almost like working for him." Spurred in part by Shira's good experiences, the fiancé gradually converted his buildings over to Airbnb, preferring the money and the minimal interaction with guests. "And now he's looking for more properties because the income is triple, if not quadruple, what you would get in just a monthly rent from one person." Shira worried that "Something's going to happen, I know that. Because it's, like, almost too good to be true."

Mehmet did one of the first nationwide studies of these effects, looking at ten major cities.[4] He found that they were at various stages of Airbnb-induced "gentrification" and that on average landlords received between two and three times as much for short-term versus long-term rentals. He found that over time, in some cities where Airbnb activity was highest, the difference in the two markets was closing because long-term rents had already risen so much and so many units had disappeared from that market. Other scholars also found evidence of these effects.[5]

By 2018 New York City had just under fifty-seven thousand active daily Airbnb listings,[6] many of them illegal, and a growing number of ghost hotels. The conservative estimate of one highly publicized study was that nine thousand apartments and homes have already been lost to short-term rentals and that this has resulted in an annual rent increase of $384.[7] The same study found that while there were plenty of hosts legitimately earning money by sharing their homes, two-thirds of the total revenue was going to landlords with illegal listings.[8] A similar dynamic also causes housing prices to rise, because properties become more valuable as a result of the income flow they can generate. While that's nice for people who already own a home, it's a barrier for anyone trying to get into the market, especially younger would-be buyers.[9]

Not surprisingly, these dynamics led to mounting opposition to Airbnb. Dissatisfaction was greatest in cities where activity has grown the most, such as San Francisco and New York, where housing was already scarce and unaffordable. Residents also identified declining quality of life in neighborhoods where Airbnb has expanded rapidly. In contrast to hotels, which are restricted by zoning laws and are often in city centers, platform listings have proliferated in residential areas, transforming their character and undermining neighborliness. In some places the rentals have brought parties, noise, and crime (chronicled at Airbnbhell.com). City governments have been trying to rein in Airbnb and similar platforms, with mixed success.

The fight for housing affordability is only one of the contentious issues raised by the sharing economy. Other platforms are also creating problems for urban residents. In chapters 2 and 3 I discussed how platforms are affecting labor conditions, racial discrimination, and social inequality. I haven't yet touched on carbon emissions and air pollution, congestion, and traffic fatalities. There are some extreme stories. One Chicago resident was reportedly renting out thirty-eight cars on Turo. He was parking them on city streets, causing havoc for his neighbors, who couldn't find spots for their own cars.[10] (We had heard about this guy years earlier, when he was starting out, during our interview with Jason, who worked for the company.) While opposition from incumbent industries (such as taxis and hotels) was to be expected, criticism has been pouring in from many directions. The idealist discourse promised efficiency, opportunity and access, social connection, and environmental benefits. A decade in, what have platforms delivered? As they remake the urban landscape, are they a malevolent invasive or a beautiful exotic?

## Economic Impacts

On the positive side of the ledger the benefits to consumers are large. The companies have brought lower-priced options in lodging and drive for hire.[11] They've also innovated with shared transport options (UberPool and LyftLine) and home sharing (renting with the host present). For those looking for household help, handymen, or babysitters, the platforms have increased availability by offering an alternative to informal, word-of-mouth markets. While there are problems—in ride-hail, safety and provisions for people with disabilities have been flashpoints—for the most part consumers have flocked to these apps for their convenience, variety, and low costs. Price has been the main motive for many consumers, and as economists begin to quantify the monetary benefits to them, they find they are substantial.[12] Cashless transacting is also a plus for many, some of whom feel awkward exchanging money. But there are more than utilitarian factors at play. On Airbnb, avoiding the sterility, predictability, and repetitiveness of hotel chains came up repeatedly in our conversations with consumers. Leah, the special education and yoga teacher, talked about having a fabulous experience in Paris, the platform's biggest market, even though face-to-face socializing didn't happen. "And just getting to drop into a stranger's life for a weekend . . . I never met the owner of the place I was staying in, but I connected with a shadow of them. . . . There's no better way to experience someplace than with a local." But cheap services are also enabling a social class dynamic that economists' analyses ignore: the new servant economy I mentioned in the last chapter. The merely well-off who want, but can't afford, a full-time housekeeper, cook, driver, or "Man Friday" can now purchase slices of these workers at very affordable prices. The buyers are whiter, richer, and more highly educated than the average American.[13] Income inequality plus technology is yielding a more pernicious division of labor.

On the supply side, another effect is on legacy businesses. I've already mentioned that the taxi industry has been badly affected, with drivers facing reduced wages and medallion owners saddled with debt.[14] The hotel industry has not suffered the same degree of adverse impact, largely because Airbnb has mainly been catering to personal travel, while hotels take the business segment. But some research shows that Airbnb is hurting lower-priced motels and bed-and-breakfasts.[15] The bigger hotels get affected during periods of peak demand, such as New Year's Eve in Manhattan or during the Super Bowl, when the supply of Airbnbs, which can be quite variable, expands and prevents room rates from going sky high.[16] Mark began his hosting during Marathon Week in Boston, and we see this swelling of listings in our national data. But the platforms have also spawned new businesses in ancillary services for lodging (cleaners and managers), raised incomes for providers, and led to tourist spending in new locations. Another entry in the economic ledger is that some providers are using platforms to start small businesses, as we saw with some of our TaskRabbits and Airbnb hosts, even if platforms' claims of widespread "micro-entrepreneurship" are overblown.[17]

While founders and venture capitalists are getting spectacularly rich, platforms are helping many in the middle class. Leah's view was one we heard a lot: "So I feel like that definitely strengthens middle-class people who are just trying to go about their lives. Yes, absolutely. I would so much rather give my money to an individual than to a company, especially a multibillion-dollar hotel chain." Earnings from the platform are helping people to stay in their homes or, in the case of the nation's underpaid teachers, to afford daily life. Our supplemental earners are using platform income to pay down debts or build retirement savings.

But these benefits are flowing disproportionately to better-off providers, as I noted in the previous chapter. For low-wage workers, platforms are making precarious work even more risky. In ride-hail, delivery, and temping, the deterioration of working conditions is well under way. A case in point is Wonolo, which stands for Work Now Locally, a platform for blue-collar warehouse labor and on-demand tasks like setting up in-store displays. The founders of Wonolo approached me for help when they were starting out. In my discussion with them they emphasized the "efficiency" of their model, its ability to give flexibility to workers, and their good intentions. When legal scholar Veena Dubal looked into the company some years later, she found a variety of insidious practices, such as mandatory, but largely undisclosed, charges for insurance; an empty promise of the right to be an employee; and default membership (with fees) in an advocacy organization controlled by the company to fight against regulatory protections for workers. Dubal concluded that "the people most likely impacted by this unprotected, precarious physical labor (that can be secured without an in-person interview) are those on the margins of the workforce: men and women of color who are disproportionately targeted by the criminal justice system; probationers, parolees, and others who may have work orders and are thus forced to work against the threat of incarceration; and immigrants without documented status."[18] In 2015, Trebor Scholz described for-profit platforms as a Trojan Horse that will destroy unions, labor protections, and regulation.[19] It's an epic that's still being written, but in the absence of organized opposition, Scholz's reference is all too apt.

## Social Connection

Early boosters of the sector had high hopes that it would foster meaningful social interactions. Peer-to-peer transactions were thought to be an alternative to isolation or ersatz corporate conversation. If neighbors were lending or even renting each other tools and equipment, wouldn't they become more trusting and better acquainted? Of respondents in the national survey that I helped field, 72 percent thought so.[20]

Our informants believe that platforms do foster a more social form of exchange, a finding that is also replicated by other researchers.[21] This was especially true of Airbnb hosts, many of whom spent time with their guests. We talked to hosts who had meals with guests, showed them around town, and became real friends. Some said they'd do reciprocal stays if they went to their guests' countries or hometowns. A repeated refrain was that hosting is like traveling without going anywhere, because it brought people from other cultures into their homes. They love learning about the places people are from. They talked about gifts that guests bring, or meals they cook for them. And they enjoy what they can offer in return. As Amelie explained: "We love to have people who are traveling the world and want to come and meet people from the city." Courtney was probably typical of this large group of hosts. The money is important, but so are the ecological and social values. "I've met some really fascinating people. They've cooked me meals, they've left me presents, they've come back, so that's been cool too." That said, the connections can also be shallow. Shira talked about enjoying her interactions with guests and about how hearing their stories was one of her motivations for hosting. But as an absent host she almost always communicated via text and explained that she rarely met guests face-to-face as the language barriers made her feel "helpless." And of course some hosts don't want social interaction. Lily recounted staying in an Airbnb on the Cape with a socially oriented host who "loved meeting people, 'blah blah blah.'" She contrasted her own attitude. "I'm not that interested in the people. . . . What I like about it is that it has been very easy. Like we have a spare bedroom. [LAUGHTER] It's a great way to make money."

There isn't much quantitative evidence on social ties and sharing platforms; however, two sophisticated studies of Couchsurfing found that the ability of the platform to create durable social ties declined over time.[22] Sociologist Paolo Parigi and colleagues were able to exploit a unique feature of this company's data collection. Users register new "friends" on the site, but in contrast to friending on a platform like Facebook, Couchsurfing asked a number of detailed questions about the depth of the friendship. The researchers could also identify reciprocal stays. When the data was analyzed, they found that the platform did create new ties and that they were friendships in the true meaning of the word. But over time, the friendship effect weakened. And curiously, it weakened as there was more information available online about potential hosts and guests through the ratings and reputation system. Apparently the uncertainty of the early days, when people were more "unknown" online, generated more trust and connection. Over time, the researchers concluded, users grew "progressively disenchanted."

Lodging platforms are obvious sites where social connection can happen, but the idealist discourse promised that other exchanges would also build ties. Goods sharing was promoted with a strong prosocial message. Most failed, however, and neighborhood versions have been the least successful. Those still in operation are more likely to be large platforms like ThredUp and other apparel sites, where used clothes travel from household to household but users only interact with the company. Many of the viable rental platforms, like RenttheRunway, have company-owned products with no P2P dimension.[23]

We did find some personalization outside of Airbnb. It was most prevalent on TaskRabbit, although only some of our respondents discussed making durable connections. Tyler, the aspiring musician, did repeated jobs for some clients and felt he'd developed real bonds. He described it as a "network of people that are counting on you that you can count on. After a certain amount of time of working for someone, it's not just work anymore. You have a relationship." For Tyler, those connections felt like a safety net. "So I know if I ever really came into a bad situation where I really fell off the wagon for some reason, I do have people that would be willing to help. And I guess that's the neighbor-to-neighbor thing that TaskRabbit really likes to market." Jerry, a lab technician who was a TaskRabbit client, found community in a serendipitous way. "I didn't even realize that my neighbors were two of the people that are actually cleaners." He hired them repeatedly and was delighted with the outcome. "It's almost like you're giving your friends money, you know?"

On Turo there was the feel-good vibe that interviewees across our cases discussed—the fact that they were helping people and really liked that, even if face-to-face interaction was minimal. In this case it was obviated by technology. Cars can be equipped with remote access, so no meeting is required. Lock boxes and keyless entry have also reduced personal contact on Airbnb. One survey of P2P car-sharing sites found that 80 percent of renters preferred *not* having to meet the owner of the vehicle.[24] We interviewed customers who felt similarly. Kelly emphasized that she preferred to not talk to the taskers she hired: "A to B flawless, minimal interaction." She laughed, then admitted, "That sounds horrible."

Kelly came to feel that the platforms were doing the opposite of what their supporters expected. Instead of fostering social connection, they were intensifying social distance. Kelly had been an employee but recently started her own software business. She had a lot of experience on platforms, having used Airbnb, Turo, and

TaskRabbit. On the consumer side, she thought that the platforms were great for people like her, "who work 100 hours a week." These people have ample disposable income but no time. So they just want somebody else to go out and do the things they need done. Having worked on both sides of TaskRabbit, Kelly believed the interactions were becoming dehumanizing. "You're paying people to do stuff for you, so you lose that touch with reality. I just think socially you start to think of people as a little more menial. . . . So it does create a little bit of that snobbishness. . . . I have noticed a lot of people who use those services can actually—especially coming from the other side and working—and I'm trying to stay mostly on the user side—you start to, yes, develop a bit of an attitude."

These findings raise a question that we don't have an answer to but that is important. As sharing platforms shift from novel to ordinary, and their P2P structures are normalized, will the social connections of the early days melt away or even evolve into the snobbishness Kelly noticed? When Lyft started, passengers sat in the front. In 2019 Uber announced what is essentially a "Mute" button passengers can push—or what one headline termed a "shut up and drive" option.[25] This "quiet" mode (Uber's term) lets drivers know the passenger prefers not to talk. It's a far cry from the early days of sharing.

## Environmental Impacts

One of the strongest claims for the sharing economy was that it would reduce ecological degradation. Recognition that we are in a climate emergency is especially high among the highly educated young adults who have been the vanguard of the sharing sector. Many were captivated by the commonsense approach to eco-impacts that the idealistic discourse offered, especially the mantra of "efficiency." If cars sit idle for twenty-three hours a day, deploying them for ridesharing will reduce the demand for new vehicles. Airbnb listings will prevent the construction of hotels. Secondhand markets transfer goods from people who have little use for them into the hands of those who want them, thereby reducing purchases.

The logic seemed unassailable to many, and quite a few of our respondents repeated it nearly verbatim. These included hosts, car renters, and ride-hail drivers. Adam, an Airbnb host, offered a typical rationale: "Personally I'm [against] overconsumption of resources in the world from either the environmental or an equity perspective. I know that's incredibly broad, but to me things like Airbnb or other sorts of sharing platforms allow people to get the same services without generally needing to [use] the same resources, natural resources, or energy, or whatever. And so things like tool libraries, or car sharing—when you own a car it sits on the road in front of your house not being used, for, like, 90 percent of its life or something." Thomas Friedman, echoing the conventional wisdom, assured his readers: "Just think how much better all this is for the environment—for people to be renting their spare bedrooms rather than building another Holiday Inn and another and another."[26] Nationally, 64 percent of respondents believed that the sharing economy lowers environmental impacts, likely because it seems like common sense.[27]

This impeccable logic turns out to be flawed. One reason is that its analysis is static. The hotel-construction example works if Airbnb doesn't increase the number of people traveling. Ride-hailing will reduce the demand for new cars if it doesn't increase the desire to ride in cars. In the world of environmental impact, things are complicated. One change leads to another and then another. Figuring out the footprint of any activity or product involves a system-wide analysis that the idealistic discourse completely missed.

Behind the ripple effects is an important economic dynamic. If an innovation lowers the price of a good or service, demand for it will generally increase.[28] And lower prices have been key to the scaling of sharing platforms. Airbnb is an alternative to exorbitant hotel prices in expensive cities. Where I live, taking a ride-hail to the airport is half the price of a taxi. In fact, the platforms' environmental claims often conflict with their economic ones. They take credit for creating increased economic activity but ignore the fact that every additional dollar of spending carries carbon and other environmental impacts.[29] The failure to address these "rebound effects"—second- and third-round behaviors—was a worrisome sign from the beginning. Rebounds are likely to have been largest in lodging and ride-hail because travel and transport are two carbon intensive activities and because those are the sectors with the most activity. In both cases there's mounting evidence of a big footprint.

One of the nice things about studying the sharing economy in the United States is that the platforms came to cities at different times. This offers researchers a "natural experiment," a situation where some places have the app and others don't, so it's possible to identify the effects they cause. Economists at the University of Chicago took advantage of the fact that ride-hailing was rolled out gradually, and they tracked before-and-after patterns as Uber and Lyft entered 2,955 cities.[30] To estimate the carbon and air pollution impacts of ride-hailing, relevant variables are the number of cars on the road and how many miles they're being driven. This study found an increase in both. Nationwide, what transportation analysts call vehicle miles traveled (VMT) increased by 3 percent as a result of ride-hailing. Fuel consumption rose an extra 1.7 percent. Car registrations went up 5 percent on average, and a whopping 9.6 percent in cities with high-population density. Another national study, by transportation expert Bruce Schaller, found that the introduction of ride-hailing apps resulted in a doubling of the "for-hire" driving segment and an estimated 5.7 billion additional miles driven.[31] Schaller calculated that for every one-mile reduction in private driving, ride-hailing led to 2.8 additional miles. And pooled services like UberPool and LyftLine barely made a difference: their additional miles are 2.6.

City-specific estimates come to similar conclusions. A San Francisco study that looked at how things changed from 2010 (before Uber and Lyft) to 2016 found that VMT rose 13 percent, half of which is attributable to the platforms.[32] By 2016, ride-hail vehicles accounted for 15 percent of all trips within the city. Even Uber and Lyft now admit they are increasing congestion. A 2019 report they funded found that while they are still a small proportion of total VMT (1 to 3 percent across six metropolitan regions), their impact can be as high as 8 percent (Boston) or 13 percent (San Francisco).[33]

These findings contrast with early claims. Ride-hailing was supposed to reduce car ownership; instead, workers are buying cars in order to drive. The software was supposed to reduce "dead-heading" (drivers riding around looking for passengers), and while that happened at first, the increased demand for rides has far outweighed that efficiency. Overall, the biggest impact of ride-hailing has been that more people are taking more trips in private cars and putting more carbon and other pollution into the atmosphere. One survey finds that 61 percent of rides are not replacing people's own driving but are substitutes for public transportation, walking, cycling, or just staying put.[34] While that's a somewhat squishy number because it's self-reported, evidence of this kind of substitution is growing.

The trend in public transportation use is particularly worrisome. After years of rising, ridership on the nation's public transport systems (excluding New York) declined 7 percent over the last decade, and studies show that ride-hail is a major culprit.[35] The San Francisco study found that bus ridership fell by a whopping 12.7 percent.[36] For years, the ride-hail companies insisted they were supportive of public provision and emphasized their utility for solving long-standing challenges for local systems. These include "first and last mile" gaps (getting from home to a station and back), routes with low ridership, and providing service during off-peak times. Some locales have been partnering with the companies to address these real needs. In 2018

Lyft committed to carbon offsetting, meaning they are paying money to compensate for the carbon emitted by their vehicles.[37] But this is a false solution. The problem is that ride-hailing is undermining the only real low-carbon transport system we have.[38] It doesn't take a crack researcher to see the threat. When UberPool and LyftLine offer fares as low as three dollars, ride-hailing is price-competitive with public transport and offers superior convenience. It may be affordable for consumers but not for the climate.[39]

There's another aspect of ride-hailing that isn't environmental but that the increased number of vehicles on the streets is responsible for: traffic accidents and, even more problematically, fatalities. The University of Chicago study discussed above found that the growth of ride-hail has resulted in between 2 and 4 percent more traffic fatalities, including for pedestrians.[40] Before ride-hailing, traffic fatalities had been declining for twenty years. That trend reversed in 2010, and deaths have climbed since then. This is true even though ride-hailing services are a popular option for people who have been drinking. Moreover, as ride-hailing has expanded, additional deaths have been rising.

We know less about how Airbnb and other accommodation platforms are affecting carbon footprints. But the assumption that they are doing wonders for the environment is questionable. In contrast to some platforms that have quietly stopped making environmental claims, Airbnb has doubled down, producing glossy reports with evidence that its listings are lower-impact than hotel stays.[41] This is likely correct, although it's also the case that there's limited overlap between Airbnb customers and guests at the big downtown hotels. There's also likely "selection bias" at work because travelers who opt for Airbnb may already lead more environmentally conscious lifestyles, wherever they stay. But whatever the outcome of that comparison, the bigger question is whether Airbnb leads to more trips because it reduces costs. We found evidence of this "induced travel" effect. Some of our informants used their rentals as an opportunity to make leisure trips, because they became so much cheaper with someone paying to stay in their home. There's also the guest side of the equation. Airbnb claims (with no documentation) that induced travel is low, only 1 to 3 percent.[42] But in one survey of U.S. and Finnish consumers, 41 percent reported that P2P accommodation increases their travel frequency, and the fraction was even higher for Americans.[43] Similarly, an economic analysis for the U.S. found that across cities, 42 percent to 63 percent of Airbnb bookings would not have been made at hotels if Airbnb wasn't an option.[44] And even if the implausibly small 1–3 percent figure were correct, the carbon released from air travel swamps the environmental differences between hotels and Airbnbs. A Nordic study estimated that one additional London–Oslo flight is equivalent to savings of 270–400 guest nights.[45]

The final segment to consider is goods sharing, where rebound effects are smaller. The limited take-up of P2P goods markets on for-profit platforms suggests their contribution to lower carbon and eco-footprints has been marginal. But there are a few bright spots. One of the most promising is food sharing, in which an app facilitates the movement of unwanted food from donors to receivers. A London company called Olio shared its data with researchers from Yale, who have done the first environmental accounting of food donation platforms.[46] Analyzing twenty-plus months of data and more than 170,000 transactions, they found that more than half of the offered items were redistributed, which resulted in a major reduction in emissions. That's because surplus food goes to landfills and as it rots, it releases methane, a potent greenhouse gas. Those gains are balanced against the impact of moving the food from place to place. The calculus was positive because in a dense urban area, pickup and drop-off are mainly via low-carbon modes of travel such as public transport and biking. Food sharing also has the beneficial effect of getting food to people who need it.

We don't have studies of newer goods-sharing platforms, but Anders Fremstad's analysis of Craigslist in California found that it was responsible for reducing daily per person solid waste by about a third of a pound.[47] We also found an analysis of the used book market that shows that once rebound effects are factored in, results are ambiguous. One reason is that secondhand outlets make markets more "liquid." This leads higher-income consumers to buy more, knowing they can easily resell their purchases. This was a point I tried hard to convey to a platform entrepreneur who wanted advice as he was launching an app that listed resale prices for prospective buyers of products. He insisted that because people will pay more for products when they can resell them, this would result in longer-lived, more sustainably produced, options. Over multiple conversations I tried to explain that his app would increase new purchases and, as a follow-on, expand the global circulation of products, thereby increasing emissions. I asked him to at least do some research. Then he stopped calling. His psychic investment in the belief that he could make money and help the planet at the same time kept him in denial about the likely climate consequences of his start-up.

## Commercialization

"Sharing" hasn't yielded its promised environmental and social benefits in part because it spurred commercial activity rather than the more intensive and friendlier use of assets that people already owned. Jason, the Turo employee we met earlier, was a bicycle commuter who didn't even own a car when he started working at the company. When he saw the opportunity to have renters pay for his lease he acquired a personal vehicle. But it was Mark, the Airbnb host with the luxury condo, who was most active in adapting his life to commercial success on the platform. When he rented out his place, he took a trip and set his nightly price high enough to pay for it. And we learned about other changes in his life during a follow-up interview. As he professed his unabated enthusiasm for sharing, he explained that he decided to "change careers [into real estate] to be more involved with this paradigm shift." After his lawyer friend forced him to stop hosting, he bought his own home in the area. He was renovating it to turn it into the perfect upscale listing. "So I purposely stayed in six hotels [when] I was traveling for work for the year . . . [to] sort of see what it was like. How it felt, glass door, with tub, without tub. . . . The length of my tub is based off the one at the Ritz Carlton that I really liked." By coincidence, Mark's neighbor was also Airbnb-ing, charging $550 a night for a nearly identical place. Mark was expecting to earn at least that much.

As full of contradictions as ever, Mark paired his commercial ambitions with environmental and social ones. He was excited about sustainable innovations in housing. Describing a recent visit to a cohousing community, he discovered "things like communal closets. . . . I saw a lobster pot, I saw a popcorn maker, I saw an iron; I saw a steamer in this closet in the hallway. The hallways were also wider, and they had a sitting area in the middle of it." Mark was coming to realize that achieving the goals he professed would require changing physical and social infrastructure. (He hadn't yet squared these ideas with his hopes of enticing weekend travelers to his pricey listing.) Mark's explorations of cohousing had led him beyond the commercial platforms, into the community sharing solutions that emerged after the financial collapse. He was enthusiastic about their future. We were too, as they began. In fact, it's where we started our research.

# 5    *Swapping with Snobs*


As the sharing economy was taking off, Shauna, a thirty-four-year-old unmarried white professional, was struggling with the volume of food from her farm share.[1] Many weeks she'd get more of an item than she could consume—corn, zucchini, or whatever vegetable was most plentiful at the time. She liked the healthful produce, and wanted to support a local farm, but was uncomfortable with the waste. Then she heard about the concept of food swapping, which had just sprung up in Brooklyn. So she founded the Northeastern Food Swap, a monthly gathering of gastronomic enthusiasts, who would bring one or two items made from scratch to trade with others. The swap started with twenty to thirty members and was a lively affair, held in a coworking space in a hipster suburban neighborhood. Participants laid out their wares on tables and the mostly white, young to middle-aged women swappers would browse and sample the offerings. There were many delectable items—granolas, jams, baked goods, exotic condiments, and soups—all homemade.

Shauna and her cofounders envisioned the swap not only as a place to use up their farm shares but as a contribution to the growing alternative food movement. They wanted to help urban residents "take back their pantries" by accessing healthful ingredients, reclaiming lost taste palates, and mastering food preparation. We learned about the food swap just as it was founded, and the research team sent Connor Fitzmaurice, our food maven, to study it. Connor attended every month, often bringing two different items to test reactions to each. When other members of the team went, they found a down-to-earth atmosphere with appealing offerings.

Yet the food swap failed. After about a year, regular attendance had dwindled to eight people. The founders were no longer willing to pay the rental fee for the coworking space, so they moved to a free venue. Membership never recovered, and by the end of the second year, the swap officially ended, after frequent last-minute cancellations and a lack of attendance. Yet it was not for lack of interest in food swapping. A holiday cookie event the founders organized annually attracted at least fifty people. They just couldn't keep them at the monthly gatherings.

The food swap was one of many community start-ups that were founded alongside the for-profit platforms. These initiatives emphasized nonmonetized exchange: lending, bartering, gifting, helping, and the reuse of goods. The financial meltdown and subsequent recession was one catalyst for these initiatives. The consumer binge that preceded the crash and its environmental imprint was another.[2] The desire to build social connections also mattered. Some participants recognized the dramatic dysfunctions of global capitalism and hoped to create an alternative. These multiple, often reinforcing, motives resulted in the formation of hundreds, perhaps thousands, of new undertakings. Some were old-fashioned and low-tech. Others employed sophisticated software like the for-profits. They were an integral part of the "sharing" movement that I discussed in chapter 1. Many of these initiatives participated in conferences and networks with for-profit companies and the connections have been especially strong in Europe. In the U.S. the split between the commercial and community players widened over time, as commitment to common good outcomes faded for many Big Share companies. But the common history is important.

A decade later, many of the nonprofits have disappeared. That's a disappointment, but it doesn't mean this part of the sharing economy has failed. All of our sites had successes, even as they faltered on some dimensions. And despite the problems we identified, we came away from this part of our research believing in the importance of these innovative economic forms. If sharing is to fulfill its promise, it will require a vibrant nonprofit segment.

Our swap was undone by a combination of foodie judgmentalism and overt snobbery. Its high cultural capital participants engaged in subtle practices of social one-upwomanship that made it almost impossible to retain members. Outwardly friendly and welcoming, swap insiders rejected newcomers' offerings according to criteria that were opaque, inconsistent, and changing. The outcome at the food swap was most extreme, but aspects of its failure plagued the four cases we researched.[3] Exclusionary behaviors also sometimes undermined the good intentions of founders and participants in the time bank, makerspace, and the open education sites. While the for-profit platforms also had their share of prejudicial behavior, the nonprofits were more homogeneous and socially exclusionary.

The community sharing efforts also suffered from another problem that differentiated them from the Big Sharing platforms. They struggled to provide economic value to their intended audiences. The for-profits offer earning opportunities and cheaper services, and those financial inducements are at the core of their rapid growth. By contrast, the nonprofits attracted many of their participants on the basis of ideological commitments. But to construct alternative markets that grow and function well, there also needs to be a "value proposition." That was often absent.

## Community Sharing

As the "Uber of x" phenomenon took off in 2008–9, a parallel burst of activity was taking place among people who wanted to make the world a better place and didn't feel the need to earn lots of money doing it. These mostly young adults created repair cafes, tool libraries, food-sharing apps, clothing and food swaps, and toy exchanges. They enrolled in time banks, social eating apps, and land sharing. They signed up for neighborhood platforms for sharing or gifting household possessions. They got interested in foraging via apps like Neighborhood Fruit, which point people to free fruit available on public land. They tried to create matches of all sorts: gardeners with landowners, cooks with eaters, people with too much food with people who didn't have enough. When we started our project, our first cases were nonprofits. They were challenging market logics, and the people who were active in them were optimistic about their possibilities. Over the next three years, we researched four cases. The food swap, the makerspace, and the time bank were place-based, noncommercial community initiatives. (We use pseudonyms for these sites.) The fourth, which we call Open Learning, studied people who were using free and low-cost resources found mainly online.

Each site organized its activities differently. The food swap used a silent auction to organize bilateral (i.e., two-person) bartering. The time bank was also a barter system, but multilateral. A member "offers" services, say, vegan baking or dog-sitting, and "receives" services, say, language tutoring or tailoring. Because she won't be baking for her tutor, she'll receive credits for her baking based on the amount of time the task takes. These credits are put into an account. Hence the concept of the "time bank." When she gets a language lesson, her account is debited for the length of time it lasts. A bedrock principle of time banks, which differentiates them from ordinary service markets, is that everyone's time is valued equally. An hour is an hour, whether the task is lawyering or driving. The time bank we studied is low-tech, so although there's a website, matches are made manually rather than algorithmically. For the food swap and time bank, the robustness, or size, of the economy is based on the volume of trades. The makerspace was a nonprofit that rented a cavernous former factory and purchased tools and machinery. People could access the space through classes, membership, and renting a personal cubby. The "economy" we studied there consisted of people helping and teaching each other. In the Open Learning case, the people we studied are nomads, who range over sites and types of resources. Therefore, we did research at many locations, on and offline.

In all four cases, we did interviews and ethnography—that is, in-person observation and participation. (See Appendix A.) Connor did two years of preparing and swapping items. Will spent eighteen months at the makerspace. Lindsey "Luka" Carfagna's ethnographic participation spanned three years and included MOOCs (large online classes), an innovative pedagogical platform called Peer-to-Peer University, and many other free or low-cost learning sites. She lurked and was an active learner and facilitator. Offline she visited hackathons, innovation labs, and meet-ups. Emilie DuBois Poteat and Luka both received and gave services in the Time Bank.

In total we interviewed 100 people for these four cases. (See Appendix B for details on the sample.) As with the for-profits, we targeted people in the eighteen-to-thirty-four age group, although at the makerspace we also included some key informants who were older. Other characteristics differed across the four sites. Participants at the time bank and food swap were almost all women. The makerspace was roughly two-thirds men, and Open Learners were evenly divided by gender. Our sample is highly educated, white, and socioeconomically privileged. It is 81 percent white, 11 Asian, 3 black, and 3 percent Latinx. Among the 100, only 1 does not have a high school degree. The fraction with a college degree is 46 percent, and nearly as many (43 percent) also have a graduate degree. They also come from highly educated parents. Among the respondents from whom we were able to collect information on parental education, we find that half of their mothers and 61 percent of their fathers have graduate degrees.

## Motives for Community Sharing

We found a fair amount of overlap in organizational purpose and participants' motives across the sites. In the mission statements accessibility was prominent. Skillshare, an offline Open Learning site where Luka spent time, declares, "Our mission is simple: provide universal access to high-quality learning." The makerspace aimed to "empower dedicated fabricators, including hobbyists, artists, and early stage entrepreneurs." Empowerment was also a theme at the food swap, whose mission included "helping swappers eat locally, sustainably, and affordably." Time banks have the most explicitly egalitarian orientation. The mission of the national organization TimeBanksUSA is "to nurture and expand a movement that promotes equality and builds caring community economies through inclusive exchange of time and talent." Our local group describes itself as working "towards a world in which neighborhoods help neighbors and every individual can contribute so that our communities are safe and vibrant." Accessibility was often discussed in terms of affordability, but it also alluded to the belief that everyone could do the activity—whether it was learning, making, preparing food, or offering services. Another theme was building social ties and fostering community. The food swap, makerspace, and time bank all had a strong emphasis on the local context.

Participants in these efforts articulated the range of motives we found among users on commercial platforms.[4] They adopted the idealist discourse but in reference to the alternative markets in this niche of the sector. Social connection and community was the most common theme. In the time bank, meeting people and building ties was a prevalent desire. Patricia (Pat), a time bank member explained: "I'm really into hunter-gatherer societies, to be honest. . . . For me, that's real community, where you're always in touch with people, and the community meets your needs, and you help the community through work, through feeding people, through—you know, if anything comes up." Dahlia, a freelance copy editor, referred to "that sort of southern way of treating your neighbors and things. . . . I'm used to knowing my neighbors and helping them." Members at the other sites also referenced social connection. Anne, one of the cofounders of the food swap, believes it "builds community around food . . . urban people who might otherwise not know each other." At the makerspace "the community" was ritually invoked and revered as a central aspect of the whole enterprise. Jen, a white woman in her late twenties who was an early member of the makerspace, stated that making in a social context is essential to well-being: "Interacting and making tangible things actually has social and cognitive impacts on human beings that are really important. The absence of those from our lives is having [adverse] effects on our society. . . . One part of the human experience is enabling that, whether somebody wants to interact with it just as a hobby . . . or as their main mode of expression and work. And then doing it in a collaborative environment."

For many, social connection was predicated on face-to-face exchange. Rohit and his wife put Craigslist and the time bank into the same category, because both offered personalization. "One of the reasons we like Craigslist is the exchange of goods and services is very human. . . . So it's a sort of emotional gain I get from interacting with a person that I really like. For some reason, when you interact with stores, there's that dehumanizing part of it that makes it feel like a transaction rather than interaction. . . . Transactions, we may walk away with a sense of, 'Yes, we got a deal,' but that's not a smile. Usually, we tend to walk away from Craigslist and other stuff high-fiving and smiling." Sarah, another time banker, was similarly critical of conventional commerce, recounting a disillusioning trip to the car mechanic: "I didn't even have to talk to him after he fixed my car. So there was so little interaction there, and there was something very important that happened. I put a lot of money into him fixing my car, and there was nothing really there afterwards. That's a lot of trust, like I had no real relationship." Food swappers also frequently mentioned their desire to participate in a local economy in which they know "their" farmer. We heard related ideas among open learners. Alexandra, a white woman in her late twenties, worked for an organization that designs open learning content and is an open learner herself. "I want people to make things that are deeply meaningful. And culturally important," she said. "If you do projects that you love, you will acquire skills that people will pay for." For Alexandra and others this space enabled a personalized entrepreneurial alternative to the conventional economy.

Another recurring theme was the rejection of consumerist lifestyles and the importance of doing things for oneself. These sentiments were common even outside of the maker community. Marco, a fitness entrepreneur from a working-class family, was using open learning to build his business. He was also designing a minihome with his uncle and wanted to learn how to build his own rainwater collection system and solar panels. For him, consumerism was a symptom of waste and cultural deficiency. "And people consume because they're lazy. . . . If you put a few hours in, you save yourself money and you help save the environment. It doesn't make sense not to do it. But everyone wants what's right there right now, it's easy." Mei also saw open learning as an antidote to hyperconsumerism. "I think we all have, for the most part, material goods that are decent, and instead of moving on to maybe social, emotional goods, like relationship, and quality of life that way, the goods consumption has just been ratcheted up to all these crazy levels of luxury. . . . I wish people valued things that were more about the heart, rather than the wallet, and these new modes of learning are an expression of moving towards the heart." Time bankers used their trades to learn new things such as languages or, in one case, how to whittle. The ethos of the food swap was oriented toward homemade foods. Makers even extended their philosophy of creativity into the commercial economy. For Evan, this meant dealing with his car, even though, in contrast to Marco's logic, DIY was a more costly option. "You change your own oil and it makes no [economic] sense. . . . But it's awesome changing your own oil. It doesn't take a lot of time, especially if you have the right tools, and it's really good for your car to, like, feel the oil. You're not talking to somebody who talked to somebody who talked to the mechanic who changed your own oil. You're, like, 'No, no, no; the oil, it feels right.'"

Many of our open learners had start-ups, and for them DIY was a pathway to a different kind of economy. As Naomi explained: "If you happen to be interested in glow in the dark yo-yos made from special imported wood from I don't know where. Maybe that's your thing. And maybe you can really go and learn about the wood and learn about glow in the dark paint materials and become an expert in that and teach somebody else and maybe make a bit of money . . . and then start selling your yo-yos to your neighbors down the street. All of that, that whole hierarchy, that whole stack of learning and creating and economics didn't used to be possible."

The DIY ethic also dovetailed with weariness with commercial provision. Molly, a social worker at a nonprofit organization that works with youth, was having her wedding dress sewn through the time bank. She could ensure that it was ethically made, didn't cost much, and that it would be a meaningful object. Time bankers were especially tired of what sociologist Arlie Hochschild has called "the outsourced self"—that is, commercial versions of services that until recently people did for themselves, from caring labor to intimate tasks.[5] An aversion to cash transactions also showed up in the practices of makers, among whom an informal "beer for work" economy had developed. Michelle, a time banker who quit a job in corporate finance and was piecing together part-time gigs, took the view that "anybody who has the sense to barter is probably a better person than somebody who just sticks to money." Aviva, another active member, spent an entire year trading work for housing and food. The only interactions she had with money were for health insurance. And our most "de-monied" respondent was Micah, who lived with eleven roommates in a cooperative house. He is able to get by with few individual cash transactions, preferring barter and cooperative provisioning, and the informal time bank that operates among his roommates. Although he earns money as a software developer, he also spends a lot of time doing things without pay, such as offering web development skills and teaching language at a community center. He believes in a "person-based" economy and thinks the time bank is a step in that direction. Ultimately, rather than earning money to support himself, he is interested in a lifestyle in which his survival needs are ensured through "a series of relationships that I was building with people . . . whether it be mentoring or skills or sharing."

Not surprisingly, given its setup, members of the time bank were most critical of the economic system, with half of our respondents articulating anticapitalist sentiments in their interviews. Speaking about the shift toward commercialized consumption, Elaina opined that "it just destroyed a lot of culture. I don't feel like it really makes us happy and fulfills us in any way." But it wasn't only among time bankers that we heard these views. Food swappers think the food system is "insane." Airbnb and Turo users talked about disliking chains and brand names. Respondents in multiple sites expressed their discomfort with global supply chains, sweatshops, and the environmental impacts of the consumer culture. Time banker Rachel believed that "we're running out of resources and . . . it's creating massive inequalities that are destabilizing our society and our democracy."

## Why the Food Swap Failed: Snobbery and Social Exclusion

Among our four sites the failure of the food swap was most spectacular.[6] Why did things go awry for the well-meaning founders? One reason is that they demanded not only "homemade goods" (the official criterion) but the "right" packaging, ingredients, eclectic pairing of tastes, and degree of quotidian usefulness. There was a Goldilocks-like dissatisfaction expressed by the core group that left many goods untraded at the end of each session and a dwindling number of participants.[7] Newcomers would often leave with most of what they brought, never to return.

Being successful at the swap required threading the needle. Items that were in demand had to be everyday foods but not ordinary ones. As one founder routinely told newbies: "I wouldn't recommend bringing brownies. . . . I mean, unless they are like the best brownies ever. But everyone here can make brownies if they want them." The insider group wanted daily use items, but they had to be exotic, like "plum vermouth jam," sweet tomato basil jelly, or a blood orange cocktail mixer. An iconic favorite was a lime marmalade someone brought early on, because it combined a common food with an unusual flavor. Furthermore, while the swap was ostensibly trying to help people learn to cook and "take back their pantries," the items the regulars desired were too complicated and time-consuming for most people to make. The core group wanted sophisticated gourmet foods, or items that were pickled or canned, which require specialized skills. Local sourcing was also a plus, and could overcome ordinariness, as the example of a popular grape jelly made with homegrown grapes made clear. But growing food is a tall order for urbanites. We also saw that rejection of someone's offerings could lead to social rejection, as one elderly woman who came to a summertime swap discovered. Her all-too-ordinary cupcakes with vanilla icing went untraded, and no one talked to her.

Another off-putting practice was the policing of ingredients. Insiders shunned foods made with anything artificial or processed. One first-time participant brought homemade "truffles" that he had put together by grinding up Oreo cookies. One of the regulars queried him: "Now, are the truffles actually made of Oreo cookies?" The first-timer replied affirmatively, proud of his creative repurposing of the cookies, only to be rebuffed: "Oh, well then I won't be able to trade with you, because I can only trade for, like, really homemade things. Like made from scratch, with no preservatives or chemicals or anything, because my friend doesn't eat any processed foods. She only eats homemade things that she makes completely herself." And while some ingredients were taboo because they were too connected to the industrial food system, others were rejected for being too alternative. Personalized versions of kombucha and sourdough starter both flopped. Despite the founders' motive of reducing farm-share waste, real leftovers did not go over well. One couple brought vegan stuffing after Thanksgiving and received the cold shoulder. The failure was compounded by their use of the wrong packaging—Ziploc bags. Tupperware and other plastic containers were also no-nos. Plastic is too associated with industrial food and reeks of artificiality rather than "real-ness," a frequently referenced criterion. Successful trades usually involved a Mason jar, the then-trendy container that symbolized good hygiene, foodie knowledge, and the right aesthetic sensibility. Creative labels merited bonus points.

So to some extent we can chalk up the food swap's failure to snobbery. Food is an area where cultural capital—preference for high-status goods and practices on the basis of knowledge and familiarity rather than cost—is legendary. The pioneering work of Josée Johnston and Shyon Baumann on "foodies" is relevant to understanding our case. Foodies are typically high in cultural capital but distinct from old-style gourmets who only value the expensive haute cuisine of France. Foodies are more omnivorous and appreciate many genres, including peasant and ethnic offerings. Johnston and Baumann find that foodies prize exotic and authentic foods, and our respondents certainly displayed these preferences. The iconic lime marmalade was "real" food, but it also had an exotic flavor. While they are open to many cuisine styles, foodies are also snobbish. They use their specialized knowledge and tastes as a way of "distinguishing" themselves and establishing their superiority to those not in the know.[8] But at the food swap there was a twist. The rhetoric of empowerment, access, and taking back the pantry, as well as the down-to-earth feel of the swap, positioned it against pretension.[9] Members identified with the alternative food movement and its progressive values, even as they acted in socially exclusionary ways. This contributed to the social opacity of the space. It would have been relatively easy to articulate, or write down, the hidden rules of the swap so that newcomers could be included. Why didn't the website warn against Ziploc bags, artificial ingredients, and overly common items? Why weren't there examples of popular offerings? By failing to make criteria transparent, the insider group unwittingly made it hard for outsiders to be accepted and undermined participation.

## Distinction at Other Sites

Social class positioning also played a role in the time bank.[10] As one of the largest volunteer time banks in the U.S. when we studied it, it was certainly not a failure. But we found a less than robust economy of trades, particularly among the younger age group we were studying.[11] One example of the lack of interest was a failed attempt to create an "emergency" service, in which people could post last-minute needs. Six months after it was begun, ten or fifteen people posted emergencies, but only one garnered a response.

One reason for low trading volume is that while members were very ideologically aligned with the idea that each person's time was equally valued, in practice many didn't really want to follow through on that radical premise. A number of them even had "aha" moments during their interviews, as they realized the contradiction in their attitudes. Some members who offered professional services, such as massage or healing arts, wanted to earn much more for their time than what less specialized skills like driving, pet-sitting, or baking typically pay in the market. Others rejected trades from people who didn't seem professional enough, especially for riskier services, such as home or car repair. At the same time, many of these more discriminating traders were perfectly comfortable with the fact that they were amateurs at the services they posted. Corie mused about her own offerings. "It reminds you about all the areas of your life that you've actually learned things in, like gardening or home repair stuff. Things you never think of as skills because they're not on your resume." Corie, who was a lawyer and social worker, failed to realize that legal advice and counseling would be more valuable to unemployed or cash-poor members than gardening. Others wanted to avoid the activities of their day jobs. For example, one software expert wanted to do "physical labor." She preferred installing thermostats to the expensive coding she was capable of and which would have benefited quite a few members.

There were also some outright expressions of social class presumption. One member, who did note that perhaps she was being a "snob," listed factors that would lead her to reject potential trading partners: grammatical errors or typos in the profile, failure to "write in complete sentences," or writing "poorly"—all class markers. Other reasons that came up were the absence of a website, external references, or testimonials. Some members treated the time bank as a charitable activity, giving services but not deigning to receive them in return.[12] These practices allowed members to position themselves as different from those who really "needed" the time bank or as high-status earners whose skills were too valuable to trade. While a public ratings system might have allayed fears and led to a higher volume of trades, members voted against it, thinking the spirit of reputation systems was not "time bank-y." But the absence of ratings likely allowed class prejudice and stereotyping to play a larger role, which in the end might have hurt less-advantaged members.

In some ways the makerspace was the most socially exclusionary of the sites we studied. On the face of it this might be surprising, because it was the most successful in conventional terms. There was a long waiting list for rental spaces, and participation in the community was robust. Classes were popular, people frequently came for tours, and representatives from makerspaces around the country visited for assistance and advice. But there was a marked social hierarchy that was deeply problematic.

"Industry," our anonymizing term for the site, was founded in 2010 by a robotics engineer, computer hackers, a costume designer, and a group of artists. It grew rapidly, and supports a wide range of tools and types of making, including 3D printers and laser cutters, robotics, woodworking, welding, jewelry making, printing, metal and digital fabrication, fabric arts, and rapid prototyping. The dominant ethic at Industry is the belief that every person has the drive and ability to be a "maker," a deeply egalitarian sensibility. References to creativity and community were ubiquitous in our conversations. In many ways Industry did fulfill its mission statements, which emphasize providing tools, instruction, and space at affordable prices in a collaborative environment.

And yet, the space developed a pronounced social hierarchy with a dominant in-group who reproduced an exclusionary culture. As at the food swap, the surface vibe was friendly and open. But during his research, Will experienced an intensity to status positioning that was far beyond what we had expected. One finding was that an exclusive group of high-status makers emerged from this ostensibly egalitarian community. Its social superiority was reflected in numerous ways. Names of the most esteemed makers were dropped casually in conversation. Social differentiation was also reflected in spatial allocations at the site. High status makers got prime spots in the center, and ordinary members were shunted to more distant locations. The in-group also took up vertical space—building extra stories onto their cubicles or, in one case, a looming tower.

But the most telling evidence for the exalted status of this group was the existence of a dual-currency system for managing exchanges among members. A big draw for participation in a community like Industry is the opportunity to learn from others. Outside of the formal classes, members helped each other on their projects—by teaching each other new skills, sharing personal tools, doing discrete tasks, or navigating the tricky bits. Among the in-group this assistance was compensated either by reciprocal help or in a "beer economy," in which payment was a case or six-pack of the recipient's favorite brand. Payment in beer came up repeatedly in our interviews with high-status makers and on the listserve that Will monitored. "Hello, this email is an offer of beer for help from my cube neighbor. I am hoping that a cog [our anonymizing term for a member] is thirsty. I have a set of fancy handlebars into which I would like to insert some Tektro bar end brakes. Unfortunately, the inside of the handlebars are not the standard diameter. Go figure! I am looking for some help to ream the internal diameter of the bars out to 20+mm. I am local and would of course pay with the requisite six-pack of your choice." The post reveals that not just anyone can participate in the beer economy, as in this case the person who needed the help enlisted his cube neighbor to make the ask, most likely because his status in this exclusive circuit of exchange was not secure.

Drinking beer is an informal activity, done among equals, particularly as it creates social vulnerabilities if enough of it is consumed. Therefore, it operates well as a medium of exchange among an elite peer group. Drinking beer is also a common gender-bonding ritual, and the in-group is almost all male. While we heard criticisms of other social hierarchies at the site (such as gender and class), and there was plenty of grousing about undemocratic governance, the beer economy was revered. Not once did anyone complain about the elitism it reflected.

## Exalting the Exotic

While creativity and community were the officially recognized traits for fabricators at Industry, there were specific kinds of making that yielded status. One marker was earning power. Some members were able to charge a lot for their time ($50–$150), which contributed to their aura. There were also some successful start-ups at the site that commanded respect. But the in-group was not oriented to money. In fact, a thread that ran through the most admired projects was their lack of connection to commercial value. High-status makers were frequently involved in esoteric, impractical, and exotic activities. In *Distinction*, Pierre Bourdieu called this quality "distance from necessity," and it is a strategy used by those with high cultural capital. At Industry it was a foundation of social esteem. Members who could waste money or time making useless things sat at the pinnacle of the social order.

The desire to demonstrate distance from necessity revealed itself in numerous ways. One was via aversion to the functional. Michelle described one of her recent projects—making beard cozies. "This one is topologically different than the rest because it's got five handles on top, so it's like a five-handled coffee cup, topologically, compared to the other ones." Kent was into making sticks for an "obscure" Japanese martial art called Shintito. "They're sticks that aren't perfectly round, they have sixteen sides. . . . I'm still working through it, but as it turns out I'm the only person in the U.S. making these things for now." Some members were part of an exclusive collective-within-the-collective, which required sponsorship to join. Michelle was hoping to get in and described some of the things they do, like bike jousting and three-legged races of two bikes side by side, with a shared pant leg between them. Other activities were just plain quirky. During his interview Larry described a typical request on the listserve: "Something today was, 'Hey, I've got 1,000 black walnuts I want to crack. How do I do that?'"

Distance from necessity was also enacted via wackiness. Woz probably wins that prize. A former repeat contestant on the TV show *Junkyard Wars* (in which teams compete building offbeat machines like bicycle powered submersibles), he was producing his own show, "Mechanical Artillery 101." "Yes, you can be a siege engineer—where I take you through 2500 years of catapult history, and then 15 years or so of the modern catapult craze and how to join it." He seemed particularly proud of being on the Science Channel with compatriots who are "involved in the fine art of hurling vegetables for distance."

The propensity for nonfunctional making was widely recognized. Val, an electrical engineer, described people at Industry as "very energetic, very smart people generally, not always practical. . . . There's just a lot of whimsy." When asked what unites the different maker groups at Industry, Brian, another electrical engineer, says it's "being excited about something . . . preferably something weird." He explained that his interest is in learning blacksmithing. When we asked him to elaborate on what he wants to make, he explained that it's "nothing I could make that's practically useful that I can't buy at Home Depot for $3." Uselessness creates the wow factor.

Perhaps the most impractical project of all was an eighteen-foot, two-ton hexapod robot that the founder and his crew worked on for years. The robot came up in a number of our conversations. As one ordinary, business-oriented maker explained: "You have people who take it to some extreme. They're building some really specific or weird project that they've devoted eight months to, like a giant robot animal. It's really single use. Like, you're going to devote so much time to this one project, and then it has one function and then you're done. Then they just move on to the next project."

The valorizing of these nonfunctional items meant that social standing at the site depended on various types of privilege. Many members were highly educated engineers, physicists, or other tech professionals, and most came from middle-class or upper-middle-class families. While a few in-group makers were from working-class origins or had dropped out of school, often to do computer work, all shared the ability to spend time and sometimes money at Industry. Mark, a talented inventor with a science PhD from MIT and highly valuable skill set with which he could earn a lot if he chose to, signaled his distance from necessity by casually mentioning his rent and his failure to monetize his inventions. "There are some things that I've come up with that I do think were adopted by larger companies. And I guess I feel a mix of pride that I had the right idea earlier than they did, but it would be nice if I, you know, had enough income to pay my rent every month; that would be convenient. Like the lights over there in the other room, they are—to the best of my knowledge—the very first lights ever to be directly controllable over Wi-Fi. It was 2007. . . . Of course, subsequently, it's probably been patented by Philips." And in case we hadn't gotten the message, he explained: "I just have a wide and strangely broad range of expertise."

In the end, the fact that the community elevated a style of making that rejected everyday, useful items and wasn't oriented to the repair of existing things meant it appealed to and was accessible for a certain elite. They didn't display their privilege through ordinary consumerism but its rejection. Liz, one of the more class-conscious members we interviewed, recounted having her clothing stolen while on a trip and buying a few replacement dresses at Walmart. When friends compliment her and ask if she made them, her truthful answer is a "conversation stopper." She explains: "You get kind of looked down on for doing the easy thing sometimes . . . because everyone assumes that because they have found the time and spare income to do x, y, or z thing that is, you know, better for the environment, or better for politics, or whatever."

## Diversity Fail

Given the levels of status jockeying we found at these sites, it's not surprising that they were unable to fulfill their stated intentions to attract a heterogenous group of participants, particularly with respect to race, gender, and class. The Boston area has a relatively white and educated population, but our sites were disproportionately so. Paradoxically, given its mission to help the unemployed, the time bank was in some ways the least diverse of the four. Its education levels were "off the charts": all our informants had a college degree, and more than half had postgraduate credentials. The irony was not lost on Amy, who was a public interest lawyer. "It originally started here for poor people, and they quickly realized that poor people have a lot of needs, but not necessarily a lot to offer. . . . And so, they consciously recruited middle-class folks who have resources, and skills, and other things to offer." So, over time, she explained, "there aren't any working-class people in [the time bank]. . . . They're all white, middle-income professionals." Some of the members, such as Pat, spoke critically about the lack of diversity. "I mean, if I'm going to be totally blunt here, there's a lot of educated white-lady skills on there, and not so many carpentry, and plumbing, and electricity, and hair stylist, and all those things that don't tend to be your stereotypical educated, white, Cambridge lady skills. And it seems like what I love about it is that we could all be helping each other out with all the things we know how to do, and getting to know each other in the process, rather than having this weird segregation which we already have all the time. . . . It's the Stuff White People Like activity."

At Industry the orientation to "Stuff White People Like" was less recognized, but stronger, as esoteric and nonfunctional making has appeal for people with racial, gender, and class privilege. In his year and a half at the site, Will encountered only one African American maker. And while its location is in a multiracial, ethnically diverse neighborhood, he recalls only one identifiable Latinx, who took a class with him. Industry is a space of overwhelming whiteness. Yet few participants talked explicitly about race. We did hear an occasional critique of attempts to be more racially diverse. But few seemed aware that the culture of the site and the disdain for functional making fostered whiteness. So we weren't surprised that our interpretation of social dynamics at the site was not always shared by participants. Bob, a forty-year-old white man with twenty years in information technology who was into making movie props, experienced Industry differently. He claimed not to be conscious of race, class, or gender issues, perhaps because he belonged to the dominant group in all three categories. "It's an epically open, supportive environment. Nobody cares are long as you're a nice person."

Industry also had a pronounced gender skew, although with 30 percent women, it was less male than many makerspaces, likely a consequence of including artists from the beginning. But there was strong gender segregation in terms of activities and space. By contrast, food swappers were almost all women. The open-learner sample was more gender balanced but disproportionately white and highly educated.

The social homogeneity we found at our nonprofit sites was present from the beginning, as founders tended to be white and middle-class. Had these initiatives started out with a more heterogeneous founder group, or even early participant population, they might have been more successful in attracting and retaining a wider range of people.[13] At the very least, early stage diversity might have created more awareness of how the cultures of these organizations deterred people in racialized, classed, and gender-specific ways. But there was another factor at work that also had diversity implications, especially for race and class. That was the "value" of the goods and services the sites were offering.

## The Missing "Value Proposition"

The rapid growth of commercial platforms like Airbnb and Uber was in large part due to the fact that they offered something of significant value to users. For consumers, that has been lower prices. For providers, the draw was earning money, as well as the ease of participation. There's plenty to criticize about the reasons these platforms have been able to offer lower prices (for example, lack of regulatory compliance and labor exploitation), but it's hard to dispute their popularity.

By contrast, the nonprofits led with ideology.[14] In the time bank it was the equal worth of every person's time. At the makerspace it was the human drive to create. Food swappers wanted to empower people in their relation to food. For open learners the motivator was belief in self-directed instruction. This is not to say there isn't "value" in these motives. But where the efforts fell short, or failed to attract participants, one reason was that they weren't offering something that had economic value to enough people. The problem was most acute at the food swap. Many would-be swappers found it difficult to make trades because their offerings lacked worth to others. By contrast, the makerspace was able to offer value to participants, but it did so under conditions that undermined solidarity and mutual respect among them.

The lack of a value proposition was most evident at the time bank. The time bank concept is based on providing needed services for people who lack the means to buy them, especially the "poor people" Lee referenced above. Expensive services such as legal help or assistance with software or technology would have been in high demand. But these weren't generally available, as the professionals with that expertise often wanted to do something different from what they did each day.[15] A similar dynamic came into play with other kinds of high-priced services. Fatima discussed her desire to trade with a woman who does "a very specific type of massage. . . . It's extremely expensive to get her because she's very talented in that and she's been doing it for many years. She won't put that trade on the [time bank], but she'll put other things on, like gardening or cleaning. . . . I asked her about it, and she said it's a very learned thing and I need to keep it for clients who pay." Similarly, blue-collar tradespeople (plumbers, electricians) weren't interested in working without pay. This accords with studies of other time banks, in which the gap between requests and offerings in this category was twice as large as for any other type of service.[16] Amateur versions of blue-collar skills could sometimes be had, but many members were unwilling to trust their wiring or plumbing to nonprofessionals.

Some people understood that they shouldn't expect top quality at the time bank and were fine with that. Others talked about services they wouldn't use the time bank for. There were also quality problems with more common competences. Melissa recounted a problematic experience. "So I don't know what style of massage that it was, like it wasn't a style, so there wasn't a chair. It was on the floor, and there was olive oil and lotion, and there was someone there. . . . It was just uncomfortable." Amy had someone do bike repair, and her problem got worse. She also recounted a recurring failure on a gardening trade. "Every single time I tried to set up appointments, they wouldn't show." The fact that a number of members only gave services, and had no desire to receive them, also reveals the lack of economic value they perceived. While we do have examples of people who were able to save significant amounts of money by repeated trades—for one member it was getting dog-sitting help—there were not many. When asked whether she'd been able to find trades that would yield big savings, Pat replied that she'd "looked for trades that would be large expenses, but . . . no one was offering them."

Part of the difficulty was that equal worth for each person's time regardless of skill level meant that professionals who could earn eighty dollars, one hundred dollars, or more per hour were being asked to trade with people whose offerings netted ten dollars or fifteen dollars on the market. That chasm may have been too wide to bridge. We wondered whether a two-tiered system would have provided more value to members, in which scarce skills might earn more than widely dispersed ones. The differential could be less than the market but not zero. That would reward people who have invested time and money in learning their craft and would make those valuable services available to people who need them. While that idea violates the strong egalitarianism of the time-bank movement, it might yield a more robust trading system. Alternatively, the bank could position itself more intentionally in the lower priced part of the market, as a place to trade for less expensive services. That might mitigate some frustration with the narrow range of offerings. Our findings accord with a number of studies of time banking. Ed Collom, an early researcher in this field, found strong ideological motivations among highly educated users.[17] Other studies have also identified the "value fail" that we discovered. Victoria Bellotti and her colleagues analyzed trading data from three large U.S. time banks and found mismatches in what people wanted, as well as an overly ideological orientation. A study of a Finnish platform called Kassi, which organized various forms of goods exchange (loans, gifts, sales) and "everyday favors," found that many who signed up discovered reasons not to use the service. Fewer than 20 percent were frequent users, and only 56 percent of those found the service personally useful, compared to 79 percent who said that the site's "values correspond to mine."[18] Of course, some community initiatives do succeed on this dimension. Sociologist Sofia Aptekar's study of the gifting platform Freecycle finds that members get instrumental value from the community, which she calls "green-washed convenience."[19] The site offers an environmentally satisfying and convenient way of solving an ongoing, guilt-inducing problem—overbuying, which leads to excessive clutter. It's not surprising that Freecycle is one of the most successful nonprofits.

Another question for some community sharing efforts is whether they are trying to fix what isn't broken. When Luka first described our project to a working-class friend, his reaction was that in his circles nonmonetized reciprocity and sharing was already frequent and normative. Some researchers have come to a similar conclusion. A study of projects in a neighborhood of London found that some formal efforts, such as a community-owned pub, a time bank connected to a primary care practice, and a "Menshed" with tools and space for older men, were providing value, albeit with considerable financial and/or volunteer support.[20] But survey data also suggested that where robust informal sharing among friends and neighbors already exists, digital platforms to enable stranger reciprocity may be unnecessary. In the presence of neighborhood ties and trust, local, placed-based sharing may develop organically.

Bellotti and her collaborators' research confirms the general argument of this section. Sharing economy initiatives often have a mismatch between providers and users. As they note, providers, on the one hand, are driven by "idealistic motivations, such as creating a better community or increasing sustainability. Users, on the other hand, are looking for services that provide what they need whilst increasing value and convenience."[21]

The difficulties we found at our sites have also plagued many of the nonprofit initiatives we mentioned at the beginning of the chapter. Goods-loaning platforms have almost all failed. A number of the food-oriented organizations, such as leftovers exchanges, and food preparation sites, have gone by the wayside. Most of the garden sharing groups we identified in 2010–11 are defunct. Tool libraries and repair cafes have been more successful but haven't expanded like the for-profits. In some ways these experiences are reminiscent of those of the New Communalists we met in chapter 1. They, too, put ideology in the lead. And they were predominantly white, male, and middle class. Both also suffered from a crucial absence—support from the state. Among the New Communalists it was by design. For the community initiatives, it has been more the unwillingness of local municipalities to see the importance of these efforts and invest in them. In Europe, where many cities are committed to community sharing, this is a vibrant sector. It can be in the U.S. as well, especially if it absorbs lessons such as the importance of diversity and providing economic value. We'll return briefly to the European efforts in the next chapter. But achieving a true sharing economy will take more than the expansion of the nonprofits. It also requires the transformation of commercial platforms into democratic entities. While that may sound utopian, it is actually starting to happen. That is the subject of our final case.

# 6   Co-ops, Commons, and Democratic Sharing

I began this book with the problems of work under capitalism—unfreedom, lousy bosses, the nine-to-five grind, excessive supervision, meaninglessness, and low wages. The sharing economy promised an escape by empowering individuals to work for themselves with the technological and market support of a platform. Many of the people we interviewed experienced it this way. But platforms haven't worked for everyone, and over time, they are working for fewer and fewer earners. At their worst, the companies have morphed into predatory employers. I also argued that achieving the promise of platforms requires specific conditions. Some we've already discussed, such as avoiding extreme earner dependence and keeping inequality in check. Regulation is another necessary condition for good outcomes. But there's also a deeper, structural innovation that is possible—the platform cooperative. It preserves the technology and basic structure of platform work but swaps out the owners and investors and gives their shares to workers. It's an innovation that can make the promise of a new way to work come true.

One of the first platform cooperatives is Stocksy United, founded in 2013 by Bruce Livingstone and Brianna Wettlaufer. Years earlier, Livingstone had started an innovative online stock photography business called iStock.[1] In 2006 iStock was acquired by Getty, the industry leader. Problems soon began to surface. Pictures were earning "pennies," the artists felt taken advantage of, and morale plummeted.[2] Livingstone and Wettlaufer grew dissatisfied with the new arrangement. So with $1.3 million in proceeds from the sale, they founded a company that puts artists first. Stocksy committed itself to "creative integrity, fair profit sharing, and co-ownership, with every voice being heard."[3] With substantial capital and know-how behind it, Stocksy quickly became one of the most successful examples of a new kind of online venture—a platform cooperative.[4]

The crux of a platform cooperative is that the providers, in this case the artists, own the company. They hire the staff who run the day-to-day operations. But major decisions rest with the producers. Rather than siphoning off a third or more of the revenue to founders and investors, as some sites do, Stocksy returns a much larger fraction to the artists. We were interested in Stocksy because it was one of the few large-scale platform cooperatives with a track record. So with Samantha Eddy taking the lead, we made it the final case in our project. While Stocksy isn't perfect, it *is* a genuine success story—with satisfied artists, strong revenue and growth, and commitment to its values.

The Stocksy experience shows that a different way to work is possible. The company offers artists meaning, autonomy, and decent earnings. Co-ops—alongside "commons" organizations, freelancers' unions, not-for-profits, and new municipal policies—can deliver on the wider promises of the idealistic discourse. These entities can be the foundation of a pluralistic economy that incorporates aspects of "Big" and "Small" Sharing. From the former it takes convenience, sophisticated ratings systems, the redistribution of value, and the ability to automate many management functions. Big Sharing finds the sweet spot of economic and noneconomic incentives that encourages widespread participation. It can also use the data it amasses to propel a learning process for reducing carbon footprints and generating interpersonal trust. There's also contribution from "Small" Sharing, the nonprofits who bring a strong social mission and trading options beyond renting and selling. Most important, a true sharing sector will operate with democratic governance and widespread ownership, to protect against exploitation, excessive wealth extraction by founders and investors, and other antisocial outcomes. To see how we might get there, it will be useful to consider the possible pathways that the sharing economy may follow in coming years.

Scholars who have written about the future of the sector have identified three likely directions: platform capitalism, a regime of state regulation, and what I call "democratic sharing."[5] Any of these three is possible because code is not destiny; that is, technology will not determine the future. In the United States we've traveled a fair way down the path of platform capitalism. But as the one-decade mark approached, cities began to pass regulations to contain the excesses of the companies. The viability of a more thoroughgoing regulatory regime can also be seen from the vantage point of Europe, where the laws governing platform behaviors are quite different. And while technology does not drive outcomes, it does affect the parameters of possibility. The fact that algorithms and ratings systems can take on tasks previously in the purview of management is one reason that the third outcome—democratic sharing—has become a serious option.

## Platform Capitalism

A future of "platform capitalism" is one in which companies grow ever larger and more powerful.[6] In this account, sharing businesses are fully integrated into the larger technology ecosystem. The tech sector has already demonstrated a tendency toward market domination by individual companies, on account of network effects, patient venture capital, and political power.[7] (That patience is what has allowed Uber and Lyft to subsidize rides for so long and other tech companies to make losses for years.) In 2018, Amazon accounted for about half of all U.S. online retail, and Google holds 88 percent of the search-engine market share.[8] The idea is that the sharing sector will be similarly monopolistic. Uber will dominate in mobility and delivery, Airbnb in accommodation, and perhaps a third platform in the remaining labor services. Innovation scholar Koen Frenken, who has sketched out three trajectories along the lines I am describing, predicts that in this pathway "super-platforms" will integrate multiple services and afford "maximum conveniences for seamless consumption."[9] Some have a more dystopian view of market dominance and see a future of predatory behavior. If Uber bests Lyft (or vice versa), will it raise fares? Once ride-hail apps have battered or eliminated the competition, including public transit, consumers may not have alternatives. Critics are fearful that platform capitalism will be a hyperexploitative system in which a few behemoths have all the power. In 2016 Martin Kenney and John Zysman penned what may be the most quoted prediction in this literature: "We are in the midst of a reorganization of our economy in which platform owners are seemingly developing power that may be even more formidable than was that of the factory owners in the early industrial revolution."[10]

Despite many observers' assumption that we're on this glide path, I'm not so sure. I'm writing these words on the day Uber went public and became the most money-losing IPO of all time.[11] One reason is that there are ongoing questions about the basic business model of the sector. One comes from advances in automation. If driverless vehicles and drone delivery become the norm, the companies will incur capital costs, in contrast to the present. Robots are starting to be used for elder care. They'll also likely be walking dogs, assembling IKEA furniture, and cleaning houses. But who will own the bots? Will it be Care.com, TaskRabbit, and DogVacay? Or will those platforms have fallen by the wayside? Another uncertainty is that the road to market dominance and profitability relies on passive workers and consumers plus captured government. Although those conditions prevailed in the United States in the first decade of the sharing economy, that may be changing. Workers are organizing. Democratic politicians and economists have been developing analyses and policies to address market power.[12] As regulatory activity and workers' resistance increase, they raise the possibility of a different future.

## Regulating Uber: How Europe Did It Differently

A second scenario is a regulatory regime in which platforms become subject to rules that constrain their actions.[13] Around the globe regulations cover compensation and benefits, taxes, consumer safety, nondiscrimination, and environmental outcomes. A robust regulatory regime would force platforms to share their revenues more fairly, limit the risk they can devolve onto workers, and hold them accountable for the impacts of their business. If Uber causes excess congestion, or Airbnb drives up rents, government would have the ability to address these consequences. Regulators in Europe have been less company-friendly than in the United States. Their experience reveals what can be accomplished with public pressure and political will. The case of Uber, which has been studied most among the sharing companies, shows how much difference the regulatory environment can make.

Uber is currently banned or barely operates in a number of European countries, including Greece, Portugal, Denmark, Hungary, and Bulgaria.[14] The company has left because its model violates local regulations on licensing, unfair competition, or treatment of labor. In Germany Uber debuted in 2014 with its tried-and-true method—break the law and figure out how to stay in business later. One of its signature strategies has been to mobilize consumers to barrage government officials with supportive messages through its app.[15] I happened to be at an academic meeting with an Uber executive on the day major injunctions were issued against the company in Germany. He was confident that consumer pressure would force the authorities to back down. We sparred a bit without resolving much. But Uber's gambit failed. As political scientist Kathleen Thelen has argued, national taxi organizations and concerns about unfair competition led the public to see Uber as a "threat to the public interest,"[16] and it was never able to overcome that opposition. To this day, Uber has only minimal presence in Germany.

Things have gone differently in other locales. In the Netherlands the company originally ignored the law with its low-cost UberPop service. But it was soon forced to switch to another model, which complied with existing regulations, a pattern it has repeated in other countries.[17] In Sweden, unions (who cover the majority of workers) welcomed Uber's technological innovation. But they opposed "social dumping"—that is, shifting risk onto workers by reducing wages and benefits and eroding working conditions, hallmarks of the platform business model. The company followed existing regulations from the get-go and was essentially forced to operate as a regular taxi service, although there was some adaptation on the part of the government as well.[18] Uber is engaged in ongoing battles across Europe, particularly in France, where taxi drivers have been militant in opposition, and London, where the company's license to operate has been revoked and only temporarily reinstated.[19] The company is on the hot seat for compensation, competition, and safety issues.

Uber isn't the only platform being regulated in Europe. Cities across the Continent have also been reining in Airbnb and other lodging sites, largely by banning commercial operators, reducing the number of days hosts can rent out their entire home, requiring licenses, and levying taxes. Where Airbnb activity has been especially problematic, authorities have gone further. In Barcelona new licenses have not been issued since 2014.[20] And despite fierce resistance, the city forced the company to hand over its data. One consequence was the removal of more than twenty-five hundred illegal listings.[21] The ability of cities, national governments, and the European Union to take on even the biggest platforms and win reveals that these companies can change their behaviors.

## The U.S. Debate about Regulation

Is it feasible to regulate platforms in the United States as they have been in Europe, with effective protections for workers and urban residents? We didn't cover this topic in most of our interviews, but occasionally it came up. Angelo was skeptical. Talking about Uber and Lyft, he believed "they [officials] waited too long to try to impose regulations and they [the companies] became too powerful. It came to the point where oh you need us more than we need you." Others, like Bill, who rented out on Turo, thought regulations would and should be put into place. He explained that even though he's a Republican, he wanted more government oversight of the sector. This was partly to promote it. But it was also to deal with what he called the "blind spot" of a system built on trust. That's because there are people who will abuse that trust. "There'll have to be regulations and laws to make sure that the consumer—or not even the consumer—the people who participate in it are protected." Legal scholars, economists, and other social scientists agree and have produced research on why and how sharing platforms should be regulated.[22] Their papers advance compelling arguments using long-standing approaches, as well as newer rationales specific to digital entities. Among the former are consumer protections, such as the need for drivers and hosts to carry insurance, or mechanisms to guarantee that homes and vehicles are safe. Background checks and licensing for providers also fall into this category. Other issues in consumer law include preventing discrimination by race, gender, disability, age, and other protected statuses. This is a weak spot of the sector because platforms have mostly been exempt from existing laws. Labor conditions have also been a major regulatory focus, with numerous lawsuits on the appropriateness of the independent contractor status for platform earners, especially in ride-hail and delivery.[23]

Another set of arguments involves market failures, which produce externalities—effects on third parties that are not included in the calculations of the transactors. George, who rented out on Turo and Airbnb, was pretty clear that eventually external effects would be internalized. "So Airbnb's been able to basically sidestep a lot of regulation and overhead costs, and they've been able to grab that profit as well as sharing some of that profit with their hosts. But either they're externalizing those costs, and it's a short-term solution and eventually it's going to catch up, or regulation is going to come in and enforce some of that overhead, and then the parity won't be there." George didn't go into detail about these costs, but there are two types. They can be limited in scope, such as the noise suffered by residents in buildings with lots of Airbnb activity or the traffic fatalities associated with ride-hailing. They can also affect a broader public, as when they reduce housing supply or raise rents. In ride-hailing these externalities include congestion and air and carbon pollution. In municipalities and courts around the country advocates are attempting to apply existing regulations to the platforms and to push for new rules and precedents.

Big Sharing companies have spent a decade evading these public protections. Legal scholars and others have argued that their actions amount to "regulatory arbitrage," or the ability to capitalize on loopholes or selective enforcement of the law.[24] This strategy is an essential feature of the business model. By not bearing the burdens of compliance, such as the obligation to serve disabled customers or pay minimum wages, these firms gain an unfair competitive advantage. There's even an eponymous law for former Uber CEO Travis Kalanick that dictates that the company should break the rules and apologize afterward. Quite a few platform companies entered markets doing just that—acting in violation of existing regulations in order to establish a foothold. They then relied on the idealist discourse to gain public support and deter regulators and politicians from opposing them. The platforms argue for dismantling existing regulatory regimes on the grounds that they stifle innovation and threaten the sector's economic viability. The companies position themselves as efficient, low-cost, and proconsumer,[25] while opponents are maligned as antiprogress, Luddite, and rent-seeking. Perhaps not surprisingly, a Koch Brothers–funded project against taxi regulation was used nearly word-for-word by Uber in its messaging.[26] The companies are using the right-wing antigovernment playbook.

In ride-hail, denigrating the competition was a bit like shooting fish in a barrel. Decades of caps on taxi licenses, racial discrimination by drivers, and coziness with regulators had eroded public support for the industry. That was partly due to widespread amnesia about why licenses were limited in the first place, which is that in the 1930s, when men were desperate for work and flooded into driving, oversupply drove incomes down to unsustainable levels. In sectors with low barriers to entry where the required skills are widely available, competition can become "ruinous" and result in poverty wages. That dynamic is the origin of taxi regulation and the basis on which driving became a viable occupation. By breaking the law, Uber and Lyft destroyed that viability, and we're now seeing their drivers subjected to a similar race-to-the-bottom.[27]

And what the ideological high ground can't accomplish, money can. The biggest platforms, again with Uber in the lead, have employed an army of lobbyists and public relations firms to fight even minor changes. In response to a modest proposed California law to fill the gap in insurance coverage when a driver has the app on but isn't on a fare, Uber hired fourteen of the fifteen biggest Sacramento lobbying firms.[28] In 2017 Uber and Lyft had more lobbyists than Amazon, Microsoft, and Walmart combined.[29]

Airbnb has also been active trying to stop laws that limit rental activity or mandate the collection of hotel and occupancy taxes. Publicly, the company presents a less oppositional face than the ride-hail platforms, claiming to be a good citizen collecting taxes and opposing commercial rentals. Behind the scenes, however, the CEO of a compliance firm says Airbnb is waging "a city-by-city, block-by-block guerrilla war" against local governments.[30] The company has filed lawsuits against ordinances in many cities and mobilized hosts with scare tactics.[31] In places where short-term rentals are illegal, it has successfully pushed to liberalize these laws. The company has also fought hard to keep listing data from regulators, which reduces tax payments and allows illegal rentals to remain on the platform. Over the years, to keep regulators at bay, Airbnb has periodically purged violators, but subsequently allows them to creep back onto the platform. It, too, is hiring armies of lobbyists. In 2017, after Nashville passed an ordinance restricting "mini-hotels," the company hired eleven lobbyists to pass a Tennessee state law taking away cities' rights to regulate short-term rentals.[32] By late 2018, six states had similarly blocked municipal authority.[33]

This strategy, which is called "preemption," has been all too successful. So far, platform activity has been concentrated in urban areas, because they provide sufficient density. To the companies' dismay, municipalities are the most progressive unit of government in the U.S. and have been most active in passing regulations. So Uber embarked on a strategy that Big Tobacco, the National Rifle Association, and the ultraright, Koch-funded American Legislative Exchange Council (ALEC) have successfully pioneered—getting state legislatures to pass laws overriding local ordinances and regulation. In a mere four years (from 2014 through 2017), using language provided by ALEC, Uber and Lyft succeeded in getting forty-two states to pass laws with preemption provisions.[34] This deregulation spree included taking away workers' rights, outlawing employee status for drivers (in thirty-two states), and blocking city-wide minimum wages.[35] Although they've been most successful in the United States,[36] the big companies have also been pursuing a deregulatory strategy in Europe.[37]

The federal government has also been disinclined to regulate the companies. The Federal Trade Commission convened a workshop in 2015 to discuss the sector. The ensuing report began with an approving nod to Josef Schumpeter's concept of the "gale of creative destruction" on account of the benefits that these "disruptive" entities will bring to consumers.[38] While the FTC did subsequently bring charges against Uber for overstating drivers' earnings and exposing consumers' data, it has defined its oversight role narrowly.[39] Perhaps most important, it has not strayed from well-worn approaches to conventional companies, meaning that the unique issues raised by digital firms have so far gone unaddressed.

## What's Special about Regulating Digital Platforms

Two regulatory issues are particularly salient in the case of digital platforms: market power and the role of data. While the tendency toward monopoly is a concern in many industries, platforms present extreme cases. Network effects and the small cost of adding new users create incentives for bigness, which is enabled by the patience of venture capital. In addition, the immense sums available to technology firms have facilitated their capture of regulators and legislators. So far the federal government, which oversees competition policy, has not been willing to break up monopolistic platforms. But in early September of 2019, fifty attorneys general from the states announced they were investigating Google. Facebook is also under scrutiny.[40]

Proprietary data, and the power it affords, is another issue. Platforms collect massive amounts of information about consumers in the course of their activities. They also reach beyond their apps to grab additional data. In 2018 Uber applied for a patent on an application that analysts think it will use to tell when a potential customer is drunk.[41] This kind of information offers enhanced opportunities for what legal scholars call "taking"—as in "taking advantage."[42] Companies can take advantage in a variety of ways. In the case of Uber's patent, the impaired state of a rider would render them willing to pay more or easier to cheat. Another way to take advantage is to exploit "cognitive biases" that behavioral science has uncovered. These include increased willingness to buy a product if it's priced one cent lower ($9.99 versus $10.00) or the tendency to make decisions on instinct rather than via deliberation. In the case of digital platforms the potential for this type of "market manipulation"[43] is greater because they are continuously experimenting with the environments in which customers and providers are exchanging. This allows the platforms to go beyond general cognitive biases, to exploit the psyches of particular individuals. They can discover the highest price each person will be willing to pay or the least they will work for. They can also adapt their algorithms to induce behaviors they want. Ride-hail companies use gaming techniques to keep workers at the wheel longer,[44] and they have learned that riders are more willing to pay surge prices when their phone batteries are low.[45] Legal scholars and others have argued that this information asymmetry gives firms immense power and provides a strong rationale for regulation.[46] Data transparency is one way to mitigate the asymmetry.

Public availability of data is crucial for other reasons, too. Without it, it's difficult to assess the extent of person-to-person discrimination. And if we want platforms to be held accountable for the carbon and other environmental impacts of their activities, access to data is imperative. So far, companies have been unwilling to provide their data to officials or the public. But some cities are asserting themselves because regulatory enforcement is impossible without this information. In Toronto, ride-hail and lodging laws now include requirements that the companies provide data, which they are doing.[47] New York, after years of fighting with Airbnb, passed an ordinance that requires accommodation platforms to provide names and addresses for listings, as well as information on rental history and bank accounts.[48] As of this writing, Airbnb and HomeAway are fighting these provisions in the courts.[49] But recent rulings on data for both ride-hail and lodging platforms have gone in favor of the public, suggesting that we may be on the road to much-needed data sharing.

## Regulation Rising?

The New York City ordinance is one of a number of steps the city took in 2018 and 2019 to protect workers and consumers and bring transparency to sharing platforms. Under state law whole apartment rentals of fewer than thirty days were already illegal,[50] but inability to enforce the law led to the demand for data. San Francisco also stepped up its oversight of short-term rentals, in the wake of severe housing shortages. Although it had restricted rentals in 2014, changes to its registration system went into effect in January of 2018 and nearly halved the number of properties listed, from ten thousand to fifty-five hundred.[51] The San Francisco regulation permits whole home rentals of primary residences for a maximum of ninety days per year, with no limits on renting rooms when hosts are present. The city also requires a license.[52] Other cities and states are following suit with regulations that legalize short-term rentals with absent hosts but limit days per year in order to keep commercial operators off the platform. The aim is to return hosting to its roots of true home sharing. The externalities associated with Airbnb activity finally pushed officials to protect public interests.

New York City also took the lead on labor conditions, when its Taxi and Limousine Commission passed landmark legislation requiring driver wages of at least $26.51 an hour (gross) or $17.22 (after expenses).[53] It's unlikely most cities will enact similar laws soon, in part because New York's ride-hail drivers are already licensed like taxi operators and because they are more likely to work full-time than in other cities (80 percent of all app-based rides are provided by full-timers).[54] There are signs, however, that platform workers are beginning to organize and demand better conditions. In early 2019 Instacart workers took to the airwaves to denounce a policy by which tips were being used to bring wages up to the guaranteed minimum. The company backed down quickly.[55] An even stronger sign came in May of 2019, two days before Uber's IPO, when ride-hail drivers staged a global work stoppage, the first of its kind. While the action was not large enough to shut down the apps, it showed the power of determined organizing using digital strategies.[56] As I mentioned in chapter 2, in September of 2019 California passed Assembly Bill 5 (AB5), which explicitly makes gig workers employees.[57] This is the most far-reaching legislation in the country and is likely to change the way ride-hail and delivery platforms operate.[58] But these developments should not blind us to the difficulty of worker organizing or the hardball tactics of the platforms. Even before the governor signed AB5, the companies publicly announced they are putting tens of millions toward a ballot initiative to overturn it.[59] TaskRabbit's Terms of Service prohibit taskers from even sharing contact information with each other,[60] taking away a right that the law guarantees regular employees.

There's no question that regulation is justified and necessary. It's almost impossible to solve problems of housing shortages, labor exploitation, illegal listings, unsafe drivers, pollution, and congestion without it. Two thousand eighteen and nineteen appeared to be a turning point in the ability of cities to regulate ride-hail and accommodation sites. But was it? Angelo warned that the regulators are too late, and he could be right. Countersuits, the legacy of preemption, and the political power of the Big Sharing entities give the companies a structural advantage.[61] Outside of New York and San Francisco they've been more successful in fighting off city governments. But even if these regulatory efforts are successful, they don't go far enough. That's because regulation is oriented to reducing harms and weighing them off against benefits.[62] But platform technology creates the possibility of doing far more than that under the right conditions. Restructuring the social relationships by which platforms operate might actually achieve the common-good outcomes that participants want. That's where democratic sharing comes in.

## Democratic Sharing

Returning to the history of cyberutopianism shows why a reboot of the sector is both desirable and possible. Early computer enthusiasts believed that digital technology would engender horizontal, empowered relations among users. By the 1990s, many in that community thought that privately owned corporations were the way to achieve those outcomes. When the sharing economy emerged, participants adopted a similar position—the idealist discourse. It consisted of claims about economic, social, and environmental benefits that would flow automatically from the combination of markets and technology. We know now that things have turned out very differently. Some platforms have become downright dystopian. Others are a mixed bag. Many of the truly socially oriented efforts have failed.

But what if the early optimism was partly right, in the sense that the technology could help satisfy those aspirations? While technology doesn't guarantee outcomes, it does open up possibilities. Digital technology is remaking the economics of many sectors by offering convenience through reducing transactions costs, creating new mechanisms for ensuring trust, and developing ways to deploy excess capacity. The enthusiasts got that part right. What they missed was that in order to realize the full benefits of the technology, the social relations under which people are "sharing" also have to change.[63] Instead of private ownership and a conventional market orientation, which have pulled the companies toward business-as-usual, the sector would need to go deeper into sharing. And perhaps not coincidentally, as these debates about cyberculture were occurring, an intellectual breakthrough reframed academic understandings of sharing and provided the foundations for transforming those very social relations.

The reigning view from economics was that sharing is an inefficient anachronism from precapitalist societies. But this conclusion is misguided. Eleanor Ostrom's work on ecosystems showed that holding ownership "in common" (i.e., sharing) could lead to efficient use and long-term sustainability.[64] Surveying research on irrigation systems, forests, fisheries, and other natural resources, Ostrom's analysis put the lie to the claim that any arrangements other than private property or state ownership led to a "tragedy of the commons," in which the resource would necessarily be degraded by overuse. This research earned Ostrom a Nobel Prize in Economics—an impressive feat given that she was a political scientist and the first woman to be selected for this award. She identified the conditions under which shared ownership and governance work well—the most important of which was democratic, community control at the smallest feasible scale. The successes, over hundreds of years, of some of Ostrom's cases led to enthusiasm for expanding "commons" to realms such as art, culture, scholarship, and of course, the digital world.[65]

The intellectual foundations for sharing also got a boost from a pair of pathbreaking contributions by legal scholar Yochai Benkler ("Sharing Nicely" from the *Yale Law Review* and his influential book *The Wealth of Networks*).[66] Benkler argued against the conventional view that there are only three choices for organizing economic life—

markets, firms, and the state. He made the case that a fourth—"social sharing"—was not only widespread but was becoming more efficient on account of digital technology. Benkler studied an activity called peer production, in which individual programmers work online to produce code together and make it freely available for anyone who follows community norms. Well-known products from this mode of production are the Linux operating system, Mozilla, and Python. Outside of software, other types of peer production began to emerge, the most famous of which is Wikipedia. People engage in these projects not for money but from intellectual engagement, wanting to contribute socially, or to enhance their professional reputations. At the core of Benkler's work is the insight that digital technology has changed the calculus about the most efficient form of social relations. He foresaw a move away from self-interested market behavior and large, autonomous firms, toward networks, collaboration, and sharing.

The scholarly work of Ostrom, Benkler, and others points the way to constructing the new social relations that can exploit the possibilities of the sharing sector. First, cooperative ownership of companies looks to be easier to develop and scale online than offline. And second, public ownership and governance of platforms has become much more feasible. There are now movements for both, which go by the names *platform cooperativism* and *sharing cities*. At the end of chapter 2 I asked whether the technology used in the sharing economy obviated the need for bosses and managers. Platform co-ops suggest an affirmative answer to that question.

## Selling through Stocksy

The essence of a platform cooperative is that it is owned and governed by the people who produce the product. In the case of Stocksy United, that's the photographers. While Stocksy has a multistakeholder structure in which founders and staff have some shares, the vast majority (valued at $1 each) belong to the artists, who number roughly a thousand.[67] They come from sixty-five countries, and like workers on other platforms they are very diverse. They differ not only by age, race, gender, and ethnicity but also in orientations to their art. Replicating the division between dependent and supplementary earners we found on the for-profit platforms, there's a divide between professionals, who make a living from photo sales, and hobbyists, or what are sometimes (snarkily) termed mom-tographers. Photography no longer requires expensive equipment because even smartphone photos can be good enough to sell, which has opened up the field to many more people. While this variation among the artists is similar to what we found on other platforms, a key difference is that Stocksy customers are businesses rather than individuals.

By almost any conventional measure, Stocksy has been wildly successful. One reason is that its compensation is far better than at the corporate firms. Instead of the literal pennies many reported getting from Getty, Stocksy pays 50 percent of the revenue from a sale to the artist, and 75 percent on an extended license. (The industry standard is more like 20 to 30 percent and 45 percent.)[68] The payment structure is one indication of the broader commitment to the artists, which in turn means that many are eager to join. For the first cohort, admission was about as competitive as getting into Harvard College, later shifting to a 10 percent acceptance rate.[69] Another indication of its success is that the platform attracted top-talent photographers who wouldn't ordinarily dream of selling in the "low-end" stock portion of the industry. They were inspired to join on account of the cooperative structure. This allowed Stocksy to carve out a profitable artistic niche, a boutique style that distinguished it from its competitors, which in turn yielded strong revenues. By the second year, the company not only paid out $4 million in royalties, but had a surplus over operating costs that was remitted to members as a dividend.

While the artists have frustrations like any group, we found that they were quite satisfied. This was true across the divides of supplemental and dependent earners, unlike on the for-profit platforms. Part-timer Christina explains that "it's really great just side money. . . . So like from bigger shoots or projects that I do outside of Stocksy, I usually like to set aside that money, the simple funds that I get each month from the payouts on Stocksy is perfect for movie theater money." Hector reports that Stocksy sales "pay for my beer, alcohol like tequila, my bourbon, occasionally my dark rum, sometimes my light rum." (Clearly, Hector has a sense of humor.) Emily, a more dependent artist is also very positive, despite a drop-off in income at the time of our interview. "So I've been with them since 2013, and I saw steady growth. Twenty fifteen was great and then it's flat-lined a little bit. So there's definitely a little worry there that it might not be worth the investment of my time to keep producing for them. . . . If it doesn't make sense financially, I won't keep doing it." At the same time she reports, "I love, love, love and adore Stocksy, and I support what they're doing."

The Stocksy team is committed to strong transparency with their data, which meant they were willing to give us the distribution of revenue across their contributors. Of the one thousand members in 2016, eighty-seven of them earned 66 percent of the total royalties. Among those eighty-seven, the top nine contributors earned 26.5 percent. This is a highly concentrated distribution, far beyond what we (or they) expected. But it's due in part to the presence of the super-talented artists who won't typically sell on stock platforms and even more to the great divergence of activity among members. The high contributors invest large sums on shoots—up to $20,000 in some cases—and produce many images. As Emily explained, "You kind of get out what you put in. So if people don't want to invest that time, that's fine. . . . They're not going to do that well. . . . There's probably ten to twenty full-time shooters, and they have thousands of images and they are killing it."

Because the artists are getting fair prices for their work, low earnings aren't a sign of exploitation or unfair treatment. We didn't hear complaints from people who put in long hours or invested significant sums without a payoff, in contrast to gig workers on for-profit platforms. Another reason the economics are not more problematic is that unlike on most platforms, there's a cap on participation. When anyone can join, you can get too many people chasing too few customers. By limiting membership, and using artistic merit as the criterion, Stocksy is able to keep quality high.[70] This in turn yields healthy customer demand and revenue. That said, they can't avoid what we've termed "the challenge of individual contribution." With a finite level of demand, the artists are inevitably partly competing against each other. And diverse effort levels can lead to lopsided outcomes. This complicates the dynamics of platform co-ops, which are typically communities of independent producers. It is also a contrast with conventional cooperatives, where the workers collaborate to make a common product and aren't in competition with each other. At Stocksy the challenge of individual contribution is more pronounced than in services where the market value of what's being produced is more uniform. This is one reason why platform cooperatives for ride-hail drivers, cleaners, delivery couriers, and care workers will have more equal revenue distributions than Stocksy and why the concentrated distribution we found didn't sour us on the platform co-op model.

Participation can be a weak point of cooperatives, as many members lack interest or time to get involved in governance. At Stocksy the usual barriers are compounded by differences in time zones and the fact that not all members speak English. Votes typically include only two hundred to three hundred of the one thousand members. And we found that some people are barely aware of or don't care much about the cooperative structure. At the same time, we found those who are paying attention give management high marks. As one photographer offered: "I think Stocksy has done a good job of still letting us make choices, even if it's not what they want. It's happened a couple times where they would put out a proposal . . . and then the feedback would come in and the co-op overwhelmingly [says] no, that's not where we want to go. And they listened."

Furthermore, members who participate appreciate the online forums, which are a space for governance and getting advice from other members. Angela reports that "all I would say is the mood on the forums is very supportive; it is very communal." For Lisa the fact that Stocksy is a cooperative makes all the difference. "We're much more engaged in what's happening overall. We have a lot more discussions and conversations. I mean and we're a family. I think that's really a big part of us. If any of us has travels we'll post on the forums and like, hey, I'm going to be in Europe and I'll be in these places and who can I meet up with? . . . Their mission is productivity, collaboration and community, and being supportive."

## Platform Cooperativism

A Spanish co-op called Las Indias is credited with first writing about the idea of platform co-ops, in 2011.[71] Three years later, the idea was percolating in the United States, with pioneers Trebor Scholz, Nathan Schneider, and Janelle Orsi beginning to organize around the concept.[72] Soon after, Scholz and Schneider held a conference in New York that attracted more than a thousand participants and revealed that cooperativism was of great interest to many in the progressive digital community. Since then, efforts to develop platform co-ops have been ongoing. Although the numbers are small, early results are promising.[73]

These kinds of ideas came up spontaneously in our interview with Tim, a twenty-seven-year-old part-time college teacher and interpreter. Tim earns about $45,000 a year with multiple gigs, has

$80,000 in student debt, and was renting out his car on Turo. He had an idea for a better system. "A cooperative of people investing in a fleet of cars so that we all own it, we all take responsibility in the car, how it's maintained, and how clean they are, filling up the gas tank—all those little details. As the owners, we decide we want to add another car to the fleet. We can vote on it, we can decide we're going to take on this additional expense. And it wouldn't be a profit motive. It would be more meeting the need of the residents." One issue he had with Turo was its 25 percent fee. "I don't know where it's going. But with a cooperative I feel that there's more transparency. People would be able to see where the expenses are going."

While few of our respondents volunteered these kinds of ideas about co-ops, much of what they did say they wanted is addressed by the structure Tim outlined. Tim's vision is different from Stocksy because it entails common ownership of a capital asset, in this case vehicles. On labor platforms there's not much capital, and producers do their work as individuals. This setup can lead to considerable inequality, as we saw with the Stocksy revenue distribution.[74] But cooperative ownership lets workers retain much more of the value they produce, because the owners' cut is remitted back to them. With predatory platforms that's a big chunk of revenue. At Stocksy this is a major benefit. There are also savings in comparison to ordinary (non-digitally managed) firms. Algorithms take over many of the functions of management, which reduces costs and raises incomes. While this can be problematic when the algorithms are constructed to make profits for owners, if they are built with workers' interests in mind, it can be a benefit. When I argued that digital technology creates the possibility of radically different, and better, outcomes, this is a major reason why. And, of course, cooperatives allow members to take control of their own work lives, with policy determined by democratic principles.[75] In 2018, tech employees' lack of power over their work became a flashpoint, with ongoing protests at Google, Amazon, and other companies about forced participation in objectionable immigration policies and drone warfare.[76]

The co-op structure makes sense for well-remunerated producers in many fields. Stocksy is an "upscale" enterprise in the sense that its photos are higher quality than run-of-the-mill stock. But co-ops may hold even more benefit in low-wage markets, such as driving, delivery, caring labor, and handywork, where earners have less market power because skills are more common. In home health or childcare, agencies can take up to 50 percent of the revenue for the work of matching and ensuring quality. Now, algorithms and public ratings systems render these "middlemen" superfluous, and that money can go to underpaid workers. Platform co-ops have already formed in some of these occupations—including Up and Go for housecleaners in New York City, Green Taxi in Denver, Shift for couriers in Vancouver, and NursesCan in California.[77] While these examples are local, as most sharing economy activities are, the technology can be shared and replicated. As proponents work on open source software for platform co-ops,[78] and pioneers in the field hone their policies and structures, it's likely that the numbers will expand. In fact, one of the most appealing things about platform cooperatives, in contrast to their offline cousins, is their ability to replicate and scale. Fora do Eixo (FdE, or the Off-Axis Circuit) is a mix of musicians, artists, producers, and venues that was founded in Brazil by three university students. It now operates in fifteen countries, comprises two hundred collectives, and has two thousand employees.[79] Other examples of existing and information co-ops include website writers, translators, web hosts, data-rights advocates, and Fairbnb, which works for community powered tourism. One of the most successful cooperatives is a freelancers' organization called Smart, which began in Belgium and now has more than thirty-five thousand members in forty cities across nine countries.[80] The co-op pools risk and provides billing, insurance, and other services.

At the same time, platform cooperatives face formidable challenges, which helps to explain why there are just a handful of them. Historically, financing has been the biggest barrier to growth, as traditional investors are wary of the cooperative form. (The availability of funding from the beginning was important for Stocksy's success.) Even the most progressive venture-capital firm in the sharing economy sector, Union Square Ventures, doesn't support this form.[81] Attracting customers is also difficult, especially if there is a powerful incumbent in the market. And with the two-sided structure of platforms, "chicken-and-egg" imbalances can develop between buyers and sellers. There are other complexities in the relation between these two groups—for example, an in-built tension over prices and quality of service. This conflict is one reason some have argued for multistakeholder platform co-ops, which include consumers in governance and can incorporate divergent points of view.[82] Other dilemmas for cooperatives, which are often started with idealistic motives, mirror what we saw in the nonprofit cases. They may not always get their "value proposition" right, which can undermine growth. Similarly, they can reinforce the same patterns of exclusion and privilege that we found.

A final issue is that because co-ops are an intervention into the structure of firms, but not markets, they are vulnerable to the tyrannies of those markets. In our research on Stocksy we found that buyers wanted pictures of affluent white Westerners—what we call a "neo-imperialist aesthetic"—and artists felt they needed to comply.[83] Another "tyranny" is excessive competition for customers, which leads to downward pressure on earnings and working conditions.

## Sharing Cities

The challenges that cooperatives face, such as financing and the tyranny of the market, suggest that collective action is necessary for this sector to reach its full potential. These considerations mean there's a public interest in structuring the environment in which all sharing platforms operate. That's where cities come in. Since the sharing economy has been largely an urban phenomenon, municipal governments have been most active in attempting to foster, regulate, and shape sharing activity. For some, the sharing sector represents an opportunity to create a new urban economy that promotes values of justice and inclusion, sustainability and carbon neutrality, and democracy and participation. By intervening at a level above the individual company, this movement aims for deeper and more structural transformation.[84]

Cities are doing this in different ways.[85] Seoul was the first to designate itself a "Sharing City," in 2012. It put values of community and developing the local economy at the center of its policies, as it set up seed funds for start-ups and banned Uber in order to incubate homegrown alternatives. One result of its orientation is an Airbnb substitute called Kozaza, which has the added mission of preserving *hanok*, traditional Korean homes.[86] Seoul is making city-owned spaces such as parking lots and buildings available for community initiatives, a practice that other governments are also adopting. Amsterdam followed suit with the sharing designation but took a more conventional approach of commonsense regulation and partnership with Big Sharing platforms to avoid the worst impacts without discouraging their growth. At the other end of the spectrum are attempts to change the basic structure of the economy by encouraging ecosystems of cooperatives and deep democratic sharing. Bologna and Barcelona have long histories of radical participatory movements, and both have taken this path.[87] In Barcelona, Mayor Ada Colau was elected on a platform called "Barcelona in Common." In addition to capping the number of short-term rentals, the city has nested its approach to the sharing economy within a larger program to promote a "social economy" that reduces territorial and economic inequalities. Policies are directed at increasing small and cooperative enterprises and relocalizing urban manufacturing through an interlocking network of businesses, especially to benefit disadvantaged groups and areas. A comprehensive "commons" approach incorporates digital openness, as well as ecological and social considerations, with enhanced citizen participation. In 2016 the City Council set up BarCola (Barcelona Collaboration), a joint working group of the municipality and representatives from the platform sector, to develop policy. Many cities in the Global South, such as Medellin and Porto Allegre, are engaged in similar justice and commons oriented participatory policies.

Other cities are prioritizing different goals. In Sweden, Gothenburg is using enthusiasm for sharing to promote activities that reduce carbon emissions. New York City has focused on labor rights and housing affordability. Whatever the orientation of an individual city, sharing policies need to incorporate racial and economic justice, whether they aim to set minimum conditions for workers, as in the Charter of the fundamental rights of digital labor put forward by Bologna, funds for community development in low-income areas, or platforms to ensure food security. Sharing initiatives should benefit marginalized and underserved communities and avoid the inequality-enhancing impacts of Big Sharing. This is the area where the nonprofits we studied most needed improvement—in broadening participation by race, class, and gender, and providing economic value for people who need it most.

Will these efforts succeed? The commons and cooperative movements that have emerged in both academia and at the municipal level are attempting to develop vibrant off- and online ecosystems that yield justice, sustainability, and democracy. That's a tall order. We saw in chapter 4 how difficult it can be to predict and control the negative consequences of successful platforms. That's why continuous learning through access to data and the ability to regulate are so important. We can't trust the technology to get things right. We've got to build our values into the software. This is true not just for sharing algorithms but for those that are increasingly in use across society. As Tawana put it forcefully, in response to the claim that technology is destroying human connection, "Damn it, it's not the tool, it's the person that wields it, I promise."

## Sharing the Planet

All this effort will be for naught if we don't deal with the accelerating impacts of climate destabilization. Scientists have done the hard work of figuring out what's going on with the atmosphere and climate and setting out the timescales on which we must respond to avoid catastrophe.[88] Now it's time for us, especially those who live in wealthy societies, to act. While deploying new technologies, especially in energy and transport, is essential, we also need new "social technology." And none is more urgent than learning how to share. Whether it's within communities of known others or stranger sharing, we're not going to get through the climate emergency unless we share atmosphere, resources, consumer goods, and ultimately scarcity. We'll need to do that at small scale and large. We need solidarity and learning. Platforms can help with that, by studying resource use and facilitating exchanges when climate disasters hit. We'll have to build carbon neutrality into Big Sharing companies, as well as into the new commons and co-ops we need to create. We also need a proliferation of platforms in the clean energy sector, as well as innovation on sites dedicated to ecological restoration and recovery. And we'll have to develop a new way of being, which prioritizes cooperation and helping.

The values of many of our participants are worth revisiting here. While they didn't always (or in some cases even usually) manage to live them out, they did envision the kind of world we need to create. Especially at our nonprofit sites, they emphasized the importance of community, doing for others, living lightly on the earth, and rejecting a global capitalist system that is destroying people and planet. In contrast to those who are running Big Sharing platforms, many of the people we met during our years of research recognize the problems we face and know which are the wrong ways forward. The contention of this book is that having wasted the first decade with a false start, we need to get moving on a collaborative revolution that's dedicated to facing that reality—and truly sharing with each other, as we share the planet.

# Appendix A

## Research Methods

*Interviews*

All interviews were semi-structured and were generally scheduled for sixty minutes, although some went longer or shorter. Most were face-to-face and took place in a variety of locales—coffee shops, our office at Boston College, and other venues. Some were done via computer or phone. A small number of interviews for the for-profit platform cases were done remotely with people who lived in other cities. For the for-profits we worked from a common script, although the conversations diverged. All interviews were professionally transcribed.

Recruitment methods varied, as noted below. For the for-profit platforms, we needed to use multiple recruitment methods, especially as time went on. We required a minimum number of trades for the time bank and for-profits. We also required that informants be within the age range of eighteen to thirty-four years old, except for the makerspace and drivers. We generally compensated people for interviews. We began at twenty-five dollars, and by the end of our interviewing were paying forty dollars.

All interviews were followed by a short survey that collected demographic and financial information. The tables in Appendix B report on some of this information. For some cases, numbers of interviews conducted as described below vary from Appendix B Tables because we have not included the consumers and do not double count re-interviews. In addition, a few people who worked on more than one for-profit platform were reclassified to another case if their primary platform differed from the one they were interviewed for.

*Ethnography*

We did ethnography for the four nonprofit cases. Methods differed and are described below by case.

*Other Research*

We also attended and spoke at conferences where platform founders, employees, workers, and consultants were present. Juliet was invited onto a membership-only listserv with founders, employees, consultants, and a few researchers. She was also approached by platform entrepreneurs and had conversations with them. She also had informal interviews and conversations with platform employees. Juliet helped to field the first national random sample U.S. poll that asked about the sharing economy, in collaboration with newdream.org and PolicyInteractive.

## How We Discuss Our Data in This Book

Anonymity: We have used pseudonyms throughout the book for informants and the food swap, makerspace, and time bank. We have altered details about some individuals to preserve their anonimity.

Quotations: Where there is no citation to a quote or piece of information, it comes from our research. We have altered quotations to take out many of the verbal fillers such as "like" and "you know" in order to make the quotes more readable. In cases where those fillers are relevant to the speaker's meaning or to convey a better sense of their conversational style, we have retained them.

## Nonprofit Cases

*Time Bank (Emilie Dubois Poteat, Lindsey "Luka" Carfagna)*

Recruitment was carried out by soliciting an interview as a trade on the platform. The organization gave us credits to do the interviews. We did twenty-nine in-depth semi-structured interviews and surveys. We also did approximately eighty-five hours of participant observation. This consisted of trades on both sides of the ledger (i.e., giving and getting services), for a total of twenty trades. These were with additional respondents. Examples of trades include copyediting, rides around Boston, dog-sitting, apartment organization, engagement photo shoots,

and personal training. We attended one conference on time banking and participated in organizational meetings and orientations.

Data collection: 2011–2012.

## Makerspace (William Attwood-Charles)

Research methods included semi-structured interviews with thirty-two participants, as well as ethnographic observation. Will took a woodworking class at the
makerspace, in addition to renting a small workstation where he could observe
the activity of makers. A total of 175 hours of field research were conducted at the
space over eighteen months. Recruitment was done by in-person requests, either
through interactions in class or casual encounters in the space, as well as through
the makerspace's listserv. For this case, because the age range was greater than
our others, we interviewed a number of people who were older than thirty-four.
In addition to interviews, Will took field notes and analyzed postings on the organization's listserve.

Data collection: July 2013–January 2015.

## Food Swap (Connor Fitzmaurice)

Research on the Northeastern Food Swap was primarily based on two years of
participant observation. Connor became a regular member of the group, attend-
ing monthly swapping events and bringing items to trade. Swaps were scheduled
for three hours, resulting in approximately eighty hours of observations. These
were recorded in field notes written immediately following each event.

Participant observation was supplemented with five semi-structured interviews with key figures in the swap: the founders and two core members of
the group. These interviews were intended to uncover motivations for participation, along with any explicit strategies interview subjects used to make good
trades and evaluate offerings. These formal interviews were supplemented
with numerous informal conversations during swapping events. The data
collection for this case followed an inductive method. As participation in the
group deepened, the struggles many participants were having securing trades
became more apparent. As a result, Connor was able to tweak offerings
to informally test how different types of goods were received by the group.
Often the researcher would bring two sets of items to judge their comparative
reception. Most important, they were able to ask more focused questions

during the events, to evaluate whether trades were meeting participants' expectations. All written field notes and interview transcripts were analyzed, along with bid sheets that were collected from many of the swaps. These bid sheets were a valuable data source. While the explicit purpose of these silent auction bid sheets was to facilitate trade and reduce face-to-face rejection, they also allowed for more accurate tracking of how the group was functioning. They documented not only participation in the group but also relative interest in the various goods on offer.

Data collection: July 2012–2014.

*Open Learning (Lindsey "Luka" Carfagna)*

This research was done in two phases. Phase 1 consisted of three hundred hours of participant observation from 2012 to 2014, thirty-four in-depth interviews, and a demographic survey of interview participants. Phase 1 entailed joining, lurking, learning, and teaching in multiple open-learning platforms, spaces, and resources in an attempt to become an open learner and examine open learning in Luka's own practices and interactions with others. Luka tailored her social media presence to the project and primarily used Twitter as a platform for engaging with other learners. Open-learning resources and environments were chosen based on popularity (the MOOC craze was happening at this time), recommendations from key innovators, and recommendations from interview participants. Interview participants were recruited throughout the participant-observation process, and Luka continued to informally interact with participants and their preferred open-learning environments after the interviews. Interviews lasted between forty-five and ninety minutes and were either conducted in person or over video chat. All participants were also asked to complete a demographic questionnaire.

Phase 2 consisted of follow-up interviews with eighteen of the original thirty-four participants in the late spring and early summer of 2015, plus in-depth internet searches for public information on the remaining sixteen original participants. Twenty-six of the original participants responded to the initial phase 2 recruitment email, but only eighteen were available to schedule a follow-up interview. Follow-up interviews lasted between thirty and seventy-five minutes and were conducted either over video chat or the phone.

Data collection: Phase 1: 2012–2014; Phase 2: late spring/early summer 2015.

For-Profit Cases

*Airbnb, Turo, TaskRabbit Wave 1 (Emilie Dubois Poteat,*
*Juliet, and undergraduates)*

For our first wave of research we recruited forty-three participants on these three platforms. We used random sampling methods until we were unable to find additional respondents. For TaskRabbit we posted the interview as a task. For Airbnb we contacted hosts via the platform and used snowball sampling. For Turo we contacted participants via the platform. We only interviewed people who had done a minimum of five completed transactions, ages eighteen to thirty-four. Interviews were approximately sixty minutes each and were compensated at about twenty-five dollars, although there was some individual variation. Interviews began with background to obtain a brief narrative of the respondent's life trajectory. We then asked a series of questions about their involvement with the platform, from initial motivations and expectations to detailed information about experiences, earnings, and satisfaction with the work. We followed this interview script in subsequent waves of data collection unless otherwise noted.

   Data collection: 2013.


*TaskRabbit Wave 2 (Robert Wengronowitz and undergraduates)*

We conducted seventeen semi-structured hour-long interviews with taskers and administered a follow-up survey. The participation requirement was a minimum of five completed transactions and being within the age range of eighteen to thirty-four. We compensated respondents at thirty-five dollars on average (more experienced taskers required higher compensation). We recruited interviewees through the TaskRabbit platform by requesting an interview as the task. We also targeted taskers who appeared to be persons of color in their profile.

   Data collection: August 2015–December 2015.


*Follow-Up Interviews: TaskRabbit and Airbnb*
*(Taylor Cain, Juliet)*

We did twelve follow-up interviews with TaskRabbits and Airbnb hosts.
Data collection: 2015.

*Airbnb Wave 2 (Isak Ladegaard)*

After reviewing the transcripts of our first set of Airbnb interviews, we decided to conduct a second phase of interviews. For this second phase we completed a total of thirty-two interviews, each one lasting between sixty and ninety minutes. This time we were particularly interested in how hosts interacted with their guests, and we limited the sample to hosts who (a) rented out space in the home they live in, rather than renting out a separate property, and (b) had hosted at least five times, to ensure that they have enough hosting experience to draw from. (One participant who had hosted only three times was also included because of her numerous relevant experiences as a guest.) Some participants were recruited within the platform. When this proved to be difficult, we reached out to hosts on various social media websites and snowballed based on previous interviews.

Data collection: September 2016–August 2017.

*Airbnb Quantitative (Mehmet Cansoy)*

The quantitative component of our research on Airbnb focused on individuals providing services on the platform. Throughout 2016 we collected information on the geographic location, prices, and various other pieces of information on roughly two hundred thousand units available for rent on the platform. In early 2017 we also acquired comprehensive data on about 475,000 listings collected by a third party. We used the scraped location of listings to match them with census tracts using the US Census's Geocoder API. We then merged the listing-level data with the 2011–2015 five-year estimates of the American Community Survey for the same census tract. This allowed us to study the patterns of participation across lines of race and class, how the economic benefits of Airbnb are distributed, the role of discrimination in the public reputation system, and the potential gentrification impacts of the platform. Details on our statistical methods can be found in our papers.

*Consumer Interviews (Robert Wengronowitz and undergraduates)*

These were interviews with people who participated on platforms as consumers. Respondents needed to have a minimum of five completed transactions and be in the age range of eighteen to thirty-four. Interviews were approximately sixty minutes and included a demographic survey. Interviews were semi-structured and began with background to obtain a brief narrative of their life trajectory. We then asked a series of questions about their involvement with the given platform, from initial motivations and expectations to detailed information about experiences. We recruited through email lists, Facebook, Twitter, Craigslist, snowballing, and fliers posted around town. This sample consisted of twenty people who had used Airbnb, TaskRabbit, or Turo.

Dates of data collection: July 2014–March 2015.

### Uber/Lyft (Isak Ladegaard)

We conducted seventeen semi-structured interviews of forty-five minutes to sixty minutes with each participant. Most interviewees were recruited through the ride-hail platforms—that is, during a ride—but we also contacted drivers on social media, ride-hailing-focused websites, and by snowballing. With the exception of one Skype interview, all interviews were conducted in person, with the majority conducted in public locations such as cafes and parks. We asked open-ended questions about their experiences, including how they got involved with ride-hailing, their best and worst rides, how they decided which rides to accept, how they manage their profiles and listings, and what kinds of experiences they have with rating customers and being rated by them. All interviews were audio-recorded, transcribed, and coded.

Dates of data collection: September 2016–August 2017.

### Postmates/Favor (William Attwood-Charles)

We conducted twenty-six semi-structured interviews and a demographic survey. Participants were recruited primarily through Craigslist advertisements requesting interviews with gig couriers, as well as official and unofficial Postmates and Favor Facebook groups. Additionally, the researcher participated in two separate "onboarding" events (similar to orientations but focused on how to use the app) for new Postmates and Favor couriers.

Dates of data collection: October 2015–May 2016.

### Stocksy (Samantha Eddy)

We conducted twenty-nine semi-structured interviews and a demographic survey. Participants were recruited through a mass email sent by the organization to its membership. Interested parties contacted us via email to arrange an interview.

Because this is a global platform, interviews were done via computer or telephone. The script focused on issues that differed from those in the other for-profit cases and included both narratives of participation and experiences on the platform, as well as discussion of governance.

Dates of data collection: April 2017–October 2017.

# *Appendix B*

Describing Our Sample

This appendix describes our sample by its demographic and socioeconomic characteristics and includes our categorization of respondents' platform dependence.

TABLE B.1 Demographic Information for Earners on For-Profit Platforms

| | Airbnb | Postmates & Favor | Turo | TaskRabbit | Uber & Lyft | Totals |
|---|---|---|---|---|---|---|
| Number of respondents | 44 | 26 | 11 | 31 | 17 | 129 |
| Mean age | 29.5 | 25.5 | 29.5 | 29.6 | 31.6 | 28.9 |
| Gender (%) | | | | | | |
|   Female | 40.1 | 26.9 | 27.3 | 38.7 | 17.6 | 33.3 |
|   Male | 56.8 | 73.1 | 72.7 | 61.3 | 82.4 | 65.9 |
|   Other | 2.3 | 0 | 0 | 0 | 0 | 0.8 |
| Race (%) | | | | | | |
|   Asian | 13.9 | 7.7 | 25 | 7.1 | 0 | 9.6 |
|   Black | 2.8 | 19.2 | 0 | 17.9 | 31.2 | 14 |
|   Hispanic | 5.6 | 7.7 | 0 | 14.3 | 25 | 10.5 |
|   White | 69.4 | 61.5 | 75 | 53.6 | 31.2 | 58.8 |
|   Other | 8.3 | 3.8 | 0 | 7.1 | 12.5 | 7 |
| Education (self) (%) | | | | | | |
|   High school or less | 2.3 | 11.5 | 0 | 3.6 | 25 | 7.3 |
|   Some college | 9.1 | 30.8 | 0 | 25 | 31.2 | 19.4 |
|   College degree | 52.3 | 46.2 | 30 | 53.6 | 37.5 | 47.6 |
|   Graduate degree | 36.4 | 11.5 | 70 | 17.9 | 6.2 | 25.8 |
| Annual income in preceding year (%) | | | | | | |
|   $0–25k | 15.2 | 60 | 12.5 | 35.7 | 23.1 | 31.8 |
|   $25–50k | 21.2 | 28 | 37.5 | 46.4 | 53.8 | 34.6 |
|   $50–75k | 30.3 | 8 | 12.5 | 10.7 | 15.4 | 16.8 |
|   $75–125k | 24.2 | 0 | 25 | 3.6 | 7.7 | 11.2 |
|   $125–250k | 9.1 | 4 | 12.5 | 3.6 | 0 | 5.6 |
| Education (mother) (%) | | | | | | |
|   High school or less | 22.2 | 38.1 | 25 | 18.5 | 42.9 | 27.4 |
|   Some college | 13.9 | 4.8 | 12.5 | 14.8 | 14.3 | 12.3 |
|   College degree | 41.7 | 42.9 | 37.5 | 22.2 | 21.4 | 34 |
|   Graduate degree | 22.2 | 14.3 | 25 | 44.4 | 21.4 | 26.4 |
| Education (father) (%) | | | | | | |
|   High school or less | 14.3 | 33.3 | 25 | 22.2 | 66.7 | 27.4 |
|   Some college | 8.6 | 20.8 | 0 | 11.1 | 0 | 10.4 |
|   College degree | 34.3 | 20.8 | 37.5 | 25.9 | 16.7 | 27.4 |
|   Graduate degree | 42.9 | 25 | 37.5 | 40.7 | 16.7 | 34.9 |

*Note*: Totals may not equal 100 as a result of rounding.

TABLE B.2 Platform Dependence of Earners by Case (in percentages)

| | Airbnb | Postmates & Favor | Turo | TaskRabbit | Uber & Lyft | Total |
|---|---|---|---|---|---|---|
| Number of respondents | 44 | 26 | 11 | 31 | 17 | 129 |
| Platform dependence (%) | | | | | | |
| Dependent | 2.3 | 26.9 | 0 | 29 | 70.6 | 22.5 |
| Partially dependent | 56.8 | 34.6 | 45.5 | 45.2 | 17.6 | 43.4 |
| Supplemental | 40.9 | 38.5 | 54.5 | 25.8 | 11.8 | 34.1 |

TABLE B.3 Demographic Information for Participants in Nonprofit Cases

| | Food Swap | Makerspace | Open Education | Time Bank | Total |
|---|---|---|---|---|---|
| Number of respondents | 5 | 32 | 34 | 29 | 100 |
| Mean age | 30.6 | 38.4 | 26.4 | 29.8 | 31.5 |
| Gender (%) | | | | | |
| Female | 100 | 31.2 | 50 | 69 | 52 |
| Male | 0 | 68.8 | 50 | 31 | 48 |
| Race (%) | | | | | |
| Asian | 0 | 3.1 | 15.2 | 18.5 | 11.3 |
| Black | 20 | 0 | 3 | 3.7 | 3.1 |
| Hispanic | 0 | 3.1 | 3 | 3.7 | 3.1 |
| White | 80 | 93.8 | 78.8 | 70.4 | 81.4 |
| Other | 0 | 0 | 0 | 3.7 | 1 |
| Education (%) | | | | | |
| High school or less | 0 | 3.1 | 0 | 0 | 1 |
| Some college | 0 | 6.2 | 24.2 | 0 | 10.2 |
| College degree | 20 | 59.4 | 36.4 | 46.4 | 45.9 |
| Graduate degree | 80 | 31.2 | 39.4 | 53.6 | 42.9 |

*Note*: Totals may not equal 100 as a result of rounding.

TABLE B.4 Demographic Information for Stocksy Artists

| | |
|---|---|
| Number of respondents | 29 |
| Mean age | 38.9 |
| Gender | |
|   Female | 19 |
|   Male | 10 |
| Race | |
|   Asian | 4 |
|   Black | 0 |
|   Hispanic | 0 |
|   White | 15 |
|   Other | 2 |
|   NA | 8 |
| Education | |
|   High school or less | 3 |
|   Some college | 3 |
|   College degree | 10 |
|   Graduate degree | 5 |
|   NA | 8 |

# Appendix C

Who Are Sharing Economy Participants?

The earliest users of sharing economy platforms were young, highly educated, and relatively privileged. Over time, the user base has diversified, but we can't be too precise about how much, because it's an ill-defined segment without official statistics. There are only a few U.S. random sample surveys. One is a Pew Research Center study of consumers done at the end of 2015 (Pew Research Center 2016b). Its most notable finding is the disproportionate representation of the young and highly educated. Eighteen- to twenty-nine-year-olds are overrepresented as consumers of ride-hailing, clothing rental, and coworking spaces; buyers of secondhand and handmade goods; and consumers of gig labor for household tasks. The twenty-nine to forty-four age group was more prominent in lodging—perhaps because it's a higher-cost service. Usage drops off significantly after age forty-five, although since 2015 more older Americans seem to be using apps, both as consumers and as ride-hail drivers. Consumers are more highly educated than the general population; our calculations from the Pew study show that more than half of college degree holders use at least one type of service. There are also racial differences. Whites are 2.5 times more likely to have used a lodging platform than blacks. Men and women consume equally, although there are differences across categories. While half the population had purchased secondhand goods online, take-up for other sharing services was much lower: 15 percent had used ride-hailing services, 11 percent lodging platforms, 4 percent coworking and task labor, and 2 percent had rented clothing from platforms. These numbers have increased in recent years.

A second Pew survey in 2016 (Pew Research Center 2016a) looked at the provider side and found that 24 percent of the population had done some form of online earning. Goods selling was the most common activity, with 18 percent of the sample participating, in comparison to 8 percent doing gig labor such as ride-hailing, cleaning, or shopping for others. Sociodemographic characteristics of earners have been hard to pin down. The Pew study found nearly equal numbers of men and women earners, in contrast to almost all the other sources, including Farrell, Greig, and Hamoudi (2018) and Burston-Marsteller (2016), which find that men make up two-thirds of earners. A key reason men predominate is their concentration in ride-hail, which is the largest category. Men predominate in ride-hail and on-demand delivery, although women make up the majority of grocery shoppers (Selyukh 2019). Platform workers are also highly educated. A widely reported survey of Uber drivers (Hall and Krueger 2018) found that 37 percent held a college degree, and 40 percent had either an associate's degree or some college (11 percent had a postgraduate degree). More recent studies show this workforce has changed, at least in the big cities. In Los Angeles (UCLA Institute for Research on Labor and Employment 2018) and New York (Parrott and Reich 2018), drivers are now almost all men, most of whom are full-time and much less educated. They are also much more likely to be foreign born. In NYC the estimate is that 90 percent are immigrants; however, outside of these services the provider workforce is generally highly educated, particularly on higher-wage platforms like TaskRabbit.

# *Appendix D*

Defining the Sharing Economy

There is considerable debate over terminology among scholars who study sharing platforms. We have discussed this issue in Schor and Fitzmaurice (2015) and Schor and Attwood-Charles (2017). The sector was originally called "collaborative consumption," a term coined by Rachel Botsman. By 2012, however, usage began to shift to the "sharing economy." There is a lack of clarity about where the term came from. Wikipedia claims that its origin is unknown (https://en.wikipedia.org/wiki/Sharing_economy) or attributable to Lawrence Lessig (2008) in his book *Remix*. But Lessig is discussing nonmonetary sharing. Benkler's influential article (2004) uses the term *social sharing*. Nicholas John (2016) finds instances of the term *sharing economy* in reference to music and software in 2007 and 2008. What does seem clear is that the term was in use before Airbnb and Uber were founded. This history supports the interpretation that the sharing economy should be seen in the context of the open source movement and collaborative online practices. In early 2012 a group in France founded "Ouishare" as a global community based on open collaborating and sharing. A few months later, there was a major sharing conference in San Francisco.

The core idea is a peer-to-peer (P2P) market in which durable assets with excess capacity are rented or loaned on a temporary basis. (Excess capacity is also the main idea of collaborative consumption.) Some scholars, such as the Dutch innovation scholar, Koen Frenken, restrict the term *sharing economy* to this kind of arrangement. Frenken et al. (2015) differentiate among the *sharing economy* (with and without payment), the *secondhand economy,* the *on-demand economy,* and the *product-service economy*. Other terms include the *access economy*, the *gig economy*, and the *platform economy*. See also (Frenken and Schor 2017).

A second aspect of the P2P structure is that peers are unknown to each other. This generally means that sites will use crowdsourced reputational information to encourage the risk-taking associated with stranger trading. As a result, some definitions of the sector include public ratings systems as a criterion. Another distinction is whether the activity is P2P or what is called Business to Consumer (B2C), or even B2B (Business to Business). We exclude B2C and B2B platforms because company ownership of goods obviates the sharing dimension. Zipcar, however, which owns the cars it rents, is often considered a pioneering sharing economy company. There is also the difference between offline and online work. Digital labor on platforms such as Amazon Mechanical Turk or Upwork is generally not included in the "sharing economy" but is termed crowdwork or microwork. In 2016 the Census Bureau provided the first official definition of the sector, using the term *digital matching firms*. It identified four characteristics: (1) the use of information technology to facilitate peer-to-peer transactions, (2) the use of ratings systems, (3) flexibility for workers to choose hours, and (4) worker-provided tools and assets necessary to do the job (Telles 2016). In comparison to what is generally meant by the sharing economy, this definition may be too restrictive, because it excludes companies who choose to employ their workers, and too broad, because it includes digital labor, which is generally not considered part of the sharing economy. Others consider secondhand markets as part of the sector, stretching the concept of "sharing" to include shared ownership or use over the life of a good. This would argue for including eBay, although in practice few do, perhaps because it was founded a decade before Uber and Airbnb. Some only include for-profit platforms, but we always include nonprofits.

In our research, we identify the sharing economy as *for-profit and non-profit peer-to-peer sites serving individuals (consumers) in offline exchanges*. All of our for-profit cases fit this definition except Stocksy, the platform cooperative. Its customers are mainly businesses, not consumers. We chose it because at the time there was not a comparably sized platform co-op that served individual consumers. The makerspace is also not a P2P organization, given that a nonprofit leases the space and owns the tools. We included it because makerspaces are one of the most vibrant organizations in the sharing space. Finally, the open-learning case is a hybrid, but we followed individuals, who were active in both P2P sites and other kinds of spaces.

In the media there is no analytic coherence to how the term *sharing economy* has been used. In practice it has mostly been a matter of self-selection, with the exception of Uber, which originally did not accept the designation but was almost always identified as a leading sharing economy platform. But a situation in which Lyft is included and Uber is not is incoherent, given how similar the companies are. Our practice has been to include P2P platforms and organizations that are oriented to consumers and mainly offer offline services. (We say *mainly* because on some platforms, such as TaskRabbit, a portion of the tasks are digital.) The offline aspect enforces a local dimension, even in cases of global companies. There are many activities and platforms that we don't include but that are close cousins— digital labor and crowdfunding are two of the biggest. Other examples include coworking and rental services.

The use of the word *sharing* has been criticized (Slee 2015; Ravenelle 2019; Reich 2015). Richardson argues the term itself has become performative (Richardson 2015). Critics have argued its purpose is to capture the positive symbolism of sharing while hiding the predatory aspects of the business model, a form of "sharewashing" (Kalamar 2013). We agree that for-profit companies benefit from the positive associations of the term. This is why we sometimes put the term in quotes, when the activities we are discussing clearly do not involve sharing. But there have always been genuine sharing entities within the sector, such as nonprofits that promote surplus food exchange, free homestays, or service barter. Their claims to the term are valid. In practice, there continues to be some mingling of for-profit and nonprofit entities at conferences such as Ouishare and within the Sharing Cities Alliance. The nonprofits derive some benefits from their alliance with well-capitalized, powerful actors, and they are committed to the terminology.

There is a simplistic position that says any activity that involves money can't be sharing, most prominently represented by consumer scholar Russell Belk (Belk 2007; 2010; 2014a; 2014b). This view ignores the array of relations of reciprocity that have sustained societies around the world for centuries and that typically pair materiality and social connection (for a full critique see Arnould and Rose 2015). Belk's sharp opposition between money and sharing comes from a capitalism-centric worldview in which the profane sphere (the monetized one) is wholly separate from the sacred one (gifting and nonmonetary relations). Zelizer (2000) calls this a "hostile worlds" view. (See also Folbre [2001]). But even the most capitalistic economies are not as segregated as this view assumes, with culturally complex mingling among gifts, intimacy, and money (Zelizer 2013). Similarly, Benkler (2004) takes the view that money is sometimes a part of social sharing. Many of the participants that we interviewed do use the term *sharing* to describe their practices, even when they involve money, although this tends to be less true among our lower-wage respondents. Ravenelle reports that among her respondents, those without assets to rent, such as Uber drivers and TaskRabbits, reject the term.

A final point is that the sharing economy exists within a larger universe. For some, that context is collaborative online relations, in particular the open-source software movement and peer production communities (Benkler 2006). To others, the relevant connection is to the major technology giants. Scholars Martin Kenney and John Zysman have argued that sharing companies should be understood as minor players in a more widespread reorganization of the economy being effected by Facebook, Google, Amazon, and other large platforms (Kenney and Zysman 2015; 2016b). In their view, to understand the sharing economy requires that broader analysis, which is why they use the term *platform economy*.

Given this terminological proliferation, and the legitimate argument that much of this activity is certainly not sharing, why do we use the term? In part it is to ground our analysis in the sector's history and its aspirations. Its origins are not merely predatory, or wholly commercial, as we discuss in chapter 1. We can see the potential of this vision more clearly outside the United States, where for-profitness is less defining, pressures for egalitarian outcomes are stronger, and the movement to create a pluralistic sharing economy is more robust. Our commitment to this ideal also explains why we have studied both the profit-oriented and community entities.

# Notes

Introduction

1. Whyte (1956) and Frank (1997).
2. Georgakas and Surkin (2012).
3. Friedan (1963).
4. By the mid-2010s, a number of books on the sharing economy were being published, by academics, journalists and practitioners. I discuss them below. Our analysis has benefited from them all. Our own contributions to the literature began in 2014, with Juliet's "Debating the Sharing Economy" (2014). Other general accounts from our team include Schor and Fitzmaurice (2015); Frenken and Schor (2017); and Schor and Cansoy (2019). We review the literature in Schor and Attwood-Charles (2017). A second review is Vallas and Schor (2020).
5. Hundreds of millions: Airbnb statistics from https://ipropertymanagement .com/airbnb-statistics; Uber www.businessofapps.com/data/uber-statistics; Lyft www.businessofapps.com/data/lyft-statistics.
6. Stranger sharing is from Schor (2014). Benkler's work a decade earlier on public carpooling sites emphasized that peers were "weakly connected" (Benkler 2004).
7. Pew Research Center (2011).
8. For a discussion of how sharing economy employees understood the discourse, see Cockayne (2016).
9. For an excellent account of the right-wing attack on the taxi industry, see Horan (2017).
10. Associated Press (2017).
11. Rosenblat (2018).

12. Paul (2019a).

13. Sundararajan (2016).

14. I discuss the peer-to-peer goods platforms in chapter 4. For-profit platforms are expanding their presence in goods rental for furniture, household goods, and clothing but with a B2C structure (Margolies 2019). The environmental impact of these rental platforms has not yet been studied.

15. Studies of the environmental impacts of ride-hail include Balding et al. (2019); Barrios, Hochberg, and Yi (2018); Clewlow and Mishra (2017); Erhardt et al. (2019); Graehler, Mucci, and Erhardt (2019); and Schaller (2018).

16. Cansoy (2019a); Wachsmuth, Combs, and Kerrigan (2019); Wachsmuth and Weisler (2018).

17. Isaac (2017a).

18. There are also books on the general economics of platforms, for example, Parker, Van Alstyne, and Choudary (2016).

19. An excellent treatment of a related subject—online digital labor—is Gray and Suri (2019).

20. Emilie Dubois Poteat was a team member in the first few years. Taylor Cain and Xiaorui Huang have also participated in the research. Undergraduate assistants are listed in the acknowledgments.

21. There were some additional activities we tried to study, but they had so little participation that we couldn't find people to interview. For example, we tried twice on eating and meal preparation apps.

22. Data on Boston Metropolitan area is from the Census Reporter, https://censusreporter.org/profiles/31000US14460-boston-cambridge-newton-ma-nh-metro-area.

23. A notable exception is Robinson (2017), who studied Uber in Boston.

24. Our project website: www.bc.edu/bc-web/schools/mcas/departments/sociology/connected.html.

25. Her book was titled *What's Mine Is Yours: The Rise of Collaborative Consumption.* Botsman and Rogers (2010).

Chapter 1

1. Elsewhere I have used the term "common good claims" for this discourse; see Schor (2014). Calo and Rosenblat (2017) argue these were "a story that proponents tell in service of some business or political purpose such as attracting participants and funding or minimizing government intervention" and that this is illegitimate. They argue the companies were posing as part of a social movement

even as they engaged in regulatory "entrepreneurship" or, worse, "arbitrage." This position is not so far from my own, although I take the view that many participants, although not necessarily all founders, had genuine, common-good motives. See also Cockayne (2016); and John (2016) on the sharing discourse.

2. See Schor (2014); and Cockayne (2016).

3. Examples include the printing press, which played an important role in the Protestant Reformation. Marshall McLuhan predicted that television was a revolutionary medium that would break down hierarchy and create a "global village." Robots were first predicted to usher in the leisured society; see Schor (1992). Of course, new technologies also spur fear. When the telephone was introduced, people worried it would break up home life and reduce the practice of visiting friends (Fischer 1992). In the 1950s some thought television was fomenting larceny by promoting consumer lifestyles (Schor 1999).

4. Technological change typically engenders both utopian and dystopian predictions, partly because it is often Janus-faced, capable of impacts that are both benign and malign, even simultaneously. The strong version of technological determinism attributes effects largely, or even solely, to the technology itself. A second camp takes the reverse view, arguing that technology is neutral, and the social context in which it is embedded determines outcomes. As I discuss in chapter 6, when Uber arrived in Sweden, it was forced to follow laws for taxi drivers, which ensured decent wages, security and other employment protections, while in the U.S. it called its drivers "independent contractors," took no responsibility for wage levels, and shifted risk onto its workforce (Söderqvist 2018; Thelen 2018). The technology is the same in both countries. A third position takes a middle ground, arguing that technology is not purely determinant, nor is it purely neutral. New technologies can change the context around them, steer outcomes in one direction or another, and have independent effects. They're just not all-powerful. See Benkler (2020) for a discussion of this point. For a theorization of platforms, and a discussion of the power of technology, see Vallas and Schor (2020).

5. These roots of the sharing economy discourse have generally not been stressed by observers, with the notable exceptions of Tom Slee (2015) and Luka Carfagna (2017).

6. Turner (2006, 11–12). When Savio railed against the "machine," he was speaking against not only actual weapons of destruction but also the information technologies that the Department of Defense and its academic allies were busy developing.

7. This memorable term is from English theorists Richard Barbrook and Andy Cameron (1996). It represents the combination of hippie counterculture and

technophilia and the view that digital technology was the route to a society free of domination. See also Turner (2006); and Thomas Frank (2000).

8. Turner (2006, 208) takes issue with Barbrook and Cameron's claim that the Californian Ideology emerged from the New Left. He argues its origins were Stewart Brand's Whole Earth network and New Communalism.

9. Tech pioneers such as John Perry Barlow (former lyricist for the Grateful Dead), Esther Dyson, and others embarked on lucrative tech-enabled careers themselves and preached the gospel of network-based financial independence.

10. The Jeffersonian vision is discussed by Barbrook and Cameron (1996). Early social networking sites populated by techno-counterculturalists did produce largely harmonious social worlds. For example, the WELL (Whole Earth 'Lectronic Link) was an example of an early harmonious online community (Turner 2006).

11. "Harmonious community" is from Turner (2006, 246). Turner's account of the development of the cyberculture in the 1980s and 1990s reveals that it already contained most of what would become the sharing economy discourse: mobilizing the "largely untapped reservoir of skills and resources that reside with the people" (115), a globalist vision of social connection, online relations as the antidote to fragmentation and isolation, "pre-industrial community" (93), and the fostering of sharing and intimacy. According to Turner, "there emerged the image of a new kind of person, one who moved from task to task pursuing information and using technical tools in an experimental manner for the advancement of himself or herself and society" (88).

12. Some believers often went even further, adopting a worldview in which systems such as markets are conceptualized as biological systems—that is, naturally occurring processes over which humans have little control. Kevin Kelly, cofounder and editor of the flagship publication of the cyberculture, *Wired*, explicitly embraced this bionomic ideology, as did others. See Turner (2006, chap. 7); and Frank (2000).

13. Joining "the free-wheeling spirit" of hippies with the "entrepreneurial zeal" of yuppies is from Barbrook and Cameron (1996, 1).

14. See Frank (2000, xiv, xii).

15. Turner (2006, 194).

16. It may seem curious that counterculturalists who came originally from the left, and who cared deeply about hierarchy and oppression, would make common cause with far-right figures such as Newt Gingrich and George Gilder, especially because the GOP is socially repressive and the party most associated with race and gender domination. But the combination of technophilia and their long-standing

critique of the state led cyberutopians into the neoliberal camp. These contradictions can be seen in the personal biographies of leading figures, such as Mitch Kapor, an early open-source advocate and cofounder of the Electronic Freedom Foundation. By the 2000s, Kapor was one of the original investors in Uber.

17. Turner (2006, 230). He also discusses the 1996 Telecom Act.

18. The Bay Area is the original location for most early sharing platforms. Individuals we have identified as connectors are Mitch Kapor, a cofounder of the Electronic Frontier Foundation and Mozilla, and Freada Klein Kapor, both key cyberculture figures who were also early Uber investors.

19. On the relation of unregulated markets and monopoly see Kahn (2017).

20. Morozov (2011). Social media has become a tool of authoritarian governments and individuals.

21. Peer production is the topic of Yochai Benkler's classic book, *The Wealth of Networks* (2006). On technology and context see also Benkler (2020).

22. See Paharia et al. (2011).

23. Leah Busque quote: www.crunchbase.com/organization/taskrabbit# section-overview.

24. Uber's origin story is detailed in Stone (2017).

25. In 2011 Couchsurfing was reorganized as a for-profit, but lodging is still gratis. Other pre-Airbnb platforms include VRBO (1995) and HomeAway (2005).

26. For the argument that Craigslist and eBay are the precursors of the sharing economy, see Schor and Fitzmaurice (2015). A number of sharing economy founders originally worked at eBay and adopted its ratings and reputation systems for their companies. Stein (2015).

27. Duhaime-Ross (2014).

28. Private communication with author from anonymous Zipcar consultant.

29. The anecdote about Chase and Harvard Business School students was from a discussion on a private listserve of sharing economy founders and others.

30. Entis (2014).

31. Wallenstein and Shelat (2017). A widely cited estimate of the size of the sector put it at $15 billion in 2013. PriceWaterHouseCoopers (2015).

32. Davis (2016b).

33. Madrigal (2019). A global analysis from 2016 identified 420, including B2B companies; see Wallenstein and Shelat (2017).

34. Airbnb logged 108 million stays in the U.S. in 2017, a decade after its founding; Detlefsen (2018).

35. Task breakdown on TaskRabbit is analyzed in Cullen and Farronato (2018).

36. Delivery is a major segment outside the U.S. In Europe, where the bicycle delivery model is popular, Deliveroo, DeliveryHero, Foodora, and UberEats are active. India has Swiggy and Zomato; the Middle East has Talabat, and China's big player is Ele.me.

37. These are just the consumer-oriented businesses. There's a whole ecosystem of platform businesses in logistics, transport, and equipment rental, as well as "digital labor" platforms that offer everything from image tagging and surveys to professional, white-collar services.

38. Our research on participants' aspirations to change the world is contained in Fitzmaurice et al. (2018).

39. We provide more detail on the characteristics of users in Appendix C.

40. See Fitzmaurice et al. (2018).

41. Cockayne (2016) found that employees of platform firms in San Francisco offered a more complex and mixed view of the sharing discourse. Some explicitly positioned themselves against Uber. Cockayne argued that the use of sharing discourse was beneficial to the for-profit, transactional firms because of its positive connotations, a point we have also made.

42. Sharing platforms also employ mapping, logistics, and payment systems that are common to many digitally enabled businesses. Users often cite the cashless, backstage financial arrangements as an appealing feature of personalized exchange.

43. The classic statement on two-sided markets is Rochet and Tirole (2003).

44. Castillo, Knoepfle, and Weyl (2018).

45. Companies also program algorithms to allocate tasks to workers who sign up for more hours or who get higher ratings.

46. For a small number of occupations, workers must post bonds to ensure their performance.

47. There's a question about how accurate the ratings are. I'll come back to this in chapter 3.

48. See, e.g., Cansoy (2019b); Ravenelle (2019); Rosenblat (2018); and Zervas, Proserpio, and Byers (2015).

49. Isaac (2019).

50. What is the optimal size for a sharing platform? For platforms with geographic reach, such as virtual labor services, network effects are stronger, and size increases choice. That has to be balanced against monopoly power, which reduces competition and welfare. By contrast, for local services, network effects dissipate more quickly. (See also Sundararajan [2016, 120] for this point.) Studying TaskRabbit, Cullen and Farronato (2018) find that network effects drop off

quickly and that doubling the number of transactions results in no efficiency gains. This is likely also true in transportation, which helps to explain why there is more robust competition in the food delivery and ride-hail sectors than lodging. It's also one reason we should be skeptical of Uber's claim that its model is Amazon—a platform where network effects are significant. Where network effects fall off quickly, smaller, local platforms are likely preferable because they avoid the problems associated with bigness, such as excessive market and political power. Furthermore, the argument that consumers need a single platform spanning geographic areas is not correct. All that's needed is network interoperability, as in highway transponders. They work across states, but states run their systems independently. Consumers and providers could be well served by an app that runs local driving, delivery, and lodging platforms across many cities.

51. Davis (2016a, 2016b); Hacker (2008); Kalleberg (2009, 2013); Pugh (2015); Standing (2011); Vallas and Kalleberg (2018) and Weil (2014), among others.

52. Weil (2014).

53. Tsotsis (2012).

54. Hill (2015, 4).

55. For an outstanding history of the taxi industry, from a gig economy scholar, see Dubal (2017).

56. For estimates of the still small size of the sector see chapter 2.

57. A possible IPO value of $120B for Uber was floated earlier in the year. Since the IPO, Uber's valuation has fallen. Uber and Lyft valuations are from Collins and Hoxie (2017). Airbnb valuation is from Lunden and Dillet (2018).

58. The most valuable, Postmates, was estimated to be worth $2 billion in late 2019 (Wilhelm 2019). A competitor, Favor, stopped operating outside of Texas in 2016–17 and thereafter merged with a retail grocer. IKEA's price for TaskRabbit was not publicly disclosed, but it is unlikely to have been much above the $38 million in funding the company had previously attracted. See www.crunchbase.com /organization/taskrabbit. Turo achieved a $311 million valuation, but the market for peer-to-peer car rental remains limited; Solomon (2015).

59. Madrigal (2019).

60. Center for a New American Dream and PolicyInteractive (2014).

61. Empson (2013).

62. For an analysis of the economics of this sector see Madden (2015).

63. Nearly $20 billion in Uber losses includes $14 billion from 2014 to 2018 (Horan 2019a), plus nearly $5 billion in the third quarter of 2019 (Newcomer 2019).

64. Horan (2019b).

65. The 41 percent subsidy is from Horan (2016).

66. Smith (2018).

67. In its IPO documents Uber named public transport as a competitor. Uber Technologies, Inc. (2019).

68. Conger (2019).

69. The oft-repeated hope that driverless cars will make ride-hail profitable ignores Uber's dismal record in this area to date, as well as the large expensive capital investment required, unlike the two-sided platform model where drivers bear the cost of vehicles.

70. Ramsey (2019).

71. Smith (2018).

72. Sustainable Economies Law Center, www.theselc.org.

73. Natalie Foster had worked for Moveon.org, the Sierra Club, and Obama's Organizing for America, and she cofounded Rebuild the Dream with Van Jones. Douglas Atkin brought a successful history with Purpose.com and All Out, which runs internet activist campaigns on LGBTQ issues.

74. When we talked before the conference, Douglas Atkin explained the goals of peers.org to me as to replace capitalism with the sharing economy and to legalize sharing to make the first goal possible. Natalie Foster's view was that we had come to a "moment where we can do it together and create more than what we have. That's what we're about: building a bottom-up economy" (Kamenitz 2014).

75. Kamenetz (2014); see also Tiku (2014).

76. Kamenetz (2014); Tiku (2014).


Chapter 2

1. Many surveys find that earners want autonomy and freedom. See Berg and Rani (2018); Forde, Stuart, and Joyce (2017); Manyika et al. (2016); Pew Research Center (2016a).

2. Scholz (2016).

3. See our papers "Dependence and Precarity in the Platform Economy" (Schor et al. 2019); "Dimensions of Platform Labor Control and the Experience of Gig Couriers" (Attwood-Charles 2019a); and "Provider Vulnerability in the Sharing Economy" (Ladegaard, Ravenelle, and Schor 2018). See also Vallas and Schor (2020), which discusses the literature on platform work and sets out our view of what's unique about it.

4. The GAO has subsequently looked into the 2017 survey and the BLS is taking steps to improve its methods for studying platform workers, as discussed here: www.gao.gov/products/GAO-19-273R#summary.

5. Estimate of 3 percent is from Board of Governors of the Federal Reserve System (2019). The 8 percent figure is from Pew Research Center (2016a). The Fed data, which is from the Survey of Household Economics and Decisionmaking, finds 16 percent of the population is involved in gig work, but the majority do not use apps or online matching. A study using tax data from 2007 to 2016 estimated the labor force on labor platforms (by designating specific platforms) and found a 1 percent rate; see Collins et al. (2019). For a discussion of the various data sources and issues of measurement see Abraham et al. (2018, 2017). Another data source is from researchers at JPMorgan Chase who have used bank account information; see Farrell and Greig (2017, 2016); and Farrell, Greig, and Hamoudi (2018). This data does not cover the entire country because the bank has not been operating in much of the Northeast, mid-Atlantic, and parts of the Midwest. Farrell et al. (2018) give details on geographic reach. Their studies break out four types of platform earnings—transport, nontransport labor services (such as dog sitting or telemedicine), selling, and leasing (or renting, as on Airbnb). Among account-holders at JPMorgan Chase only 4.5 percent of households received money from any type of platform in 2018; see Farrell et al. (2018). One reason their figure may be lower than some survey data is that not all online earnings are routed through banks. See Abraham et al. (2018) for a discussion of this point. Another feature of this data is that if multiple earners use the same bank account, 4.5 percent will be an underestimate of the fraction of the population that is participating. Transport is by far the largest segment, comprising 1 percent of earners. It includes driving, delivery, and moving.

6. Katharine Abraham, former commissioner of the Bureau of Labor Statistics, calls the increase in drivers "phenomenal" (Abraham et al. 2018). Tax data suggests the increase in other occupations is much smaller. But the tax data may be understated because more of these workers are part-timers, whose earnings are less likely to be reported to tax authorities. Provisions for reporting vary by platform.

7. Farrell, Greig, and Hamoudi (2018, 12). In any given month only 1.6 percent of households are participating and only 10 percent of earners are active for ten to twelve months a year. Transport workers, most of whom are drivers, are most likely to be active throughout the year.

8. Farrell, Greig, and Hamoudi (2018, 4).

9. After the first round of interviews on TaskRabbit yielded insufficient numbers of taskers of color, we intentionally targeted that group. Over time, on some platforms we also reverted to snowball sampling and advertising, as it became harder to find informants.

10. The gender breakdown is partly due to the platforms we chose. Another factor may be the Boston labor market, which is favorable for women given the prevalence of health and educational institutions.

11. We cannot compare the demographics of our sample to the true platform workforce because that sample has not been adequately described. We report on our demographics as context for our discussion. The most likely unrepresentative aspect of our sample is that our respondents are more highly educated than in the country as a whole.

12. Turo, https://turo.com/list-your-car.

13. We found that both homeowners and renters link to Facebook although for the latter there are risks if landlords do not permit short-term rentals.

14. There is considerable ambiguity about how past criminal records affect eligibility across platforms. Postmates turns down candidates who have been convicted of some of the more serious criminal offenses, but does not exclude others. Written policies by most platforms are ambiguous. A catalog and discussion is provided by Armstrong (2018). On the barriers to employment for those with a criminal record see Pager (2007).

15. Solomon (2017).

16. Another platform feature is that the payment system is controlled via the app. Customers must use electronic payments, and earners receive their money cashlessly. This puts the monetary logistics "backstage" and separates them from the performance of the service.

17. There is a large legal literature on classification and misclassification. See, e.g., V. Dubal (2017a); Cherry (2016); Kennedy (2017); Rogers (2015, 2017); Kuhn and Maleki (2017); and Rogers (2016).

18. In 2016, when the Census Bureau came up with the government's first suggested definition of what it termed "digital matching firms," two key aspects of the definition were criteria used to differentiate independent contractors from employees—flexibility for workers to choose hours and worker-provided tools and assets necessary to do the job. The other two parts of the census definition were the use of information technology (i.e., algorithms) to match customers with providers and the use of ratings systems. See Telles (2016, 3–4).

19. Scheiber (2018).

20. Conger and Scheiber (2019b). Uber's IPO states that "Our business would be adversely affected if Drivers were classified as employees instead of independent contractors" (Uber Technologies, Inc. 2019).

21. For a discussion of social contact among Uber drivers see Robinson (2017).

22. Miller and Bernstein (2017); Robinson (2017); Rosenblat (2018).

23. While a few of our taskers started businesses, and Airbnb is known for attracting commercial operators, most entrepreneurially inclined earners in our sample are engaged in off-platform businesses and rely on their own efforts on-platform.

24. Our analysis of dependency is from Schor et al. (2019). Other researchers have noted the heterogeneity of the platform labor force, although they have not generally made the argument we are making here. Alexandrea Ravenelle (2019) identifies three categories, although she mostly does not analyze differences among them. H.C. Robinson (2017) uses hours worked to differentiate between part-time and full-time workers and developed a typology of subgroups within each group. Alex Rosenblat (2018) categorizes Uber workers into full-timers, part-timers, and hobbyists. Manriquez (2019) differentiates among Mexican Uber drivers, distinguishing between professional and precarious workers. Malin and Chandler (2017) find heterogeneity among Uber drivers in Pittsburgh, including their privileged position in comparison to drivers in the informal, cash segment of the industry. Peticca-Harris (2018) finds three groups among Canadian Uber drivers. Another difference is that with the exception of Ravenelle, these are all studies that include only ride-hail drivers. Large-scale studies, noted below, also differentiate among workers on similar bases.

25. Analysis of our sample finds that earners do not vary significantly across dependency statuses by gender, race, and age. There is some variation by educational status, although this finding may be because the "some college" category includes current students, as well as those who did not complete degrees.

26. Board of Governors of the Federal Reserve System (2019).

27. Pew Research Center (2016a).

28. Forde et al. (2017) and Pesole, Brancati, and Fernandez-Macias (2018) both found a similar percentage of dependent workers as we did—25 percent and 24 percent respectively, using the definition of earning 50 percent or more of income from platform work. The former surveyed only microworkers (on platforms such as Amazon Mechanical Turk and Crowdflower) and the latter included both microworkers and offline service providers. Forde et al. did latent class analyses of the three groups and found significant differences among them, especially on income. Similar results were found by Broughton et al. (2018) for the U.K. An International Labour Organization study on crowdwork finds that it is a "main source of income" for only 32 percent of respondents. See Berg and Rani (2018, 41).

29. Ladegaard (2018).

30. Ravenelle (2019).

31. Uber researchers include Rosenblat (2018); Robinson (2017); Parrott and Reich (2018); UCLA Institute for Research on Labor and Employment (2018); Wells, Attoh, and Cullen (2019); Mishel (2018); and Hill (2015).

32. See our discussion of Boston in the introduction.

33. Isaac (2017b).

34. Robinson (2017).

35. For general treatments of the use of algorithms see O'Neil (2016); Pasquale (2015); Noble (2018); and Eubanks (2018).

36. Bodie et al. (2016).

37. Pasquale (2015).

38. Accounts of algorithmic control on platforms include Rosenblat (2018); Calo and Rosenblat (2017); Cameron (2019); Wood et al. (2019); Griesbach et al. (2019); Rahman (2018); Rosenblat and Stark (2016); Shapiro (2018); and Robinson (2017). These scholars attribute varying levels of control to algorithms, as I discuss below.

39. O'Connor (2016).

40. A classic statement on methods of workplace control is Edwards (1980). Technical control, which I discuss below, is Edwards's third type.

41. Griesbach et al. (2019).

42. Cameron (2018) identifies five functions of algorithms in ride-hail: matching work assignments, pricing, incentives, evaluation, and work instructions. See also Cameron (2019) and Rosenblat (2018).

43. Rosenblat and Stark (2016); Calo and Rosenblat (2017); Lee et al. (2015); Robinson (2017). Griesbach et al. (2019) find considerable dissatisfaction with the algorithm among food delivery workers, especially on Instacart.

44. Rosenblat and Stark (2016); Rosenblat (2018); Shapiro (2018) and Griesbach et al. (2019).

45. Attwood-Charles (2019a). See also Shapiro (2018); and Griesbach et al. (2019).

46. Connor went through the orientation process and was cleared for Task-Rabbit but over a month failed to get any tasks.

47. Allen-Robertson (2017).

48. The term is from Edwards (1980).

49. Edwards (1980).

50. Noble (2017). See also Skott and Guy (2007).

51. An account that assumes the company has extreme control is from K. Sabeel Rahman, who claims that "Uber exercises even more direct control and

authority over its drivers than many conventional managers do over their employ-ees, governing everything from take-home pay to the greeting that drivers must give to customers upon hire." Rahman (2016, 657). This seems dubious to us, given that other low-wage employers dictate customer scripts and pay, as well as hours, schedules, dress, and other aspects of work. Furthermore, Rahman fails to ac-count for the ways in which drivers carve out autonomy and resist management.

52. Shapiro (2018).

53. Attwood-Charles (2019a); Schor et al. (2019).

54. Other researchers have also noted the importance of human work in AI situations. See, e.g., Gray and Suri (2019); Shestakofsky (2017); and Robinson (2017).

55. Cameron (2018).

56. Shapiro (2018, 2965).

57. Robinson (2017, chap. 2). When Uber caught on, and the action wasn't suc-cessful, drivers went in person to the company's office.

58. Chen (2018, 2705). Other discussions of resistance include Ivanova et al. (2018); and Wood et al. (2019).

59. Although they don't make this argument, it's notable that in their study of algorithmic control in food delivery, Griesbach et al. (2019) find that the app with the most onerous algorithm (Instacart) also has the longest average hours among its workers (thirty-two per week). This is consistent with our argument about how dependency affects algorithmic control.

60. Bowles (1985); Schor and Bowles (1987); Schor (1988).

61. U.S. estimates are from Schor and Bowles (1987). U.K is Schor (1988). See also Pacitti (2011) on the cost of job loss and the Great Recession.

62. Kalleberg (2009, 2).

63. "Precariat" is from Guy Standing (2011); "fissuring" from David Weil (2014); "responsibilization" from Foucault originally, but for this context see Rose (1999); great "risk shift" from Jacob Hacker (2008). See also Kalleberg (2009, 2018); Pugh (2015); and Vallas and Kalleberg (2018). For an analysis of pre-carity and exploitation in the platform economy, which also addresses racial and gender differences, see van Doorn (2017).

64. Davis (2016b).

65. See, e.g., Sundararajan (2016); and Hall and Krueger (2018).

66. Ticona (2020). On the role of the smartphone see also Robinson (2017).

67. Farrell and Greig (2016).

68. The companies began leasing cars to drivers or arranging for leases. The arrangements have been fluid.

69. Griesbach et al. (2019).

70. Shapiro (2018).

71. https://payup.wtf/blog/2019/5/29/postmates-workers-are-fighting-back.

72. Uber analysis in Horan (2019b, pt. 18).

73. Lyft analysis in Horan (2019b, pt. 18).

74. Uber Technologies, Inc. (2019).

75. Dubal (2019b).

76. UCLA Institute for Research on Labor and Employment (2018).

77. Wells et al. (2019). Wells found that half of drivers would still recommend the job to a friend.

78. Mishel (2018).

79. Farrell et al. (2018).

80. For a different perspective, which highlights the ways in which platforms use financial penalties to control workers, see van Doorn (2018), who reports on the extensive use of fines by Handy, a housecleaning platform.

81. For true independent contractors who operate as self-employed, moving to a platform may decrease control and autonomy because they have to follow platform policies. However, they may also benefit from higher customer demand and support with billing and payment.

82. Rosenblat (2018).

83. Cameron (2018).

84. Wood et al. (2019, 64).

85. We discuss these varying strategies in Schor (2015). See also Li, Moreno, and Zhang (2016), who find that professional and nonprofessional hosts use different pricing strategies, with the latter profit-maximizing, in contrast to the former. Robinson (2017) also addresses this issue.

86. Shapiro (2018).

87. Sheldon (2016).

88. Ritzer (2007).


Chapter 3

1. Parkinson (2016).

2. Edelman, Luca, and Svirsky (2017).

3. Hempel (2018).

4. Benner (2016); Njus (2018).

5. For a discussion of these competing perspectives, see Cansoy and Schor (2019), "Who Gets to Share in the 'Sharing Economy': Understanding the Patterns of Participation and Exchange in Airbnb."

6. Sperling (2015).

7. Sundararajan (2016): "Democratization of opportunity" (123) and "already turning the tables" (124).

8. With Samuel Fraiberger, Sundararajan conducted a simulation using data from Getaround, a peer-to-peer car rental scheme similar to Turo. They concluded that "below median-income consumers will enjoy a disproportionate fraction of the eventual welfare gains from this kind of 'sharing economy' through broader inclusion, higher-quality rental based consumption, and new ownership facilitated by rental supply revenues." Fraiberger and Sundararajan (2015, 1) (in Abstract). To put the point in plainer language, they are predicting that poorer people will gain more than others by getting access to these new economies, on account of lower prices when they rent cars, and by purchasing vehicles from which they can then earn money.

9. Author's calculation from US Census. www.census.gov/content/dam /Census/library/publications/2018/demo/p60-263.pdf.

10. Arrow (1971). Positive stereotypes will produce the reverse outcome—all members of a group will be advantaged.

11. For a discussion of this law in the context of Airbnb see McLaughlin (2018). If the landlord is not present, antidiscrimination law does apply.

12. The Getaround website says that most cars are rented by the hour with rates at five to eight dollars. The platform takes 40 percent. Assume the individual has to borrow to finance a late model car, which is a reasonable assumption given the situation of most low-income urban dwellers. At a 3 percent interest rate, the monthly payment for a Toyota Camry is $444 at the time I am writing this. But with a low credit score, which many low-income borrowers have, the payment rises to $570 a month. On average this would require renting out between twenty-seven and thirty-four hours per week just to break even.

13. Einav, Farronato, and Levin (2016).

14. It charges another 3 percent to use its payments system; www.etsy.com /sell.

15. Perea (2016).

16. Cui, Li, and Zhang (2016).

17. Edelman and Luca (2014).

18. Laouénan and Rathelot (2016).

19. Hannák et al. (2017). The reason for this finding is not clear, but it may be due to the lower ratings given to workers of color rather than explicit bias in the software.

20. Thebault-Spieker, Terveen, and Hecht (2015). This study also found that taskers were less willing to travel to serve customers in the poorer, blacker South Side of the city, and they required higher prices to do so.

21. Ge et al. (2016). Cancellation rates for black men in low density areas were three times higher.

22. Uber has been using the argument that it is fairer to African American riders, in order to gain the support of civil rights groups in its fight against regulation. Mays (2018).

23. Cook et al. (2018).

24. Disability is an understudied area. For exceptions see Ameri et al. (2019); and Dillahunt and Malone (2015).

25. Ravenelle (2019, 36, 168–71).

26. Rosenblat (2018, 11–12, 148–49). See also Rosenblat et al. (2016).

27. Cui, Li, and Zhang (2016).

28. Laouénan and Rathelot (2016).

29. Abrahao et al. (2017).

30. Ayres, Banaji, and Jolls (2015); Nunley, Owens, and Howard (2011).

31. Mehmet's detailed findings are contained in his PhD dissertation, "'Sharing' in Unequal Spaces" (Cansoy 2018), and various papers, such as "Gentrification and Short-Term Rentals: Re-assessing the Rent Gap in Urban Centers" (Cansoy 2019a); "The Fault in the Stars: Public Reputation and the Reproduction of Racial Inequality on Airbnb" (Cansoy 2019b); and "Who Gets to Share in the 'Sharing Economy': Understanding the Patterns of Participation and Exchange in Airbnb" (Cansoy and Schor 2019). For pioneering research on Airbnb also using scraped data, see Slee (2015) and the work of Murray Cox, who posts research on the website Inside Airbnb, http://insideairbnb.com.

32. The "average" Airbnb listing in this example is an entire unit up for rental that cannot be instantly booked, is located in New York City, with all other listing properties (distance to city center, number of people accommodated, number of days the unit was available to be booked, average nightly price, number of listings by the same host, number of listings in the same area) and neighborhood properties (number of Airbnb listings in the area and population of the area) at the sample mean. When further area characteristics are introduced (per capita income, income inequality, median age, homeownership rate, housing values, and educational attainment) the gap in the probabilities attributed to the racial makeup of

the area decreases but remains significant. These are also the controls we use in our subsequent analysis.

33. Zervas, Proserpio, and Byers (2015).

34. Hannák et al. (2017). These authors conclude that "real-world biases can manifest in online labor markets."

35. The EEOC filing is discussed in Collier, Dubal, and Carter (2018, 930).

36. For a general discussion of discrimination in ratings see Rosenblat et al. (2016).

37. For a discussion of this literature see Cansoy and Schor (2019).

38. Mitchell and Franco (2018).

39. At the end of the first quarter of 2017 the homeownership rate among non-Hispanic whites stood at 72.2 percent, compared to 56.5 percent for Asians, 45.5 percent for Hispanics, and 42.3 percent for blacks. US Census Bureau (2017).

40. Details of our analysis can be found in Cansoy and Schor (2019). The statistical technique is hierarchical linear modeling.

41. Quattrone et al. (2016).

42. Cox (2017).

43. Three richest Americans and top four hundred from Collins and Hoxie (2017).

44. Wolff (2017, table 2).

45. Saez (2019).

46. Travis Kalanick net worth: https://en.wikipedia.org/wiki/Travis_Kalanick; Brian Chesky: https://en.wikipedia.org/wiki/Brian_Chesky; Nathan Blecharczyk : https://en.wikipedia.org/wiki/Nathan_Blecharczyk; Joe Gebbia: https://en.wikipedia.org/wiki/Joe_Gebbia.

47. See Schor (2017).

48. Educational attainment figures are author's calculations from BLS data for 2017: www.bls.gov/emp/tables/educational-attainment.htm.

49. Iqbal (2019). The exact number was 48 percent.

50. https://www.cnbc.com/id/100414962.

51. Airbnb (2018).

52. Zaarly introductory video: https://vimeo.com/24022320.

53. One study of Uber and its impact on employment and incomes for drivers (taxis plus ride-hail) is Berger, Chen, and Frey (2018); however, it lumps all drivers together. It finds total employment expanded (as expected, given the reduction in fares). Wages for taxi employees fell while those for self-employed drivers rose. These findings cover 2009 to 2015 and are likely out of date now, given the

ride-hail companies' increases in commissions and fare cuts in recent years. Earnings on platforms were considerably higher in the early years.

54. Schneider (2019).

55. Rosenthal (2019).

56. Zervas, Proserpio, and Byers (2017).

57. Federal Reserve Bank of New York (2019).


## Chapter 4

1. Gokey (2014).

2. Pressler (2014).

3. Ferré-Sadurni (2018). City authorities filed suit against a large illegal hotel ring in early 2019, alleging the owners had illegally hosted seventy-five thousand guests between 2015 and 2018, using a variety of ruses and false identities.

4. Cansoy (2018, 2019a).

5. Wachsmuth and Weisler (2018). A Boston study is Horn and Merante (2017). See also Barron, Kung, and Proserpio (2017); Cox and Slee (2016); Slee (2015); Wachsmuth et al. (2018, 2019). For a review of costs and benefits of Airbnb see Bivens (2019).

6. Wachsmuth et al. (2019).

7. Wachsmuth, Combs, and Kerrigan (2019). Funding for this study was provided by the hotel industry; however, its conclusions are similar to our independent research.

8. Slee (2015) had similar findings years earlier.

9. Impacts are smaller in neighborhoods where there is more home ownership because those hosts typically rent out rooms rather than whole properties. Barron et al. (2017).

10. Johnson (2018).

11. In ride-hail and delivery, prices may well rise in the future, as investors lose patience with lack of profitability.

12. Farronato and Fradkin (2018) studied the "consumer surplus," or additional value of benefit to consumers, associated with adding Airbnb to the stock of hotel and motels. They estimated it is worth forty-one dollars per consumer per night.

13. In ride-hailing, consumers are two to three times more likely to be highly educated, high-income earners, and young. Schaller (2018). Cullen and Farronato (2018, 6) report that the model TaskRabbit customer has a $150,000–$175,000 annual income, compared to $50,000–$75,000 for taskers.

14. Reduced wages from Berger et al. (2018). Medallion owners saddled with debt from Rosenthal (2019).

15. Zervas, Proserpio, and Byers (2017).

16. Farronato and Fradkin (2018).

17. See Ravenelle (2019) and Rosenblat (2018) for more discussion of this discourse.

18. Dubal (2019a). On parolees and others forced to work, see Zatz (2016).

19. Author's notes from Platform Cooperativism conference.

20. This 72 percent agreed or strongly agreed that the sharing economy "builds friendships and social relationships." Center for a New American Dream and PolicyInteractive (2014).

21. Ikkala and Lampinen (2015); Ladegaard (2018b); Lampinen (2014); Lampinen and Cheshire (2016).

22. Parigi et al. (2013); Parigi and State (2014).

23. Margolies (2019).

24. Shaheen (2018, 6).

25. Paul (2019a). Speculation abounded that Lyft was also considering such an option, but in line with its friendlier veneer, its term is "Zen" mode.

26. Friedman (2013).

27. Center for a New American Dream and PolicyInteractive (2014).

28. I say "generally" because there is a class of goods that are considered "inferior." It is possible that people buy fewer of them when their purchasing power increases.

29. For estimates of the relationship between GDP and carbon emissions see Knight, Rosa, and Schor (2013) and Knight and Schor (2014).

30. Barrios et al. (2018). The researchers conducted what is called a difference in differences analysis, which compares data before and after an event. A study of ride-hail in China using a similar methodology found an 8 percent increase in new car registrations. Gong, Greenwood, and Song (2017).

31. Schaller (2018).

32. Erhardt et al. (2019).

33. Balding et al. (2019, 8). Boston figure is 7.7 percent; San Francisco is 12.8 percent.

34. Clewlow and Mishra (2017).

35. Mallett (2018); Graehler et al. (2019).

36. Erhardt et al. (2019).

37. Anzilotti (2019).

38. And in some places they're taking public transport money to do it (Conger 2019).

39. There are other environmental impacts that haven't yet been studied much. One is that cities have regulated the emissions of taxis, requiring hybrids in some cases, for example. There's nothing comparable for ride-hailing, and the companies and drivers would be likely to oppose it.

40. Barrios et al. (2018).

41. Cleantech Group (2104). This analysis finds that in the United States there is less difference between hotels and Airbnbs than in Europe.

42. Cleantech Group (2014). The 1–3 percent figure accords with Bivens's claim that only 2 percent of Airbnb guests would not have traveled in its absence (Bivens 2019).

43. Tussyadiah and Pesonen (2016).

44. Farronato and Fradkin (2018, 29–30).

45. Skjelvik, Erlandsen, and Haavardsholm (2017).

46. Markov (2019). The dynamics of Olio differ from conventional donations to food banks, as the offerings are typically already prepared foods—sandwiches, baked goods, etc. This also reduces its distributional effect across income groups.

47. Fremstad (2017). This amounted to a 1.7 percent reduction.


Chapter 5

1. A farm share is a portion of a farm's produce, via an arrangement called Community Supported Agriculture, or CSA. In a CSA, members pay an amount in advance of the growing season and get weekly allotments of food as it is harvested.

2. Schor (2010, chap. 2).

3. Individual case studies are written up in a variety of our papers. These include "Distinction at Work: Status Practices in a Community Production Environment" (Attwood-Charles and Schor 2019 [makerspace]); "We Are Creatives: Symbolic Inefficacy and the Decoupling of Meaning from Practice" (Attwood-Charles 2019b [makerspace]); "Creativity as Organizational Myth and Practice" (Attwood-Charles 2020 [makerspace]); "Homemade Matters: Logics of Opposition in a Failed Food Swap" (Fitzmaurice and Schor 2018 [food swap]); "The Pedagogy of Precarity: Laboring to Learn in the New Economy" (Carfagna 2017 [open learning]); and "New Cultures of Connection in a Boston Time Bank" (Dubois, Schor, and Carfagna 2014 [time bank]). Papers with cross-case analysis are "Paradoxes of Openness and Distinction in the Sharing Economy" (Schor et

al. 2016); and "An Emerging Eco-habitus: The Reconfiguration of High Cultural Capital Practices among Ethical Consumers" (Carfagna et al. 2014).

4. We make this argument in more detail in Fitzmaurice et al. (2018).

5. Hochschild (2012).

6. For an account of a more successful food preparation exchange in Australia see Rowe (2017). She finds more instrumental value and less social positioning, but there are tensions as well.

7. Fitzmaurice and Schor (2018).

8. Foodies replicate the strategic behavior enacted by people high in cultural capital, as described by Pierre Bourdieu in *Distinction* (1984).

9. Johnston and Baumann (2007).

10. We discuss this in more detail in Dubois et al. (2014).

11. See Shih et al. (2015) for a similar finding.

12. Shih et al. (2015) also found charity trading.

13. I discuss this issue in Schor (2016).

14. Schor (2016). See also the excellent work of Victoria Bellotti and colleagues who have similar findings (Bellotti et al. 2015).

15. See also Bellotti et al. (2014, 2015) and Shih et al. (2015) on this issue.

16. Shih et al. (2015, table 2).

17. Collom (2011). Collom's respondents were lower income than ours, partly because his study was done in Maine; ours was in Boston.

18. Suhonen et al. (2010, 6). Respondents were twice as likely to feel that the service was a generally "useful" service than "personally useful."

19. Aptekar (2016).

20. Light and Miskelly (2014). See also Light and Miskelly (2015).

21. "Idealistic motivations" quote is from Bellotti et al. (2015, 1).


Chapter 6

1. Stock photography sites maintain an inventory of images they make available to customers. iStock was a microstock site, which sold exclusively online, and accepted images from nonprofessionals. Originally the images were free. It is considered the pioneer of microstock.

2. Cortese (2016).

3. Stocksy website: www.stocksy.com/service/about.

4. Sulakshana, Eddy, and Schor (2018); Schor (forthcoming).

5. For discussions of the future of the sector see Pasquale (2016); Frenken (2017); Kenney and Zysman (2015); Scholz (2016); and Srnicek (2016).

6. The term *platform capitalism* is generally attributed to Sascha Lobo, a technology blogger for *Der Spiegel*; see Lobo (2014). Martin Kenney and John Zysman (2016a) introduced the term *platform economy,* which has become common. Kenney and John Zysman's point, as well as that of Lobo, is that the platforms represent a new stage of capitalism. See also Srnicek (2016).

7. Calo and Rosenblat (2017); Kahn (2017); Pasquale (2013, 2015); Rahman (2016). See also Dube et al. (2018) on their monopsony position.

8. On Amazon see Lunden (2018). On Google's market share see http://gs.statcounter.com/search-engine-market-share/all/united-states-of-america.

9. Frenken (2017, 2, 8). Frenken himself is not an advocate for this monopolistic future.

10. Kenney and Zysman (2016, 62). For critical accounts of this trajectory see also Slee (2015); Scholz (2016); Rosenblat (2018); Hill (2015); and Srnicek (2016).

11. Ramsey (2019). It was also one of the worst in percentage terms.

12. For these analyses see Kahn (2017); Sitaraman (2018); and Dube et al. (2018).

13. An alternative to regulation is voluntary codes of conduct. A recent attempt to induce better treatment of workers via a voluntary code is the Fair Work Foundation, a new project from researchers at the Oxford Internet Institute. They are hoping to establish a certification system that signals adherence to a set of principles ensuring fair treatment of gig workers. See Graham et al. (2019).

14. https://en.wikipedia.org/wiki/Legality_of_TNCs_by_jurisdiction.

15. Uber's use of consumers to block regulations worked in New York City in 2015, when Mayor de Blasio attempted to cap the number of Uber vehicles. He backed down then. But this tactic was no longer effective in 2018. On consumer pressure see Walker (2016) and Culpepper and Thelen (2019).

16. Thelen (2018).

17. Pelzer, Frenken, and Boon (2019). UberPop was equivalent to what was called UberX in the U.S.

18. Thelen (2018).

19. Chan (2019).

20. Burgen (2018).

21. O'Sullivan (2018).

22. See, e.g., Acevedo (2016); Calo and Rosenblat (2017); Collier, Dubal, and Carter (2017); V.B. Dubal (2017b); V. Dubal (2017); Edelman and Geradin (2015); Edelman and Stemler (2018); Kuhn and Maleki (2017); Rahman (2016); and Rogers (2015). See also Sarah Light (2017) on precautionary federalism.

23. Veena Dubal (2017); V.B. Dubal (2017a); Cherry (2016); Rogers (2015, 2017); Eisenbrey and Mishel (2016). See also de Stefano (2016).

24. Stemler, Perry, and Haugh (2019); Calo and Rosenblat (2017). Robinson develops the concept of "regulatory breach," by which platforms enroll people *en masse* and avoid contact with regulatory interfaces. Robinson (2017, chap. 4).

25. In addition to the discussion in chapter 1, see Collier et al. (2018) and Thelen (2018).

26. Horan (2017).

27. For an excellent account of how labor organizing in San Francisco prevented the race-to-the-bottom before the 1930s, and how Uber has degraded drivers, see V.B. Dubal (2017b).

28. Collier et al. (2018, 927).

29. Borkholder et al. (2018).

30. Ulrik Binzer, CEO of Host Compliance, quoted in Martineau (2019).

31. Martineau (2019).

32. Martineau (2019).

33. Gilmore (2018).

34. Borkholder et al. (2018) provide a comprehensive study of preemption. They report forty-one states; an update from Racabi (2018) adds one more.

35. Borkholder et al. (2018).

36. For an analysis of why the U.S. has a more "permissive" regulatory landscape, see Rahman and Thelen (2019), who argue that the regulatory apparatus is more fragmented and weaker than in Europe, that there are few "societal" backstops (unions or business organizations) to oppose the power of firms, and that the U.S. has a supportive legal regime (for example, in antitrust law).

37. Airbnb has been successful in London, however. See Ferreri and Sanyal (2018).

38. See FTC Staff (2016). The White House also took a positive attitude to the sector during this time. In 2014 I was invited to a small workshop to address the federal role. A number of agencies and cabinet departments were present, but I noticed that one was missing: the Department of Labor. When I asked about it, I was told they were more likely to be critical and had not been invited.

39. Calo and Rosenblat (2017).

40. Lohr (2019).

41. Mahdawi (2018). See also Attoh, Wells, and Cullen (2019) on how Uber is using data collected in a collaboration with the city of Washington, DC.

42. Calo and Rosenblat (2017).

43. Hanson and Kysar (1999).

44. Scheiber (2017).

45. Vedantam (2016). Uber claims it does not use this information for pricing decisions.

46. See Calo and Rosenblat (2017); Stemler et al. (2019).

47. Data compliance in Toronto from private conversation with Executive Director of Municipal Licensing and Standards Tracey Cook, Nov. 2018.

48. Ferré-Sadurni (2018).

49. Weiser and Goodman (2019).

50. NYC Office of Special Enforcement, "About Illegal Short-Term Rentals," www1.nyc.gov/site/specialenforcement/enforcement/illegal-short-term-rentals.page.

51. Said (2018b, 2018a).

52. Fishman (n.d.).

53. Brustein (2018).

54. Parrott and Reich (2018).

55. Roose (2019). A similar campaign against DoorDash was not originally successful. DoorDash subsequently said it will remit tips to workers, but as of this writing it is unclear whether it has done so. Kerr (2019).

56. See Dubal (2019b) for an analysis of the strike.

57. Conger and Scheiber (2019a).

58. For a discussion of how #AB5 is likely to change the nature of gig work, see Dubal and Paul (2019).

59. Conger and Scheiber (2019a).

60. Miller and Bernstein (2017).

61. For an analysis of the structural advantage of Uber see Collier et al. (2018).

62. Regulation will also likely push the companies toward more conventional business models; for example, minimum wages and worker protections may lead companies to institute regular employment and retract flexible schedules. There is some evidence of this happening already.

63. For the argument that technological outcomes are linked to context, see Benkler (2020).

64. Ostrom (1990).

65. Hess and Ostrom (2011).

66. See also Benkler (2002, 2013, 2017a, 2017b). On cooperation see Bowles and Gintis (2011), as well as the pioneering work of Michel Bauwens on peer-to-peer production.

67. The board also has the possibility of vetoing proposals that have passed the membership. Governance is carried out through an online forum to which

all members have access. Employees of the platform are paid from general revenues.

68. Industry compensation information from Margaret Vincent, Stocksy VP of Governance and Legal.

69. Gordon-Farleigh (2018).

70. Soon after we did our research, management attempted to lift the cap and increase membership. In a follow-up with Margaret Vincent, Stocksy's lawyer, we learned how things had played out. The management's proposal was voted down by the members. After a couple of tries, the membership agreed to a slow growth strategy that also gave them an annual right to "freeze" the numbers for a year. After about a year, they had added eighty-six members, and when we contacted her, Vincent was putting together information for the annual vote on freezing.

71. Schneider (2018a). They later criticized the idea, explaining that their initial advocacy of the concept was due to the economic crisis. They decided the platform cooperative concept did not create real community. Ugarte (2017).

72. The phrase *platform cooperativism* was coined by Trebor Scholz in a blog post in December of 2014 (Scholz 2014). At that time Schneider wrote an article about cooperative ownership (Schneider 2014). And Orsi produced a video (www .youtube.com/watch?v = xpg4PjGtbu0). I discussed co-ops in the sharing economy in my 2014 piece (see Schor 2014). Scholz and Schneider produced an edited volume (Scholz and Schneider 2016). Other important work on co-ops and alternative governance in this space includes Benkler (2016); Chase (2015); van Doorn (2017); Fedosov et al. (2019); and Lampinen et al. (2018). See also Belloc (n.d.). In 2019 Scholz founded the Institute for the Cooperative Digital Economy at the New School for Social Research. (I am a member of the Council of Advisors.)

73. Schneider maintains a list of platform cooperatives at his site entitled Internet of Ownership. http://ioo.coop/. For details on the co-ops see https://docs .google.com/spreadsheets/d/1RQTMhPJVVdmE7Yeop1iwYhvj46kgvVJQnn11EP GwzeY/edit#gid=674927682.

74. Another issue is that it may be difficult to maintain democratic governance when economic contributions are highly skewed.

75. Advocates believe platform co-ops should embody open source software, transparent data, protective legal framework for workers (e.g., privacy and surveillance), etc. See Schneider (2018a).

76. Fang (2019); Shaban (2018).

77. See www.upandgo.coop; http://greentaxico-op.com; www.shift.coop. The NursesCan Cooperative is discussed in https://truthout.org/articles/nurses-join-forces-with-labor-union-to-launch-health-care-platform-cooperative.

78. One example of open source code for cooperatives is Origin: www
.originprotocol.com/en.

79. See http://foradoeixo.org.br.

80. See https://smart.coop.

81. Schneider (2018b, 156–57). Schneider reports that although Union Square
Ventures managing partner Brad Burnham has attended the platform cooperative conferences, he can't imagine investing in cooperatives.

82. Chase (2015).

83. Schneider (2018a) raises an important issue that has not gotten enough attention in the literature: how will the cooperative structure function in the era of
robots and artificial intelligence?

84. A comprehensive and valuable account of sharing in the urban context is
McLaren and Agyeman (2015).

85. In 2015 the office of Alicia Glen, deputy mayor of New York, brought together a network of cities from around the world that are engaged in fostering sharing activity to form the Sharing Cities Alliance. I attended and spoke at their Third
Annual Summit in 2018. For more on this group see www.sharingcitiesaction.net
/cities-task-force/sharing-cities-action-task-force-a-network-of-global-cities.

86. See www.kozaza.com.

87. On Bologna see especially the work of Christian Iaione and Sheila Foster,
https://labgov.city/about-people; see also Foster and Iaione (2017). For a discussion of Barcelona see Morell (2018).

88. For a comprehensive analysis of climate pathways see IPCC (2018).

# References

Abraham, Katharine G., John C. Haltiwanger, Kristin Sandusky, and James Spletzer. 2017. "Measuring the Gig Economy: Current Knowledge and Open Issues." In . Washington, DC: NBER. http://www.vox.lacea.org/?q=abstract /measuring_gig_economy.

———. 2018. "The Rise of the Gig Economy: Fact or Fiction." In . Atlanta, GA. https://www.aeaweb.org/conference/2019/preliminary/paper/4r9TeS37.

Abrahao, Bruno, Paolo Parigi, Alok Gupta, and Karen S. Cook. 2017. "Reputation Offsets Trust Judgments Based on Social Biases among Airbnb Users." *Proceedings of the National Academy of Sciences* 114 (37): 9848–53.

Acevedo, Deepa Das. 2016. "Regulating Employment Relationships in the Sharing Economy." *Employment Rights and Employment Policy Journal* 20:1–35.

Airbnb. 2018. "Celebrating Our Community of Teacher Hosts." 180814B. San Francisco, CA: Airbnb. https://press.airbnb.com/wp-content/uploads /sites/4/2018/08/PC0470_TeachersReport_180814B.pdf.

Allen-Robertson, James. 2017. "The Uber Game: Exploring Algorithmic Management and Resistance." http://repository.essex.ac.uk/20603/.

Ameri, Mason, Sean Rogers, Lisa Schur, and Douglas Kruse. 2019. "No Room at the Inn? Disability Access in the New Sharing Economy." *Academy of Management Discoveries,* February. https://doi.org/10.5465/amd.2018.0054.

Anzilotti, Eillie. 2019. "Lyft Has Spent Enough Money to Offset More Than 2 Million Tons of CO2. Is It Enough?" *Fast Company,* May 29, 2019.

Aptekar, Sofya. 2016. "Gifts among Strangers: The Social Organization of Freecycle Giving." *Social Problems* 63 (2): 266–83.

Armstrong, Mia. 2018. "Workers with Criminal Records Struggle to Find a Place in the Gig Economy." *Slate*, December 7.

Arnould, Eric J., and Alexander S. Rose. 2016. "Mutuality: Critique and Substitute for Belk's 'Sharing.'" *Marketing Theory* 16 (1): 75–99.

Arrow, Kenneth. 1971. "The Theory of Discrimination." Working Papers 403, Princeton University, Department of Economics. https://dataspace .princeton.edu/jspui/bitstream/88435/dsp014t64gn18f/1/30a.pdf.

Associated Press. 2017. "Uber to Pay $20m over Claims It Misled Drivers over How Much They Would Earn." *The Guardian*, January 19, 2017.

Attoh, Kafui, Katie Wells, and Declan Cullen. 2019. "'We're Building Their Data': Labor, Alienation, and Idiocy in the Smart City." *Environment and Planning D: Society and Space*, June. https://doi.org/10.1177/0263775819856626.

Attwood-Charles, William. 2019a. "Dimensions of Platform Labor Control and the Experience of Gig Couriers." Unpublished paper. Boston College.

———. 2019b. "We Are Creatives: Symbolic Inefficacy and the Decoupling of Meaning from Practice." Unpublished paper. Boston College.

———. 2020. "Creativity as Organizational Myth and Practice." Unpublished paper. Boston College.

Attwood-Charles, William, and Juliet B. Schor. 2019. "Distinction at Work: Status Practices in a Community Production Environment." Unpublished paper. Boston College.

Ayres, Ian, Mahzarin Banaji, and Christine Jolls. 2015. "Race Effects on eBay." *RAND Journal of Economics* 46 (4): 891–917.

Balding, Melissa, Teresa Whinery, Eleanor Leshner, and Eric Womeldorff. 2019. "Estimated Percent of Total Driving by Lyft and Uber: In Six Major US Regions." Fehr and Peers. https://drive.google.com/file/d/1FIUskVkj9ls AnWJQ6kLhAhNoVLjfFdx3/view.

Barbrook, Richard, and Andy Cameron. 1996. "The Californian Ideology." *Science as Culture* 6 (1): 44–72.

Barrios, John M., Yael V. Hochberg, and Livia Hanyi Yi. 2018. "The Cost of Convenience: Ridesharing and Traffic Fatalities." *New Working Paper Series*, Stigler Center University of Chicago, #27. https://papers.ssrn.com/sol3 /papers.cfm?abstract_id=3259965.

Barron, Kyle, Edward Kung, and Davide Proserpio. 2017. "The Sharing Economy and Housing Affordability: Evidence from Airbnb." *SSRN Electronic Journal*. https://ssrn.com/abstract=3006832.

Belk, Russell. 2007. "Why Not Share Rather Than Own?" *The ANNALS of the American Academy of Political and Social Science* 611 (1): 126–40.

———. 2010. "Sharing." *Journal of Consumer Research* 36 (5): 715–34.

———. 2014a. "Sharing versus Pseudo-Sharing in Web 2.0." *The Anthropologist* 18 (1): 7–23.

———. 2014b. "You Are What You Can Access: Sharing and Collaborative Consumption Online." *Journal of Business Research* 67 (8): 1595–1600.

Belloc, Filippo. 2019. "Why Isn't Uber Worker-Managed? A Model of Digital Platform Cooperatives." *SSRN Electronic Journal.* https://ssrn.com/abstract=3418632.

Bellotti, Victoria, Alexander Ambard, Daniel Turner, Christina Gossmann, Kamila Demkova, and John M. Carroll. 2015. "A Muddle of Models of Motivation for Using Peer-to-Peer Economy Systems." In *CHI '15: Proceedings of the 33rd Annual ACM Conference on Human Factors in Computing Systems,* 1085–94. New York: ACM Press. https://doi.org/10.1145/2702123.2702272.

Bellotti, Victoria, Sara Cambridge, Karen Hoy, Patrick C. Shih, Lisa Renery Handalian, Kyungsik Han, and John M. Carroll. 2014. "Towards Community-Centered Support for Peer-to-Peer Service Exchange: Rethinking the Timebanking Metaphor." In *Proceedings of the SIGCHI Conference on Human Factors in Computing Systems,* 2975–84. New York: ACM Press. https://doi.org/10.1145/2556288.2557061.

Benkler, Yochai. 2002. "Coase's Penguin, or, Linux and 'The Nature of the Firm.'" *Yale Law Journal* 112 (3): 369–446.

———. 2004. "Sharing Nicely: On Shareable Goods and the Emergence of Sharing as a Modality of Economic Production." *Yale Law Journal* 114 (2): 273–358.

———. 2006. *The Wealth of Networks: How Social Production Transforms Markets and Freedom.* New Haven, CT: Yale University Press.

———. 2013. "Practical Anarchism: Peer Mutualism, Market Power, and the Fallible State." *Politics & Society* 41 (2): 213–51.

———. 2016. "The Realism of Cooperativism." In *Ours to Hack and to Own: The Rise of Platform Cooperativism, a New Vision for the Future of Work and a Fairer Internet,* edited by Trebor Scholz and Nathan Schneider. New York: OR Books.

———. 2017a. "Peer Production, the Commons, and the Future of the Firm." *Strategic Organization* 15 (2): 264–74.

———. 2017b. "Law, Innovation, and Collaboration in Networked Economy and Society." *Annual Review of Law and Social Science* 13 (1): 231–50.

———. Forthcoming. "Power and Productivity: A Political Economy of Technology." In *New Goals for a Just Economy,* edited by Danielle Allen, Yochai Benkler, and Rebecca Henderson.

Benner, Katie. 2016. "Federal Judge Blocks Racial Discrimination Suit against Airbnb." *New York Times,* November 1, 2016.

Berg, Janine, and Uma Rani. 2018. "Digital Labour Platforms and the Future of Work: Towards Decent Work in the Online World." Geneva: International Labour Organization. www.ilo.org/global/publications/books/WCMS_645337/lang--en/index.htm.

Berger, Thor, Chinchih Chen, and Carl Benedikt Frey. 2018. "Drivers of Disruption? Estimating the Uber Effect." *European Economic Review* 110 (November): 197–210.

Bivens, Josh. 2019. "The Economic Costs and Benefits of Airbnb." 157766. Washington, DC: Economic Policy Institute. www.epi.org/publication/the-economic-costs-and-benefits-of-airbnb-no-reason-for-local-policymakers-to-let-airbnb-bypass-tax-or-regulatory-obligations.

Board of Governors of the Federal Reserve System. 2019. "Report on the Economic Well-Being of U.S. Households in 2018." Survey of Household Economics and Decision Making. Washington, DC: Federal Reserve Bank. www.federalreserve.gov/publications/2019-economic-well-being-of-us-households-in-2018-employment.htm.

Bodie, Matthew T., Miriam A. Cherry, Marcia McCormick, and Jintong Tang. 2016. "The Law and Policy of People Analytics." *University of Colorado Law Review* 88 (4): 961–1042.

Borkholder, Joy, Mariah Montgomery, Miya Saika Chen, and Rebecca Smith. 2018. "Uber State Interference: How TNCs Buy, Bully, and Bamboozle Their Way to Deregulation." New York: National Employment Law Project. www.nelp.org/publication/uber-state-interference.

Botsman, Rachel, and Roo Rogers. 2010. *What's Mine Is Yours: The Rise of Collaborative Consumption.* New York: Harper Business.

Bourdieu, Pierre. 1984. *Distinction: A Social Critique of the Judgement of Taste.* Translated by Richard Nice. Cambridge, MA: Harvard University Press.

Bowles, Samuel. 1985. "The Production Process in a Competitive Economy: Walrasian, Neo-Hobbesian, and Marxian Models." *American Economic Review* 75 (1): 16–36.

Bowles, Samuel, and Herbert Gintis. 2011. *A Cooperative Species: Human Reciprocity and Its Evolution.* Princeton, NJ: Princeton University Press.

Broughton, Andrea, Rosie Gloster, Rosa Marvell, Martha Green, Jamal Langley, and Alex Martin. 2018. "The Experiences of Individuals in the Gig Economy." Hove, England: Institute for Employment Studies. https://assets .publishing.service.gov.uk/government/uploads/system/uploads/attachment_data/file/679987/171107_The_experiences_of_those_in_the_gig_ economy.pdf.

Brustein, Joshua. 2018. "New York Sets Nation's First Minimum Wage for Uber, Lyft Drivers." *Bloomberg News,* December 4, 2018.

Burgen, Stephen. 2018. "Barcelona Continues Crackdown on Illegal Holiday Apartments." *The Guardian,* July 27, 2018.

Burston-Marsteller. 2016. "The On-Demand Economy Survey." www .slideshare.net/Burson-Marsteller/the-ondemand-economy-survey.

Calo, Ryan, and Alex Rosenblat. 2017. "The Taking Economy: Uber, Information, and Power." *Columbia Law Review* 117 (6): 1623–90.

Cameron, Lindsey D. 2018. "Making Out While Driving: Control, Coordination, and Its Consequences in Algorithmic Work." Unpublished paper. University of Michigan.

———. 2019. "The Rise of Algorithmic Work: Implications for Managerial Control and Career Pathways." Unpublished paper. University of Michigan.

Cansoy, Mehmet. 2018. "'Sharing' in Unequal Spaces: Short-Term Rentals and the Reproduction of Urban Inequalities." PhD diss., Boston College.

———. 2019a. "Gentrification and Short-Term Rentals: Re-assessing the Rent Gap in Urban Centers." Unpublished paper. Boston College.

———. 2019b. "The Fault in the Stars: Public Reputation and the Reproduction of Racial Inequality on Airbnb." Unpublished paper. Boston College.

Cansoy, Mehmet, and Juliet B. Schor. 2019. "Who Gets to Share in the 'Sharing Economy': Understanding the Patterns of Participation and Exchange in Airbnb." www.bc.edu/content/dam/files/schools/cas_sites/sociology/pdf /SharingEconomy.pdf.

Carfagna, Lindsey B., Emilie A. Dubois, Connor Fitzmaurice, Monique Y. Ouimette, Juliet B. Schor, Margaret Willis, and Thomas Laidley. 2014. "An Emerging Eco-habitus: The Reconfiguration of High Cultural Capital Practices among Ethical Consumers." *Journal of Consumer Culture* 14 (2): 158–78.

Carfagna, Lindsey B. 2017. "The Pedagogy of Precarity: Laboring to Learn in the New Economy." PhD diss., Boston College. https://dlib.bc.edu /islandora/object/bc-ir%3A107564.

Carfagna, Lindsey "Luka." 2014. "Beyond Learning-as-Usual: Connected Learning among Open Learners." Connected Learning Working Papers. Irvine, CA: Digital Media and Learning Research Hub. http://dmlhub.net /wp-content/uploads/files/BeyondLearningAsUsual_v3.pdf.

Castillo, Juan Camilo, Dan Knoepfle, and E. Glen Weyl. 2018. "Surge Pricing Solves the Wild Goose Chase." *SSRN Electronic Journal.* https://doi.org /10.2139/ssrn.2890666.

Center for a New American Dream and PolicyInteractive. 2014. "Analysis Report: New American Dream Survey 2014." Center for a New American Dream. https://newdream.org/downloads/New_Dream_2014_Poll_Final_ Analysis.pdf.

Chan, Kelvin. 2019. "London Keeps Uber on Short License as It Scrutinizes Firm." *Associated Press,* September 24, 2019.

Chase, Robin. 2015. *Peers Inc: How People and Platforms Are Inventing the Collaborative Economy and Reinventing Capitalism.* New York: Headline/ PublicAffairs.

Chen, Julie Yujie. 2018. "Thrown under the Bus and Outrunning It! The Logic of Didi and Taxi Drivers' Labour and Activism in the On-Demand Economy." *New Media & Society* 20 (8): 2691–2711.

Cherry, Miriam A. 2016. "Beyond Misclassification: The Digital Transformation of Work." *Comparative Labor Law & Policy Journal* 37 (3): 577–602.

Cleantech Group. 2014. "Environmental Impact of Homesharing: Phase 1 Report." San Francisco: Cleantech Group.

Clewlow, Regina R., and Gouri Shankar Mishra. 2017. "Disruptive Transportation: The Adoption, Utilization, and Impacts of Ride-Hailing in the United States." UCD-ITS-RR-17-07. Davis, CA: UC Davis Institute of Transportation Studies. https://itspubs.ucdavis.edu/wp-content/themes/ucdavis /pubs/download_pdf.

Cockayne, Daniel G. 2016. "Sharing and Neoliberal Discourse: The Economic Function of Sharing in the Digital On-Demand Economy." *Geoforum* 77 (December): 73–82.

Collier, Ruth Berins, V. B. Dubal, and Christopher Carter. 2017. "Labor Platforms and Gig Work: The Failure to Regulate." *IRLE Working Paper* 106 (17).

Collier, Ruth Berins, V. B. Dubal, and Christopher L. Carter. 2018. "Disrupting Regulation, Regulating Disruption: The Politics of Uber in the United States." *Perspectives on Politics* 16 (4): 919–37.

Collins, Brett, Andrew Garin, Emilie Jackson, Dmitri Koustas, and Mark Payne. 2019. "Is Gig Work Replacing Traditional Employment? Evidence from Two Decades of Tax Returns." www.irs.gov/pub/irs-soi/19rpgigworkreplacing traditionalemployment.pdf.

Collins, Chuck, and Josh Hoxie. 2017. "Billionaire Bonanza: The *Forbes* 400 and the Rest of Us." Washington, DC: Institute for Policy Studies. https://inequality.org/wp-content/uploads/2017/11/BILLIONAIRE-BONANZA-2017-Embargoed.pdf.

Collom, Ed. 2011. "Motivations and Differential Participation in a Community Currency System: The Dynamics within a Local Social Movement Organization." *Sociological Forum* 26 (1): 144–68.

Conger, Kate. 2019. "Uber Wants to Sell You Train Tickets. And Be Your Bus Service, Too." *New York Times,* August 7, 2019.

Conger, Kate, and Noam Scheiber. 2019a. "California Labor Bill, Near Passage, Is Blow to Uber and Lyft." *New York Times,* September 9, 2019.

———. 2019b. "California's Contractor Law Stirs Confusion Beyond the Gig Economy." *New York Times,* September 11, 2019.

Cook, Cody, Rebecca Diamond, Jonathan Hall, John List, and Paul Oyer. 2018. "The Gender Earnings Gap in the Gig Economy: Evidence from over a Million Rideshare Drivers." NBER Working Paper w24732. Cambridge, MA: National Bureau of Economic Research. https://doi.org/10.3386/w24732.

Cortese, Amy. 2016. "A New Wrinkle in the Gig Economy: Workers Get Most of the Money." *New York Times,* July 20, 2016.

Cox, Murray. 2017. "Airbnb as a Racial Gentrification Tool." New York: Inside Airbnb. http://insideairbnb.com/reports/the-face-of-airbnb-nyc.pdf.

Cox, Murray, and Tom Slee. 2016. "How Airbnb Hid the Facts in New York City." http://tomslee.net/how-airbnb-hid-the-facts-in-nyc.

Cui, Ruomeng, Jun Li, and Dennis Zhang. 2016. "Discrimination with Incomplete Information in the Sharing Economy: Field Evidence from Airbnb." *SSRN Electronic Journal.* https://doi.org/10.2139/ssrn.2882982.

Cullen, Zoë, and Chiara Farronato. 2018. "Outsourcing Tasks Online: Matching Supply and Demand on Peer-to-Peer Internet Platforms." Working Paper. Harvard Business School. www.hbs.edu/faculty/Pages/item.aspx?num=50051.

Culpepper, Pepper D., and Kathleen Thelen. 2019. "Are We All Amazon Primed? Consumers and the Politics of Platform Power." *Comparative Political Studies* 53 (2): 288–318. doi/10.1177/0010414019852687.

Davis, Gerald F. 2016a. *The Vanishing American Corporation: Navigating the Hazards of a New Economy.* San Francisco: Berrett-Kohler.

———. 2016b. "What Might Replace the Modern Corporation? Uberization and the Web Page Enterprise." *Seattle University Law Review* 39:501–15.

Detlefsen, Hans. 2018. "Airbnb's Market Share of U.S. Lodging Demand Increasing at a Decelerating Rate." *Hotel Online: The B2B News Source,* April 25, 2018. www.hotel-online.com/press_releases/release/airbnbs-market-share-of-u.s.-lodging-demand-increasing-at-a-decelerating-ra/.

Dillahunt, Tawanna R., and Amelia R. Malone. 2015. "The Promise of the Sharing Economy among Disadvantaged Communities." In *CHI '15: Proceedings of the 33rd Annual ACM Conference on Human Factors in Computing Systems,* 2285–94. New York: ACM Press. https://doi.org/10.1145/2702123.2702189.

Doorn, Niels van. 2017. "Platform Labor: On the Gendered and Racialized Exploitation of Low-Income Service Work in the 'On-Demand' Economy." *Information, Communication & Society* 20 (6): 898–914.

———. 2018. "Late for a Job in the Gig Economy? Handy Will Dock Your Pay." *Quartz at Work* (blog). October 3, 2018. https://qz.com/work/1411833/handy-charges-fees-to-its-workers-for-being-late-or-canceling-jobs/.

Dubal, V. B. 2017a. "Winning the Battle, Losing the War: Assessing the Impact of Misclassification Litigation on Workers in the Gig Economy." *Wisconsin Law Review* 4:739–802.

———. 2017b. "The Drive to Precarity: A Political History of Work, Regulation & Labor Advocacy in San Francisco's Taxi & Uber Economies." *Berkeley Journal of Employment and Labor Law* 38 (1): 73–135.

Dubal, Veena. 2017. "Wage-Slave or Entrepreneur? Contesting the Dualism of Legal Worker Categories." *California Law Review* 105 (February): 65–126.

———. 2019a. "The Digitalization of Day Labor as Gig Work." *On Labor* (blog). May 7, 2019. https://onlabor.org/the-digitalization-of-day-labor-as-gig-work.

———. 2019b. "Why the Uber Strike Was a Triumph." *Slate,* May 10.

Dubal, Veena, and Sanjukta Paul. 2019. "Law and the Future of Gig Work in California: Problems and Potentials (Part 1)." *On Labor* (blog). September 9, 2019. https://onlabor.org/law-and-the-future-of-gig-work-in-california-problems-and-potentials-part-1.

Dube, Arindrajit, Jeff Jacobs, Suresh Naidu, and Siddharth Suri. 2018. "Monopsony in Online Labor Markets." NBER Working Paper w24416. Cambridge,

MA: National Bureau of Economic Research. https://doi.org/10.3386
/w24416.

Dubois, Emilie A., Juliet B. Schor, and Lindsey B. Carfagna. 2014. "New Cultures
of Connection in a Boston Time Bank." In *Sustainable Lifestyles and the Quest
for Plentitude: Case Studies of the New Economy,* edited by Juliet B. Schor and
Craig J. Thompson, 95–124. New Haven, CT: Yale University Press.

Duhaime-Ross, Arielle. 2014. "Driven: How Zipcar's Founders Built and Lost a
Car-Sharing Empire." *The Verge,* April 1, 2014. www.theverge.com/2014
/4/1/5553910/driven-how-zipcars-founders-built-and-lost-a-car-sharing-
empire.

Edelman, Benjamin, and Michael Luca. 2014. "Digital Discrimination: The
Case of Airbnb.com." Working Paper 14-054. Harvard Business School.
www.west-info.eu/files/airbnb_research.pdf.

Edelman, Benjamin, Michael Luca, and Dan Svirsky. 2017. "Racial Discrimination in the Sharing Economy: Evidence from a Field Experiment." *American
Economic Journal: Applied Economics* 9 (2): 1–22.

Edelman, Benjamin, and Abbey Stemler. 2018. "From the Digital to the
Physical: Federal Limitations on Regulating Online Marketplaces." *SSRN
Electronic Journal.* https://doi.org/10.2139/ssrn.3106383.

Edelman, Benjamin G., and Damien Geradin. 2016. "Efficiencies and Regulatory Shortcuts: How Should We Regulate Companies like Airbnb and Uber?"
*Stanford Technology Law Review* 19:293–328.

Edwards, Richard. 1980. *Contested Terrain: The Transformation of the Workplace
in the Twentieth Century.* New York: Basic Books.

Einav, Liran, Chiara Farronato, and Jonathan Levin. 2016. "Peer-to-Peer
Markets." *Annual Review of Economics* 8 (1): 615–35.

Eisenbrey, Ross, and Lawrence Mishel. 2016. "Uber Business Model Does
Not Justify a New 'Independent Worker' Category." Washington, DC:
Economic Policy Institute. www.epi.org/publication/uber-business-model-
does-not-justify-a-new-independent-worker-category/?utm_content=
bufferd2001&utm_medium=social&utm_source=facebook.com&utm_
campaign=buffer.

Empson, Rip. 2013. "Zaarly Shutters Its Reverse Craigslist Marketplace, Goes
All In on Virtual Storefronts, as Co-founder Exits." *Tech Crunch,* March 9, 2013.

Entis, Laura. 2014. "'We're the Uber of X!'" *Entrepreneur,* August 12, 2014.

Erhardt, Gregory D., Sneha Roy, Drew Cooper, Bhargava Sana, Mei Chen, and
Joe Castiglione. 2019. "Do Transportation Network Companies Decrease or
Increase Congestion?" *Science Advances* 5 (5): eaau2670.

Eubanks, Virginia. 2018. *Automating Inequality: How High-Tech Tools Profile, Police, and Punish the Poor.* New York: St. Martin's.

Fang, Lee. 2019. "Google Hired Gig Economy Workers to Improve Artificial Intelligence in Controversial Drone-Targeting Project." *The Intercept,* February 4, 2019.

Farrell, Diana, and Fiona Greig. 2016. "Paychecks, Paydays, and the Online Platform Economy: Big Data on Income Volatility." JPMorgan Chase & Co. Institute. https://papers.ssrn.com/sol3/papers.cfm?abstract_id=2911293.

———. 2017. "The Online Platform Economy: Has Growth Peaked?" JPMorgan Chase & Co. Institute. https://papers.ssrn.com/sol3/papers.cfm?abstract_id=2911194.

Farrell, Diana, Fiona Greig, and Amar Hamoudi. 2018. "The Online Platform Economy in 2018: Drivers, Workers, Sellers, and Lessors." JPMorgan Chase & Co. Institute. www.jpmorganchase.com/corporate/institute/document/institute-ope-2018.pdf.

Farronato, Chiara, and Andrey Fradkin. 2018. "The Welfare Effects of Peer Entry in the Accommodation Market: The Case of Airbnb." NBER Working Paper w24361. Cambridge, MA: National Bureau of Economic Research. https://doi.org/10.3386/w24361.

Federal Reserve Bank of New York. 2019. "Quarterly Report on Household Debt and Credit." New York: Center for Microeconomic Data, Federal Reserve Bank of New York. www.newyorkfed.org/medialibrary/interactives/householdcredit/data/pdf/hhdc_2019q1.pdf.

Fedosov, Anton, Airi Lampinen, Tawanna R. Dillahunt, Ann Light, and Coye Cheshire. 2019. "Cooperativism and Human-Computer Interaction." In *Extended Abstracts of the 2019 CHI Conference on Human Factors in Computing Systems—CHI EA '19,* 1–4. Glasgow, Scotland: ACM Press. https://doi.org/10.1145/3290607.3311751.

Ferreri, Mara, and Romola Sanyal. 2018. "Platform Economies and Urban Planning: Airbnb and Regulated Deregulation in London." *Urban Studies* 55 (15): 3353–68.

Ferré-Sadurni, Luis. 2018. "To Curb Illegal Airbnbs, New York City Wants to Collect Data on Hosts." *New York Times,* June 26, 2018.

Fischer, Claude S. 1992. *America Calling: A Social History of the Telephone to 1940.* Berkeley: University of California Press.

Fishman, Stephen. n.d. "Overview of Airbnb Law in San Francisco." In *NOLO.* www.nolo.com/legal-encyclopedia/overview-airbnb-law-san-francisco.html.

Fitzmaurice, Connor J., Isak Ladegaard, William Attwood-Charles, Mehmet Cansoy, Lindsey B. Carfagna, Juliet B. Schor, and Robert Wengronowitz. 2018. "Domesticating the Market: Moral Exchange and the Sharing Economy." *Socio-Economic Review.* https://doi.org/10.1093/ser/mwy003.

Fitzmaurice, Connor, and Juliet B. Schor. 2018. "Homemade Matters: Logics of Opposition in a Failed Food Swap." *Social Problems* 66 (1): 144–61.

Folbre, Nancy. 2001. *The Invisible Heart: Economics and Family Values.* New York: New Press.

Forde, Chris, Mark Stuart, and Simon Joyce. 2017. "The Social Protection of Workers in the Platform Economy." PE614.184. Brussels: European Parliament. www.europarl.europa.eu/RegData/etudes/STUD/2017/614184/IPOL_STU(2017)614184_EN.pdf.

Foster, Sheila, and Christian Iaione. 2017. "Ostrom in the City: Design Principles for the Urban Commons." www.thenatureofcities.com/2017/08/20/ostrom-city-design-principles-urban-commons.

Fraiberger, Samuel P., and Arun Sundararajan. 2017. "Peer-to-Peer Rental Markets in the Sharing Economy." *SSRN Electronic Journal.* https://doi.org/10.2139/ssrn.2574337.

Frank, Thomas. 1997. *The Conquest of Cool: Business Culture, Counterculture, and the Rise of Hip Consumerism.* Chicago: University of Chicago Press.

———. 2000. *One Market under God: Extreme Capitalism, Market Populism, and the End of Economic Democracy.* New York: Doubleday.

Fremstad, Anders. 2017. "Does Craigslist Reduce Waste? Evidence from California and Florida." *Ecological Economics* 132:135–43.

Frenken, Koen. 2017. "Political Economies and Environmental Futures for the Sharing Economy." *Philosophical Transactions of the Royal Society A: Mathematical, Physical and Engineering Sciences* 375 (2095): 1–15.

Frenken, Koen, Toon Meelen, Martijn Arets, and Pieter van de Glind. 2015. "Smarter Regulation for the Sharing Economy." *The Guardian,* May 20, 2015.

Frenken, Koen, and Juliet B. Schor. 2017. "Putting the Sharing Economy into Perspective." *Environmental Innovation and Societal Transitions* 23 (June): 3–10.

Friedan, Betty. 1963. *The Feminist Mystique.* New York: Norton.

Friedman, Thomas L. 2013. "Welcome to the 'Sharing Economy.'" *New York Times,* July 20, 2013.

FTC Staff. 2016. "The 'Sharing' Economy—Issues Facing Platforms, Participants & Regulators." Washington, DC: Federal Trade Commission. www.ftc.gov/reports/sharing-economy-issues-facing-platforms-participants-regulators-federal-trade-commission.

Ge, Yanbo, Christopher R. Knittel, Don MacKenzie, and Stephen Zoepf. 2016. "Racial and Gender Discrimination in Transportation Network Companies." NBER Working Paper 22776. Cambridge, MA: National Bureau of Economic Research. www.nber.org/papers/w22776?utm_campaign=ntw&utm_medium=email&utm_source=ntw.

Georgakas, Dan, and Marvin Surkin. 2012. *Detroit, I Do Mind Dying: A Study in Urban Revolution.* Chicago: Haymarket Books.

Gilmore, Savannah. 2018. "More States Taking Action on Short-Term Rentals." National Conference of State Legislators. www.ncsl.org/research/fiscal-policy/more-states-taking-action-on-short-term-rentals.aspx.

Gokey, Malarie. 2014. "Airbnb's New Ad Campaign Aims to Convince New Yorkers It's Good for Their City." *Digital Trends,* July 14. www.digitaltrends.com/mobile/airbnbs-new-ad-campaign-new-york-city.

Gong, Jing, Brad N. Greenwood, and Yiping Song. 2017. "Uber Might Buy Me a Mercedes Benz: An Empirical Investigation of the Sharing Economy and Durable Goods Purchase." *SSRN Electronic Journal.* https://doi.org/10.2139/ssrn.2971072.

Gordon-Farleigh, Jonny. 2018. "Brianna Wettlaufer & Nuno Silva on Stocksy United." *P2PFoundation* (blog). May 13, 2018. https://blog.p2pfoundation.net/brianna-wettlaufer-nuno-silva-on-stocksy-united/2018/05/13.

Graehler, Michael, Jr., Richard Alexander Mucci, and Gregory D. Erhardt. 2019. "Understanding the Recent Transit Ridership Decline in Major US Cities: Service Cuts or Emerging Modes?" Transportation Research Board 98th Annual Meeting, Washington, DC, January 13–17, 2019. https://trid.trb.org/view/1572517.

Graham, Mark, Jamie Woodcock, Richard Heeks, Sandra Fredman, Darcy Du Toit, Jean-Paul Van Belle, Paul Mungai, and Abigail Osiki. 2019. "The Fairwork Foundation: Strategies for Improving Platform Work." In *Proceedings of the Weizenbaum Conference* 2019 *"Challenges of Digital Inequality: Digital Education, Digital Work, Digital Life."* Washington, DC, January 13–17, 2019. https://doi.org/10.34669/wi.cp/2.13.

Gray, Mary L., and Siddharth Suri. 2019. *Ghost Work: How to Stop Silicon Valley from Building a New Global Underclass.* Boston: Houghton Mifflin.

Griesbach, Kathleen, Adam Reich, Luke Elliott-Negri, and Ruth Milkman. 2019. "Algorithmic Control in Platform Food Delivery Work." *Socius: Sociological Research for a Dynamic World* 5 (January). https://doi.org/10.1177/2378023119870041.

Hacker, Jacob S. 2008. *The Great Risk Shift: The New Economic Insecurity and the Decline of the American Dream.* 2nd ed. New Haven, CT: Yale University Press.

Hall, Jonathan V., and Alan B. Krueger. 2018. "An Analysis of the Labor Market for Uber's Driver-Partners in the United States." *ILR Review* 71 (3): 705–32.

Hannák, Anikó, Claudia Wagner, David Garcia, Alan Mislove, Markus Strohmaier, and Christo Wilson. 2017. "Bias in Online Freelance Marketplaces: Evidence from TaskRabbit and Fiverr." In *CSCW '17: Proceedings of the 2017 ACM Conference on Computer Supported Cooperative Work and Social Computing,* 1914–33. New York: ACM Press. https://doi.org/10.1145/2998181.2998327.

Hanson, Jon D., and Douglas A. Kysar. 1999. "Taking Behavioralism Seriously: The Problem of Market Manipulation." *New York University Law Review* 74:101–217.

Hempel, Jessi. 2018. "Airbnb's Slow Moving Mission to Win Over African-Americans." *Wired,* July 26, 2018.

Hess, Charlotte, and Elinor Ostrom. 2011. *Understanding Knowledge as a Commons: From Theory to Practice.* Cambridge, MA: MIT Press.

Hill, Steven. 2015. *Raw Deal: How the "Uber Economy" and Runaway Capitalism Are Screwing American Workers.* New York: St. Martin's.

Hochschild, Arlie Russell. 2012. *The Outsourced Self: Intimate Life in Market Times.* New York: Metropolitan.

Horan, Hubert. 2016. "Can Uber Ever Deliver? Part One: Understanding Uber's Bleak Operating Economics." *Naked Capitalism* (blog). November 30, 2016. www.nakedcapitalism.com/2016/11/can-uber-ever-deliver-part-one-understanding-ubers-bleak-operating-economics.html.

———. 2017. "Can Uber Ever Deliver? Part Nine: The 1990s Koch Funded Propaganda Program That Is Uber's True Origin Story." *Naked Capitalism* (blog). March 15, 2017. www.nakedcapitalism.com/2017/03/can-uber-ever-deliver-part-nine-1990s-koch-funded-propaganda-program-ubers-true-origin-story.html.

———. 2019a. "Can Uber Ever Deliver? Part Nineteen." *Naked Capitalism* (blog). April 15, 2019. www.nakedcapitalism.com/2019/04/hubert-horan-can-uber-ever-deliver-part-nineteen-ubers-ipo-prospectus-overstates-its-2018-profit-improvement-by-5-billion.html.

———. 2019b. "Can Uber Ever Deliver? Part Eighteen: Lyft's IPO Prospectus Tells Investors That It Has No Idea How Ridesharing Could Ever Be

Profitable." *Naked Capitalism* (blog). March 5, 2019. www.nakedcapitalism
.com/2019/03/hubert-horan-can-uber-ever-deliver-part-eighteen-lyfts-ipo-
prospectus-tells-investors-no-idea-ridesharing-ever-profitable.html.

Horn, Keren, and Mark Merante. 2017. "Is Home Sharing Driving Up Rents?
Evidence from Airbnb in Boston." *Journal of Housing Economics* 38 (December): 14–24.

Ikkala, Tapio, and Airi Lampinen. 2015. "Monetizing Network Hospitality:
Hospitality and Sociability in the Context of Airbnb." In *CSCW '15 Proceedings of the ACM 2015 Conference on Computer Supported Cooperative Work*,
1033–44. New York: ACM Press. https://doi.org/10.1145/2675133.2675274.

IPCC. 2018. "Global Warming of 1.5°C: An IPCC Special Report on the Impacts
of Global Warming of 1.5°C above Pre-industrial Levels and Related Global
Greenhouse Gas Emission Pathways, in the Context of Strengthening the
Global Response to the Threat of Climate Change, Sustainable Development, and Efforts to Eradicate Poverty." United Nations. www.ipcc.ch/site
/assets/uploads/sites/2/2019/06/SR15_Full_Report_High_Res.pdf.

Iqbal, Mansoor. 2019. "Uber Revenue and Usage Statistics (2019)." *Business
of Apps* (blog). May 10, 2019. www.businessofapps.com/data/uber-
statistics/#4.

Isaac, Mike. 2017a. "Uber's CEO Plays with Fire." *New York Times,* April 23, 2017.

———. 2017b. "Uber Engaged in 'Illegal' Spying on Rivals, Ex-Employee Says."
*New York Times,* December 15, 2017.

———. 2019. "Which Tech Company Is Uber Most Like? Its Answer May
Surprise You." *New York Times,* April 28, 2019.

Ivanova, Mirela, Joanna Bronowicka, Eva Kocher, and Anne Degner. 2018. "The
App as a Boss? Control and Autonomy in Application-Based Management."
*Arbeit | Grenze | Fluss—Work in Progress Interdisziplinärer Arbeitsforschung.*
https://doi.org/10.11584/arbeit-grenze-fluss.2.

John, Nicholas A. 2016. *The Age of Sharing.* Cambridge: Polity.

Johnson, Dick. 2018. "38 Cars Neighbor Rents Out through App Clog North
Side Street, Alderman Says." *CNBC Chicago,* November 13, 2018. www
.nbcchicago.com/news/local/uptown-car-rental-parking-problem-
500442242.html.

Johnston, Josée, and Shyon Baumann. 2007. "Democracy versus Distinction: A
Study of Omnivorousness in Gourmet Food Writing." *American Journal of
Sociology* 113 (1): 165–204.

Kahn, Lina M. 2017. "Amazon's Antitrust Paradox." *Yale Law Journal* 126 (3):
710–805.

Kalamar, Anthony. 2013. "Sharewashing Is the New Greenwashing." OpEdNews. May 13, 2013.

Kalleberg, Arne L. 2009. "Precarious Work, Insecure Workers: Employment Relations in Transition." *American Sociological Review* 74 (1): 1–22.

———. 2013. *Good Jobs, Bad Jobs: The Rise of Polarized and Precarious Employment Systems in the United States, 1970s to 2000s.* American Sociological Association's Rose Series in Sociology. New York: Russell Sage.

———. 2018. *Precarious Lives: Job Insecurity and Well-Being in Rich Democracies.* Cambridge: Polity.

Kamenetz, Anya. 2014. "Is Peers the Sharing Economy's Future or Just a Great Silicon Valley PR Stunt?" *Fast Company,* June 10, 2014.

Kennedy, Elizabeth J. 2017. "Employed by an Algorithm: Labor Rights in the On-Demand Economy." *Seattle University Law Review* 40 (3): 987–1048.

Kenney, Martin, and John Zysman. 2015. "Choosing a Future in the Platform Economy: The Implications and Consequences of Digital Platforms." In *Kauffman Foundation New Entrepreneurial Growth Conference,* 156–60. www .brie.berkeley.edu/wp-content/uploads/2015/02/PlatformEconomy2 DistributeJune21.pdf.

———. 2016. "The Rise of the Platform Economy." *Issues in Science and Technology* 32 (3): 61–69.

Kerr, Dara. 2019. "DoorDash Still Stalling on Giving Delivery Workers Their Tips." *CNET,* August 21, 2019.

Knight, Kyle W., Eugene A. Rosa, and Juliet B. Schor. 2013. "Could Working Less Reduce Pressures on the Environment? A Cross-National Panel Analysis of OECD Countries, 1970–2007." *Global Environmental Change* 23 (4): 691–700.

Knight, Kyle W., and Juliet B. Schor. 2014. "Economic Growth and Climate Change: A Cross-National Analysis of Territorial and Consumption-Based Carbon Emissions in High-Income Countries." *Sustainability* 6 (6): 3722–31.

Kuhn, Kristine M., and Amir Maleki. 2017. "Micro-Entrepreneurs, Dependent Contractors, and Instaserfs: Understanding Online Labor Platform Workforces." *Academy of Management Perspectives* 31 (3): 183–200.

Ladegaard, Isak. 2018. "Hosting the Comfortably Exotic: Cosmopolitan Aspirations in the Sharing Economy." *Sociological Review* 66 (2): 381–400.

Ladegaard, Isak, Alexandrea Ravenelle, and Juliet B. Schor. 2018. "Provider Vulnerability in the Sharing Economy." Unpublished paper. Boston College.

Lampinen, Airi. 2014. "Account Sharing in the Context of Networked Hospitality Exchange." In *CSCW '14: Proceedings of the 17th ACM Conference on*

*Computer Supported Cooperative Work & Social Computing,* 499–504. New York: ACM Press. https://doi.org/10.1145/2531602.2531665.

Lampinen, Airi, and Coye Cheshire. 2016. "Hosting via Airbnb: Motivations and Financial Assurances in Monetized Network Hospitality." In *CHI '16: Proceedings of the 2016 CHI Conference on Human Factors in Computing Systems,* 1669–80. New York: ACM Press. www.mobilelifecentre.org/sites /default/files/Airbnb%20Submitted%20Camera.pdf.

Lampinen, Airi, Moira McGregor, Rob Comber, and Barry Brown. 2018. "Member-Owned Alternatives: Exploring Participatory Forms of Organising with Cooperatives." *Proceedings of the ACM on Human-Computer Interaction* 2 (CSCW): 1–19. https://doi.org/10.1145/3274369.

Laouénan, Morgane, and Roland Rathelot. 2016. "Ethnic Discrimination in an Online Marketplace of Vacation Rentals." Working Paper. http:// rolandrathelot.com/wp-content/uploads/Laouenan.Rathelot.Airbnb.pdf.

Lee, Min Kyung, Daniel Kusbit, Evan Metsky, and Laura Dabbish. 2015. "Working with Machines: The Impact of Algorithmic and Data-Driven Management on Human Workers." In *CHI '15: Proceedings of the 33rd Annual ACM Conference on Human Factors in Computing Systems,* 1603–12. New York: ACM Press. https://doi.org/10.1145/2702123.2702548.

Lessig, Lawrence. 2008. *Remix: Making Art and Commerce Thrive in the Hybrid Economy.* New York: Penguin.

Li, Jun, Antonio Moreno, and Dennis J Zhang. 2016. "Pros vs Joes: Agent Pricing Behavior in the Sharing Economy," Ross School of Business Working Paper Series, No. 1298. *SSRN Electronic Journal.* https://doi.org/10.2139/ ssrn.2708279.

Light, Ann, and Clodagh Miskelly. 2014. "Design for Sharing." Northumbria University: EPSRC Digital Economy. https://designforsharingdotcom.files .wordpress.com/2014/09/design-for-sharing-webversion.pdf.

———. 2015. "Sharing Economy vs Sharing Cultures? Designing for Social, Economic and Environmental Good." In special issue, *Interaction Design and Architecture(s),* no. 24, 49–62.

Light, Sarah E. 2017. "Precautionary Federalism and the Sharing Economy." *Emory Law Journal* 66:333–94.

Lobo, Sascha. 2014. "S.P.O.N.—Die Mensch-Maschine: Auf Dem Weg in Die Dumpinghölle." *Der Spiegel Online,* March 9, 2014. www.spiegel.de /netzwelt/netzpolitik/sascha-lobo-sharing-economy-wie-bei-uber-ist-plattform-kapitalismus-a-989584.html.

Lohr, Steve. 2019. "Google Antitrust Investigation Outlined by State Attorneys General." *New York Times,* September 9, 2019.

Lunden, Ingrid. 2018. "Amazon's U.S. Sales Exceeded Those of All Other Online Retailers Combined." *Tech Crunch,* July 13, 2018.

Lunden, Ingrid, and Romaine Dillet. 2018. "Airbnb Aims to Be 'Ready' to Go Public for June 30, 2019, Creates Cash Bonus for Staff." *Tech Crunch,* June 29, 2018.

Madden, Sam. 2015. "Why Homejoy Failed . . . And the Future of the On-Demand Economy." *Tech Crunch,* July 31, 2015.

Madrigal, Alexis C. 2019. "The Servant Economy." *The Atlantic,* March 6, 2019.

Mahdawi, Arwa. 2018. "Uber Developing Technology That Would Tell If You're Drunk." *The Guardian,* June 11, 2018.

Malin, Brenton J., and Curry Chandler. 2017. "Free to Work Anxiously: Splintering Precarity among Drivers for Uber and Lyft." *Communication, Culture & Critique* 10 (2): 382–400.

Mallett, William J. 2018. "Trends in Public Transportation Ridership: Implications for Federal Policy." R45144. Washington, DC: Congressional Research Service.

Manriquez, Mariana. 2019. "The Uberization of the Labor Market: A Case Study of Monterrey, Mexico." In *Work and Labor in the Digital Age,* ed. Steven P. Vallas and Anne Kovalainen, 165–88. Bingley, UK: Emerald.

Manyika, James, Susan Lund, Jacques Bughin, Kelsey Robinson, Jan Mischke, and Deepa Mahajan. 2016. "Independent Work: Choice, Necessity and the Gig Economy." New York: McKinsey Global Institute. www.mckinsey.com /featured-insights/employment-and-growth/independent-work-choice-necessity-and-the-gig-economy.

Margolies, Jane. 2019. "Speed-Dating Your Sofa." *New York Times,* May 6, 2019.

Markov, Tamar. 2019. "Who Wants My Half-Eaten Sandwich? Food Waste in the Sharing Economy." Unpublished paper. Yale University.

Martineau, Paris. 2019. "Inside Airbnb's 'Guerilla War' against Local Governments." *Wired,* March 20, 2019.

Mays, Jeffery C. 2018. "Uber Gains Civil Rights Allies against New York's Proposed Freeze: 'It's a Racial Issue.'" *New York Times,* July 29, 2018.

McLaren, Duncan, and Julian Agyeman. 2015. *Sharing Cities: A Case for Truly Smart and Sustainable Cities.* Cambridge, MA: MIT Press.

McLaughlin, Brenna R. 2018. "#AirbnbWhileBlack: Repealing the Fair Housing Act's Mrs. Murphy Exemption to Combat Racism on Airbnb." *Wisconsin Law Review* 149:156–58.

Miller, Michelle, and Eric Harris Bernstein. 2017. "New Frontiers of Worker Power: Challenges and Opportunities in the Modern Economy." New York: Roosevelt Institute. https://rooseveltinstitute.org/new-frontiers-worker-power.

Mishel, Lawrence. 2018. "Uber and the Labor Market." 145552. Washington, DC: Economic Policy Institute. www.epi.org/publication/uber-and-the-labor-market-uber-drivers-compensation-wages-and-the-scale-of-uber-and-the-gig-economy.

Mitchell, Bruce, and Juan Franco. 2018. "HOLC 'REDLINING' MAPS: The Persistent Structure of Segregation and Economic Inequality." Washington, DC: NCRC. https://ncrc.org/wp-content/uploads/dlm_uploads/2018/02/NCRC-Research-HOLC-10.pdf.

Morell, Mayo Fuster, ed. 2018. *Sharing Cities: A Worldwide Cities Overview on Platform Economy Policies with a Focus on Barcelona.* Barcelona: Universitat Oberta de Catalunya.

Morozov, Evgeny. 2011. *The Net Delusion: The Dark Side of Internet Freedom.* New York: PublicAffairs.

Newcomer, Eric. 2019. "Uber and Lyft Investors Are Looking for Signs of a Détente." *Bloomberg News,* August 2, 2019.

Njus, Elliot. 2018. "Oregon Airbnb Discrimination Suit Can Proceed, Judge Rules." *The Oregonian,* October 30, 2018.

Noble, David F. 2017. *Forces of Production: A Social History of Industrial Automation.* New York: Routledge.

Noble, Safiya Umoja. 2018. *Algorithms of Oppression: How Search Engines Reinforce Racism.* New York: New York University Press.

Nunley, John M., Mark F. Owens, and R. Stephen Howard. 2011. "The Effects of Information and Competition on Racial Discrimination: Evidence from a Field Experiment." *Journal of Economic Behavior and Organization* 80 (3): 670–79.

O'Connor, Sarah. 2016. "When Your Boss Is an Algorithm." *Financial Times,* September 8, 2016.

O'Neil, Cathy. 2016. *Weapons of Math Destruction: How Big Data Increases Inequality and Threatens Democracy.* New York: Crown.

Ostrom, Elinor. 1990. *Governing the Commons: The Evolution of Institutions for Collective Action.* Cambridge: Cambridge University Press.

O'Sullivan, Feargus. 2018. "Barcelona Finds a Way to Control Its Airbnb Market." *CityLab,* June 6, 2018.

Pacitti, Aaron. 2011. "The Cost of Job Loss and the Great Recession." *Journal of Post Keynesian Economics* 33 (4): 597–620.

Pager, Devah. 2007. *Marked: Race, Crime, and Finding Work in an Era of Mass Incarceration.* Chicago: University of Chicago Press.

Paharia, Neeru, Anat Keinan, Jill Avery, and Juliet B. Schor. 2011. "The Underdog Effect: The Marketing of Disadvantage and Determination through Brand Biography." *Journal of Consumer Research* 37 (5): 775–90.

Parigi, Paolo, and Bogdan State. 2014. "Disenchanting the World: The Impact of Technology on Relationships." *Social Informatics* 8851:166–82.

Parigi, Paolo, Bogdan State, Diana Dakhlallah, Rense Corten, and Karen Cook. 2013. "A Community of Strangers: The Dis-embedding of Social Ties." *PLoS ONE* 8 (7): e67388.

Parker, Geoffrey, Marshall Van Alstyne, and Sangeet Paul Choudary. 2016. *Platform Revolution: How Networked Markets Are Transforming the Economy and How to Make Them Work for You.* New York: Norton.

Parkinson, Hannah Jane. 2016. "#AirBnBWhileBlack Hashtag Highlights Potential Racial Bias on Rental App." *The Guardian,* May 5, 2016.

Parrott, James A., and Michael Reich. 2018. "An Earnings Standard for New York City's App-Based Drivers." New York: The New School: Center for New York City Affairs.

Pasquale, Frank. 2015. *The Black Box Society: The Secret Algorithms That Control Money and Information.* Cambridge, MA: Harvard University Press.

———. 2016. "Two Narratives of Platform Capitalism." *Yale Law and Policy Review* 35. http://ylpr.yale.edu/sites/default/files/YLPR/pasquale. final_.2.pdf.

Pasquale, Frank A. 2013. "Paradoxes of Digital Antitrust." *Harvard Journal of Law & Technology Occasional Paper Series,* July. https://jolt.law.harvard.edu /assets/misc/Pasquale.pdf.

Paul, Kari. 2019a. "The Uber Drivers Forced to Sleep in Parking Lots to Make a Decent Living." *The Guardian,* May 8, 2019.

———. 2019b. "'Shut up and Drive'? Option for Uber Riders to Avoid Small Talk Divides Drivers." *The Guardian,* May 18, 2019.

Pelzer, Peter, Koen Frenken, and Wouter Boon. 2019. "Institutional Entrepreneurship in the Platform Economy: How Uber Tried (and Failed) to Change the Dutch Taxi Law." *Environmental Innovation and Societal Transitions,* 33: 1–12 (November).

Perea, Christian. 2016. "What's The Real Commission That Uber Takes from Its Drivers? [Infographic]." *The Rideshare Guy* (blog). July 25, 2016. https:// therideshareguy.com/whats-the-real-commission-that-uber-takes-from-its-drivers-infographic.

Pesole, A., Urzi Brancati, and E. Fernandez-Macias. 2018. "Platform Workers in Europe." EUR 27275 EN. Luxembourg: Publications Office of the European Union.

Peticca-Harris, Amanda, Nadia deGama, and M. N. Ravishankar. 2018. "Postcapitalist Precarious Work and Those in the 'Drivers' Seat: Exploring the Motivations and Lived Experiences of Uber Drivers in Canada." *Organization.* https://doi-org.proxy.bc.edu/10.1177/1350508418757332.

Pew Research Center. 2011. "Little Change in Public's Response to 'Capitalism,' 'Socialism.'" Washington, DC: Pew Research Center. www.people-press.org/2011/12/28/little-change-in-publics-response-to-capitalism-socialism.

———. 2016a. "Gig Work, Online Selling and Home Sharing." www.pewinternet.org/2016/11/17/gig-work-online-selling-and-home-sharing.

———. 2016b. "Shared, Collaborative and On Demand: The New Digital Economy." www.pewinternet.org/2016/05/19/the-new-digital-economy.

Pressler, Jessica. 2014. "'The Dumbest Person in Your Building Is Passing Out Keys to Your Front Door!'" *New York Magazine,* September 23, 2014.

PriceWaterHouseCoopers. 2015. "Sharing or Paring? Growth of the Sharing Economy." PriceWaterhouseCoopers. www.pwc.com/hu/en/kiadvanyok/assets/pdf/sharing-economy-en.pdf.

Pugh, Allison J. 2015. *The Tumbleweed Society: Working and Caring in an Age of Insecurity.* Oxford: Oxford University Press.

Quattrone, Giovanni, Davide Proserpio, Daniele Quercia, Licia Capra, and Mirco Musolesi. 2016. "Who Benefits from the 'Sharing' Economy of Airbnb?" In *WWW '16: Proceedings of the 25th International Conference on World Wide Web,* 1385–1394. Republic and Canton of Geneva, Switzerland: International World Wide Web Conferences Steering Committee. https://doi.org/10.1145/2872427.2874815.

Racabi, Gali. 2018. "State TNC and MC Legislation: Preemption and Employment Status of Drivers." *On Labor* (blog). October 19, 2018. https://onlabor.org/state-tnc-and-mc-legislation-preemption-and-employment-status-of-drivers.

Rahman, Hatim. 2018. "From Iron Cages to Invisible Cages: Algorithmic Evaluations in Online Labor Markets." Unpublished paper. Stanford University.

Rahman, K. Sabeel. 2016. "The Shape of Things to Come: The On-Demand Economy and the Normative Stakes of Regulating 21st-Century Capitalism." *European Journal of Risk Regulation* 7 (4): 652–63.

Rahman, K. Sabeel, and Kathleen Thelen. 2019. "The Rise of the Platform Business Model and the Transformation of Twenty-First-Century Capitalism." *Politics & Society* 47 (2): 177–204.

Ramsey, Lydia. 2019. "Uber Had the Worst First-Day Dollar Loss Ever of Any US IPO." *Business Insider,* May 11, 2019.

Ravenelle, Alexandrea J. 2019. *Hustle and Gig: Struggling and Surviving in the Sharing Economy.* Berkeley: University of California Press.

Reich, Robert B. 2015. "The Share-the-Scraps Economy." *Robert Reich,* February 2, 2015. http://robertreich.org/post/109894095095.

Richardson, Lizzie. 2015. "Performing the Sharing Economy." *Geoforum 67* (December): 121–29.

Ritzer, George. 2007. *The McDonaldization of Society.* 2nd ed. Thousand Oaks, CA: Pine Forge.

Robinson, H.C. 2017. "Making a Digital Working Class: Uber Drivers in Boston, 2016–2017." PhD diss., MIT Program in Science, Technology and Society.

Rochet, Jean-Charles, and Jean Tirole. 2003. "Platform Competition in Two-Sided Markets." *Journal of the European Economic Association* 1 (4): 990–1029.

Rogers, Brishen. 2015. "The Social Costs of Uber." *University of Chicago Law Review* 82:85–102.

———. 2016. "Employment Rights in the Platform Economy: Getting Back to Basics." *Harvard Law and Policy Review* 10:479–520.

———. 2018. "Fissuring, Data-Driven Governance, and Platform Economy Labor Standards." In *Cambridge Handbook of the Law of the Sharing Economy,* ed. Nestor B. Davidson, Michèle Finck, and John J. Infarca, 304–15. Cambridge, UK: Cambridge University Press.

Roose, Kevin. 2019. "After Uproar, Instacart Backs Off Controversial Tipping Policy." *New York Times,* February 6, 2019.

Rose, Nikolas. 1999. *Powers of Freedom: Reframing Political Thought.* Cambridge: Cambridge University Press.

Rosenblat, Alex. 2018. *Uberland: How Algorithms Are Re-writing the Rules of Work.* Berkeley: University of California Press.

Rosenblat, Alex, Solon Barocas, Karen Levy, and Tim Hwang. 2016. "Discriminating Tastes: Customer Ratings as Vehicles for Bias." *Intelligence and Autonomy* (October): 1–21.

Rosenblat, Alex, and Luke Stark. 2016. "Algorithmic Labor and Information Asymmetries: A Case Study of Uber's Drivers." *International Journal of Communication* 10:3758–84.

Rosenthal, Brian M. 2019. "'They Were Conned': How Reckless Loans Devastated a Generation of Taxi Drivers." *New York Times,* May 19, 2019.

Rowe, Pia C. M. 2017. "Beyond Uber and Airbnb: The Social Economy of Collaborative Consumption." *Social Media + Society* 3 (2): 205630511770678.

Saez, Emmanuel. 2019. "Striking It Richer: The Evolution of Top Incomes in the United States (Updated with 2017 Final Estimates)." https://eml.berkeley .edu/~saez/saez-UStopincomes-2017.pdf.

Said, Carolyn. 2018a. "Airbnb Loses Thousands of Hosts in SF as Registration Rules Kick In." *San Francisco Chronicle,* January 14, 2018.

———. 2018b. "Airbnb Lists in San Francisco Plunge by Half." *San Francisco Chronicle,* January 18, 2018.

Schaller, Bruce. 2018. "The New Automobility: Uber, Lyft and the Future of American Cities." Brooklyn, NY: Schaller Consulting. www.schallerconsult .com/rideservices/automobility.htm.

Scheiber, Noam. 2017. "How Uber Uses Psychological Tricks to Push Its Drivers' Buttons." *New York Times,* April 2, 2017.

———. 2018. "Gig Economy Business Model Dealt a Blow in California Ruling." *New York Times,* April 30, 2018.

Schneider, Nathan. 2014. "Owning Is the New Sharing." Shareable. December 21, 2014. www.shareable.net/blog/owning-is-the-new-sharing.

———. 2018a. "An Internet of Ownership: Democratic Design for the Online Economy." *Sociological Review Monographs* 66 (2): 320–40.

———. 2018b. *Everything for Everyone: The Radical Tradition That Is Shaping the Next Economy.* New York: Nation Books.

Schneider, Todd W. 2019. "Dashboard: Taxi and Ridehailing Usage in New York City." *Todd W. Schneider* (blog). 2019. https://toddwschneider.com /dashboards/nyc-taxi-ridehailing-uber-lyft-data.

Scholz, Trebor. 2014. "Platform Cooperativism vs. the Sharing Economy." *Trebor Scholz* (blog). December 5, 2014. https://medium.com/@trebors /platform-cooperativism-vs-the-sharing-economy-2ea737f1b5ad.

———. 2016. *Uberworked and Underpaid: How Workers Are Disrupting the Digital Economy.* Cambridge: Polity.

Scholz, Trebor, and Nathan Schneider, eds. 2016. *Ours to Hack and to Own: The Rise of Platform Cooperativism, a New Vision for the Future of Work and a Fairer Internet.* New York: OR Books.

Schor, Juliet B. 1988. "Does Work Intensity Respond to Macroeconomic Variables? Evidence from British Manufacturing, 1970–1986." Harvard Institute for Economic Research Discussion Paper #1379, April 1988.

———. 1992. *The Overworked American: The Unexpected Decline of Leisure.* New York: Basic Books.

———. 1999. *The Overspent American: Why We Want What We Don't Need.* New York: HarperPerennial.

———. 2010. *Plenitude: The New Economics of True Wealth.* New York: Penguin.

———. 2014. "Debating the Sharing Economy." www.greattransition.org /publication/debating-the-sharing-economy.

———. 2015. "Homo Varians: Diverse Motives and Economic Behavior in the Sharing Economy." Unpublished paper. Boston College.

———. 2016. "'Old Exclusion in Emergent Spaces.'" In *Ours to Hack and to Own: The Rise of Platform Cooperativism,* edited by Trebor Scholz and Nathan Schneider, 38–42. New York: OR Books.

———. 2017. "Does the Sharing Economy Increase Inequality within the Eighty Percent? Findings from a Qualitative Study of Platform Providers." *Cambridge Journal of Regions, Economy and Society* 10 (2): 263–79.

———. Forthcoming. "The Just and Democratic Platform? Possibilities of Platform Cooperativism," In *New Goals for a Just Economy,* edited by Danielle Allen, Yochai Benkler, and Rebecca Henderson.

Schor, Juliet B., and William Attwood-Charles. 2017. "The Sharing Economy: Labor, Inequality and Sociability on For-Profit Platforms." *Sociology Compass* 11 (8): 1–16.

Schor, Juliet B., William Attwood-Charles, Mehmet Cansoy, Isak Ladegaard, and Robert Wengronowitz. 2019. "Dependence and Precarity in the Platform Economy." www.bc.edu/bc-web/schools/mcas/departments /sociology/connected.html.

Schor, Juliet B., and Samuel Bowles. 1987. "Employment Rents and Incidence of Strikes." *Review of Economics and Statistics* 69 (4): 584–92.

Schor, Juliet B., and Mehmet Cansoy. 2019. "The Sharing Economy." In *The Oxford Handbook of Consumption,* edited by Frederick F. Wherry and Ian Woodward, 51–74. New York: Oxford University Press.

Schor, Juliet B., Connor Fitzmaurice, William Attwood-Charles, Lindsey B. Carfagna, and Emilie Dubois Poteat. 2016. "Paradoxes of Openness and Distinction in the Sharing Economy." *Poetics* 54:66–81.

Schor, Juliet B., and Connor J. Fitzmaurice. 2015. "Collaborating and Connecting: The Emergence of the Sharing Economy." In *Handbook of Research on Sustainable Consumption,* edited by Lucia A. Reisch and Jon Thogersen, 410–25. Cheltenham, UK: Edward Elgar.

Selyukh, Alina. 2019. "Why Suburban Moms Are Delivering Your Groceries." *All Things Considered*. National Public Radio. www.npr.org/2019/05/25/722811953 /why-suburban-moms-are-delivering-your-groceries.

Shaban, Hamza. 2018. "Amazon Employees Demand Company Cut Ties with ICE." *Washington Post,* June 22, 2018.

Shaheen, Susan. 2018. "Peer-to-Peer (P2P) Carsharing: Understanding Early Markets, Social Dynamics, and Behavioral Impacts." Institute of Transportation Studies, Berkeley. https://doi.org/10.7922/g2fn14bd.

Shapiro, Aaron. 2018. "Between Autonomy and Control: Strategies of Arbitrage in the 'On-Demand' Economy." *New Media & Society* 20 (8): 2954–71.

Sheldon, Michael. 2016. "Income Targeting and the Ridesharing Market." https://static1.squarespace.com/static/56500157e4b0cb706005352d/t /56da1114e707ebbe8e963ffc/1457131797556/IncomeTargetingFeb16 .pdf.

Shestakofsky, Benjamin. 2017. "Working Algorithms: Software Automation and the Future of Work." *Work and Occupations* 44 (4): 376–423.

Shih, Patrick C., Victoria Bellotti, Kyungsik Han, and John M. Carroll. 2015. "Unequal Time for Unequal Value: Implications of Differing Motivations for Participation in Timebanking." In *CHI '15: Proceedings of the 33rd Annual ACM Conference on Human Factors in Computing Systems,* 1075–84. New York: ACM Press. https://doi.org/10.1145/2702123.2702560.

Sitaraman, Ganesh. 2018. "Taking Antitrust Away from the Courts." New York: Roosevelt Institute. https://greatdemocracyinitiative.org/wp-content /uploads/2018/09/Taking-Antitrust-Away-from-the-Courts-Report- 092018-3.pdf.

Skjelvik, John Magne, Anne Maren Erlandsen, and Oscar Haavardsholm. 2017. *Environmental Impacts and Potential of the Sharing Economy.* TemaNord. Nordic Council of Ministers. https://doi.org/10.6027/TN2017-554.

Skott, Peter, and Frederick Guy. 2007. "A Model of Power-Biased Technological Change." *Economics Letters* 95 (1): 124–31.

Slee, Tom. 2015. *What's Yours Is Mine: Against the Sharing Economy.* New York: OR Books.

Smith, Yves. 2018. "Uber Is Headed for a Crash." *New York Magazine,* December 4, 2018.

Söderqvist, Frederick. 2018. "Sweden: Will History Lead the Way in the Age of Robots and Platforms?" In *Work in the Digital Age: Challenges of the Fourth Industrial Revolution,* edited by Max Neufeind, J. O'Reilly, and Florian Ranft, 295–304. London: Rowman and Littlefield.

Solomon, Brian. 2015. "The Hottest On-Demand Start-Ups of 2015." *Forbes,* December 29, 2015.

Solomon, Dan. 2017. "One Year After Fleeing Austin, Uber and Lyft Prepare a Fresh Invasion." *Wired,* May 7, 2017.

Sperling, Gene. 2015. "How Airbnb Combats Middle Class Income Stagnation." Airbnb and Sperling Economic Strategies. www.stgeorgeutah.com/wp-content/uploads/2015/07/MiddleClassReport-MT-061915_r1.pdf.

Srnicek, Nick. 2016. *Platform Capitalism.* Theory Redux. Cambridge: Polity.

Standing, Guy. 2011. *The Precariat: The New Dangerous Class.* London: Bloomsbury.

Stefano, Valerio de. 2016. "The Rise of the 'Just-in-Time Workforce': On-Demand Work, Crowdwork, and Labor Protection in the 'Gig Economy.'" *Comparative Labor Law & Policy Journal* 37 (3): 471–504.

Stein, Joel. 2015. "Baby, You Can Drive My Car, and Do My Errands, and Rent My Stuff . . ." *Time,* January 29, 2015.

Stemler, Abbey, Joshua E. Perry, and Todd Haugh. Forthcoming. "The Code of the Platform." *Georgia Law Review.*

Stone, Brad. 2017. "Uber: The App That Changed How the World Hails a Taxi." *The Guardian,* January 29, 2017.

Suhonen, Emmi, Airi Lampinen, Coye Cheshire, and Judd Antin. 2010. "Everyday Favors: A Case Study of a Local Online Gift Exchange System." In *Proceedings of the 16th ACM International Conference on Supporting Group Work,* 11–20. New York: ACM Press. http://dl.acm.org/citation.cfm?id=1880074.

Sulakshana, Elana, Samantha Eddy, and Juliet B. Schor. 2018. "Democratic Governance in the Sharing Economy: A Case Study of a Platform Cooperative, Stocksy United." Unpublished Paper. Oxford University.

Sundararajan, Arun. 2016. *The Sharing Economy: The End of Employment and the Rise of Crowd-Based Capitalism.* Cambridge, MA: MIT Press.

Telles, Rudy, Jr. 2016. "Digital Matching Firms: A New Definition in the 'Sharing Economy' Space." ESA issue brief no. 16–01 (June 3). Economics and Statistics Administration. Office of the Chief Economist: U.S. Department of Commerce.

Thebault-Spieker, Jacob, Loren G. Terveen, and Brent Hecht. 2015. "Avoiding the South Side and the Suburbs: The Geography of Mobile Crowdsourcing Markets." In *Proceedings of the 18th ACM Conference on Computer Supported Cooperative Work & Social Computing,* 265–75. New York: ACM Press. https://doi.org/10.1145/2675133.2675278.

Thelen, Kathleen. 2018. "Regulating Uber: The Politics of the Platform Economy in Europe and the United States." *Perspectives on Politics* 16 (4): 938–53.

Ticona, Julia. 2020. *Left to Our Own Devices: Coping with Work in an Insecure Age.* New York: Oxford University Press.

Tiku, Nitasha. 2014. "Airbnb Lobbyist Is Charging $800 for Tickets to a 'Sharing' Conference." *Gawker,* May 8, 2014. http://valleywag.gawker.com /airbnb-lobbyist-is-charging-800-for-tickets-to-a-shar-1572254090.

Tsotsis, Alexia. 2012. "TaskRabbit Gets $13M from Founders Fund and Others to 'Revolutionize the World's Labor Force,'" 2012. *Tech Crunch,* July 23, 2012.

Turner, Fred. 2006. *From Counterculture to Cyberculture: Stewart Brand, the Whole Earth Network, and the Rise of Digital Utopianism.* Chicago: University of Chicago Press.

Tussyadiah, Iis P., and Juho Pesonen. 2016. "Impacts of Peer-to-Peer Accommodation Use on Travel Patterns." *Journal of Travel Research* 55 (8): 1022–40.

Uber Technologies, Inc. 2019. "Form S-1 Registration Document." Securities and Exchange Commission. www.sec.gov/Archives/edgar/data/1543151 /000119312519103850/d647752ds1.htm.

UCLA Institute for Research on Labor and Employment. 2018. "More Than a Gig: A Survey of Ridehailing Drivers in Los Angeles." Los Angeles: UCLA.

Ugarte, David. 2017. "Platform Cooperativism: A Truncated 'Cooperativism' for Millennials?" *P2PFoundation* (blog). January 31, 2017. https://blog .p2pfoundation.net/platform-cooperativism-a-truncated-cooperativism- for-millennials/2017/01/31.

US Census Bureau. 2017. "Quarterly Residential Vacancies and Homeowner- ship, First Quarter 2017." Washington, DC: US Census Bureau. www.census .gov/housing/hvs/files/currenthvspress.pdf.

Vallas, Steven P., and Arne L. Kalleberg. 2018. "Probing Precarious Work: Theory, Research, and Politics." In *Precarious Work,* edited by Arne L. Kalleberg and Steven P. Vallas, 1–30. Bingley, UK: Emerald.

Vallas, Steven P., and Juliet B. Schor. Forthcoming. "What Do Platforms Do? Understanding the Gig Economy." *Annual Review of Sociology* 46.

Vedantam, Shankar. 2016. "This Is Your Brain on Uber." *Hidden Brain: A Conversation about Life's Unseen Patterns.* National Public Radio. www.npr .org/templates/transcript/transcript.php?storyId=478266839.

Wachsmuth, David, David Chaney, Danielle Kerrigan, Andrea Shillolo, and Robin Basalaev-Binder. 2018. "The High Cost of Short-Term Rentals in New

York City." Montreal: Urban Politics and Governance Research Group, School of Urban Planning, McGill University.

Wachsmuth, David, Jennifer Combs, and Danielle Kerrigan. 2019. "The Impact of New Short-Term Rental Regulations on New York City." Montreal: Urban Politics and Governance Research Group, School of Urban Planning, McGill University. www.sharebetter.org/wp-content/uploads/2019/01/Impact-of-New-STR-Regs-2019.pdf.

Wachsmuth, David, and Alexander Weisler. 2018. "Airbnb and the Rent Gap: Gentrification through the Sharing Economy." *Environment and Planning A: Economy and Space* 50 (6): 1147–70.

Walker, Edward T. 2016. "Between Grassroots and 'Astroturf': Understanding Mobilization from the Top-Down." In *The SAGE Handbook of Resistance,* edited by David Courpasson and Steven Vallas, 269–79. Los Angeles: SAGE.

Wallenstein, Judith, and Urvesh Shelat. 2017. "Hopping Aboard the Sharing Economy." BCG Henderson Institute. www.bcg.com/en-us/publications/2017/strategy-accelerating-growth-consumer-products-hopping-aboard-sharing-economy.aspx.

Weil, David. 2014. *The Fissured Workplace: Why Work Became So Bad for So Many and What Can Be Done to Improve It.* Cambridge, MA: Harvard University Press.

Weiser, Benjamin, and J. David Goodman. 2019. "Judge Blocks New York City Law Aimed at Curbing Airbnb Rentals." *New York Times,* January 3, 2019.

Wells, Kathryn, Kafui Attoh, and Declan Cullen. 2019. "The Uber Workplace in D.C." Washington, DC: Kalmanowitz Initiative for Labor and the Working Poor, Georgetown University. https://lwp.georgetown.edu/wp-content/uploads/Uber-Workplace.pdf.

White, Andy, and Dana Olsen. 2018. "Here's Where Uber and Lyft Would Rank among the Decade's Most Valuable VC-Backed IPOs." *Pitchbook: News and Analysis,* October 16, 2018. https://pitchbook.com/news/articles/heres-where-uber-and-lyft-would-rank-among-the-decades-most-valuable-vc-backed-ipos.

Whyte, William H. 1956. *The Organization Man.* New York: Simon and Schuster.

Wilhelm, Alex. 2019. "Postmates Raises $225M More at $2.4B Valuation Despite Private IPO Filing." *Crunchbase,* September 19, 2019. https://news.crunchbase.com/news/postmates-raises-225m-more-at-2-4b-valuation-despite-private-ipo-filing.

Wolff, Edward. 2017. "Household Wealth Trends in the United States, 1962 to 2016: Has Middle Class Wealth Recovered?" NBER Working Paper w24085.

Cambridge, MA: National Bureau of Economic Research. https://doi.org/10.3386/w24085.

Wood, Alex J., Mark Graham, Vili Lehdonvirta, and Isis Hjorth. 2019. "Good Gig, Bad Gig: Autonomy and Algorithmic Control in the Global Gig Economy." *Work, Employment and Society* 33 (1): 56-75.

Zatz, Noah D. 2016. "A New Peonage: Pay, Work, or Go to Jail in Contemporary Child Support Enforcement and Beyond." *Seattle University Law Review* 39:927-55.

Zelizer, Viviana A. 2005. *The Purchase of Intimacy.* Princeton, NJ: Princeton University Press.

———. 2013. *Economic Lives: How Culture Shapes the Economy.* Princeton, NJ: Princeton University Press.

Zervas, Georgios, Davide Proserpio, and John Byers. 2015. "A First Look at Online Reputation on Airbnb, Where Every Stay Is Above Average." *SSRN Electronic Journal.* https://doi.org/10.2139/ssrn.2554500.

Zervas, Georgios, Davide Proserpio, and John W. Byers. 2017. "The Rise of the Sharing Economy: Estimating the Impact of Airbnb on the Hotel Industry." *Journal of Marketing Research* 54 (5): 687-705.

# Index

Uber *(continued)*
    regulation, 152–53; gender
    discrimination, 87; labor competi-
    tor, 59; lobbying, 156–57; network
    effect, 32; origin story, 25; quiet
    mode, 114; as sharing economy
    platform, 193; taking (advantage),
    159; traffic congestion, 117;
    transaction fees, 86; UberPool, 108,
    118; worker experience, 58, 62, 76
*Uberland*, 13
Uber of x, 26, 125
UberPop, 153
*Uberworked and Underpaid*, 12
unemployment, 3
Union Square Ventures, 171
Up and Go, 170
Upwork, 41
urban sharing, 172
UrbanSitter, 27
used book market, 120

Val, 139
Valeria, 98
value proposition, 124, 143–47
values, 174–75
vehicle miles traveled (VMT), 116
Vinni, 31

Wang, Charley, 38
wealth inequality, 95
*Wealth of Networks, The*, 163
Wells, Katie, 76
Wengronowitz, Robert, 14, 181–82

Werbach, Adam, 27
Wettlaufer, Brianna, 148–49
*What's Mine Is Yours*, 12
*What's Yours Is Mine*, 13
"When Your Boss Is an Algorithm," 66
*Whole Earth Catalog*, 22
Wikipedia, 164
Will, 53–54
women: discrimination, 87; platform
    participation, 190; ratings, 92
Wonolo, 110
Wood, Alex, 77
work: and capitalism, 3–4; and
    corporate culture, 3, 6, 12–13; and
    digital technology, 1, 6–7; employ-
    ment classification, 47, 71; and
    for-profit platforms, 2, 6–11, 13; and
    labor control, 80; and person-to-
    person economy, 2; precarious,
    70–71
workforce, sharing, 43–45, 77, 190
Woz, 139

xenophobia, 89

Yerdle, 27, 34

Zaarly, 35, 99
Zack, 98
Zelizer, Viviana, 193
Zimmer, John, 25
Zimride, 25
Zipcar, 26, 192
Zysman, John, 194

Founded in 1893,
UNIVERSITY OF CALIFORNIA PRESS
publishes bold, progressive books and journals
on topics in the arts, humanities, social sciences,
and natural sciences—with a focus on social
justice issues—that inspire thought and action
among readers worldwide.

The UC PRESS FOUNDATION
raises funds to uphold the press's vital role
as an independent, nonprofit publisher, and
receives philanthropic support from a wide
range of individuals and institutions—and from
committed readers like you. To learn more, visit
ucpress.edu/supportus.